Designs of Selfhood

Designs of Selfhood

Edited by
Vytautas Kavolis

Rutherford ● Madison ● Teaneck
Fairleigh Dickinson University Press
London and Toronto: Associated University Presses

© 1984 by Associated University Presses, Inc.

Associated University Presses
440 Forsgate Drive
Cranbury, N.J. 08512

Associated University Presses
25 Sicilian Avenue
London WC1A 2QH, England

Associated University Presses
2133 Royal Windsor Drive
Unit 1
Mississauga, Ontario, Canada L5J 1K5

Library of Congress Cataloging in Publication Data
Main entry under title:

Designs of selfhood.

Includes bibliographical references.
1. Individuality. 2. Self. 3. Identity (Psychology)
I. Kavolis, Vytautas, 1930–   .
HM136.D383   1984   302.5'4   82-48616
ISBN 0-8386-3161-4

Printed in the United States of America

I will try in plain terms to sketch a criticism, and therefore a history, of myself. . . .

My mind hangs in suspense . . . like a reflection upon stormy waters.

Benedetto Croce,
An Autobiography

Contents

Preface

The extraordinary preoccupation in the English-speaking world with is-sues of selfhood and personal identity has deep roots both in the history of Western civilization and in the universal need of the psyche to regain its bearings whenever a primordial, or at least taken-for-granted, unity of experience has been shaken by painful events or vivid breakthroughs in human insight, imagination, or sympathy.

Mountains of trivial data, incomparable subtleties of self-perception, and the most substantial theories of human psychological organization have emerged from this drive to self-understanding. We who live on the mountains, subsist by the subtleties, and wield, exploit, run to ground, and resurrect the theories can only be grateful for the profusion of efforts to advance our self-understanding.

But we do not live alone in the world, and, contrary to what Max Weber once said, it is not only the history of the West that has universal significance. Our experience of ourselves and our efforts to construct a civilization do not possess a privileged centrality in the accumulated experi-ence of humanity as a whole, even though it is only we who have acquired the negative technical capacity to terminate all of this experience. We must begin with ourselves, but we cannot stop there.

Virtually all the perspectives that are available to help us grasp the various experiences of our diverse selfhoods—whether offered by religion, by psychology and psychoanalysis, by sociology, by philosophy, or by litera-ture—have been conceived within one or another civilizational tradition and constructed of the intellectual equipment provided by this tradition. In some cases, the intellectual categories themselves are non-Western, but it does not advance our understanding to substitute a non-Western exoticism for a Western parochialism or to oscillate disconsolately from one to the other.

Even the efforts of anthropologists suffer (insofar as they are not merely descriptive) from the importation of categories of analysis that are not only Western, but, in addition, characteristic even of the Western con-sciousness only in a particular phase of its mainstream historical trajectory (roughly, for most anthropologists, from the second half of the nineteenth century on). Anthropologists are more aware of the problems raised here

9

than are most other social scientists. But their comparative inattentiveness to the actual *Geistesgeschichten*—or, in William J. Bouwsma's recent translation, "histories of meaning"—of those traditions, including the Western, which have had the major impact in shaping the world of contemporary experience, has reduced the contributions of anthropology to the problem area of self-understanding far below the signal services it has rendered in the analysis of social structures, ritual processes, and collective responses to societal change.

Social psychology, which ought to have been the central discipline gathering all strains of evidence illuminating the complex relationships between the empirical range of "souls" and the varieties of "society," recognizes neither soul nor society, let alone the tremendous historical diversity of psyches and social organizations, as dynamic wholes. Whatever the recent, mainly methodological advances in cross-cultural psychology, the basic thrust of social psychology remains an effort to find universally valid formulations about human behavior studied in artificial laboratory or real-life, but small-group, settings. Of the three categories of thought that are central to the comprehension of human conduct anywhere—"Histories, Structures, Civilizations"—at least two are entirely unknown in the territories claimed by the main schools of social psychology.

As a consequence, what has been historically constructed by a particular people in a specific period of its history becomes normatively universal as it tends to do in the more "scientific" branches of psychology. Or else it begins to dissolve in "humanistic," literary, and purely subjectivistic modes of self-interpretation in endless refinements of the detail, or in the vanished shadow, of self-analysis, since it seems that there is nothing else than one's own self (mistakenly identified with the universal self) to analyze. But one's own self is both less interesting and less fruitfully studied than the experience of mankind in matters of selfhood.

Even cross-cultural psychology asks, on the whole, only Western questions of both Western and non-Western psyches. Efforts to develop non-Western psychologies out of the heart of non-Western experiences and from within the linguistic universes by which these experiences have been structured are rarely (mainly in Japan and in India) beyond elementary beginnings.

We have reached a point in our joint intellectual development at which significant advances in our grasp of human identity (as well as our sense of worldwide scholarly responsibility) require that the central problems be posed in the context of the experience of humanity as a whole; viewed carefully and in dynamic detail within their various historical trajectories, and, where appropriate, in contemporary field settings; and analyzed not only from the perspectives of a diversity of academic disciplines (all creations and therefore expressions mainly of Western civilization) but also from the standpoints of the various civilizational traditions in which the bulk of recorded human experience has been organized, both those that have already spoken a great deal about themselves and the rest of the world and those which have been, thus far, comparatively silent. Not only the neglected traditions but also the suppressed elements of recognized traditions need to be given special attention by students of self-comprehensions: this is the magic forest of the history of culture in which what has been suppressed and neglected in the dominant streams and formations of development of our various civilizations is most likely to be alive. Above all, the expanded framework that we might, with Benjamin Nelson, designate as *the civilization-analytic approach* requires a type of mind which consciously responds and intuitively resonates to all these perspectives in its own activity.

To promote scholarly projects of this nature, to nurture minds of this kind of sensibility, the International Society for the Comparative Study of Civilizations, originally founded under the leadership of Pitirim A. Sorokin and Arnold J. Toynbee and mainly active in Europe, was revived at a meeting of the American Association for the Advancement of Science in Philadelphia, on December 29, 1971. Earlier versions of most of the studies collected in this volume were all presented at the annual meetings of the Society in 1977 at Bradford College, 1979 at California State University at Northridge, in 1980 at Syracuse University, and in 1981 at the University of Indiana. "On the Self-Person Differentiation" was read at the 1976 meeting of the American Sociological Association in New York.

The volume brings together the perspectives and insights of a psychoanalyst, a sociologist, two literary scholars, and two historians—all united in their respect for ideas, histories, languages, and the person. The book offers contributions to the comparative historical study of autobiographical modes of self-consciousness and to the practice of psychotherapy in culturally diverse settings; to the understanding of the pressures that particular languages exert on experiences of selfhood and personhood and on the "universal categories of the mind;" to a deeper grasp of the relevance to self-perception of religious and literary countertraditions both ancient and modern; and to a sharpened vision of linkages and disjunctions between political experience, legal thought, and literary images of selfhood.

All of these modes of analysis and linkages of meaning need to be simultaneously grasped in comparative historical and civilizational perspective if we are to attain an adequate understanding of the human experience with the structures and energies of human selfhood.

Designs of Selfhood

I

Beginnings and Endings

1

Histories of Selfhood, Maps of Sociability

Vytautas Kavolis

I

In 1115, a medieval churchman began his *Memoirs:*

> I confess to Thy Majesty, O God, my endless wanderings from Thy paths, and my turning back so often to the bosom of Thy Mercy, directed by Thee in spite of all. I confess the wickedness that yet boils up in my mature years, and my ingrained love of crookedness, which still lives on in the sluggishness of my worn body,

and concluded:

> Let us now place the name of the most excellent Mary, Queen of heaven and earth, together with that of Denis, lord of all France, as a conclusion to this book.[1]

This is still the Augustinian format of seven hundred and thirty years ago: the self begins with God, falls into wickedness, or what Guibert de Nogent calls "stinking willfulness," which he seeks to suppress by ascetic practices, and in the end returns, or tries to return, to God. Selfhood is placed within a perpetually recurring circular motion built into the inevitable experience of man on the temporary periphery from his eternal center.

Within this durable scheme, Guibert distinguishes himself from Saint Augustine by accents suggestive of themes that will become prominent later. Where Saint Augustine began with a recognition of the objective state of affairs: *"Great art thou, O Lord,"* Guibert puts his own religious act: *"I confess* to Thy Majesty. . . ." And where Saint Augustine had concluded by speaking to *God alone,* Guibert, in a community of worshipers ("let *us*"), recalls not only "the most excellent Mary" but also the saint who was the "lord of *all France.*"[2] In contrast to the Christian of late antiquity, the medieval man is an individual with his own intentions, and in coming back to God he does not wholly forget the political society of which he is a part.

The history of selfhood is a history of empirically established forms of self-understanding. The forms emerge most clearly in literary texts that explicitly center on a person's efforts to describe or better understand his own self or the meaning of his own life as a whole. Such texts illuminate the experience of the lived-in self more faithfully than do theoretical or normative writings formulating a general conception of what the self is or should be.

It is not always clear when a form a self-understanding emerges and how far and how deeply it extends its hold over a population. Moreover, there is change within a symbolic form over historical time (as well as conflicts between different forms at any one time). One form is not replaced by the next at some bus stop of the historical process. An older form may provide elements for a new self-comprehension. It may continue to exist side by side with the new, and may even be reconstituted from the experienced fragments of the new and the learned memories of the old, as happened in the case of the medieval man of the twentieth century, Thomas Merton.

Thomas Merton had started:

> On the last day of January 1915, under the sign of the Water Bearer, in a year of a great war, and down in the shadow of some French mountains on the Borders of Spain, I came into the world. Free by nature, in the image of God, I was nevertheless the prisoner of my own violence and my own selfishness, in the image of the world into which I was born. That world was the picture of Hell, full of men like myself, loving God and yet hating Him; born to love him, living instead in fear and hopeless self-contradictory hungers.

Merton concluded with God speaking to him:

> "But you shall taste the true solitude of my anguish and my poverty and I shall lead you into the high places of my joy and you shall die in Me and find all things in My mercy which has created you for this end. . . . That you may become the brother of God and learn to know the Christ of the burnt men."[3]

There are "modern" elements in the frames within which Merton has placed his life. He locates the story to be told in relation to historical events and the geographical environment before mentioning either himself or God, and he paints, at the beginning, not himself alone, but the moral and psychological condition of the world of which he is a part. In the beginning is not God alone, as it was for Saint Augustine, or an individual in contact with God, as it was for Guibert, but *a sociological world* unaware of missing God. Merton concludes with the recovered image of God, not as the classical restfulness in perfection of Saint Augustine or the medieval rulership of Guibert, but as the embodiment of personal suffering and salvation—"my anguish and my poverty" and "the Christ of the burnt men." But the basic medieval scheme for the comprehension of selfhood, the withdrawal-and-return circularity of man in relation to God, has retained its continuity (though not for very many) into the present.

II

An Indologist might note that, in spite of the importance of spiritual guidance in the medieval scheme of things, the medieval man does not begin his own story by a relationship to a human master, as does the twentieth-century Hindu, Paramahansa Yogananda:

> The characteristic features of Indian culture have long been a search for ultimate verities and the concomitant disciple-guru relationship.
> My own path led to a Christlike sage: his beautiful life was chiseled for the ages. He was one of the great masters who are India's truest wealth. Emerging in every generation, they have bulwarked their land against the fate of ancient Egypt and Babylonia.[4]

In China, both a Ming Neo-Confucian, Kao P'an-lung (1562–1626), and a twentieth-century Buddhist, Chen-hua, begin by encountering a spiritual authority. The Confucian then authorizes himself; the Buddhist is authorized by a human master:

> At the age of twenty-five years, when I heard magistrate Li Yüan-chung and Ku Ching-yang discuss learning, I resolved to pursue the quest of sagehood.[5]
> Although I left home to become a monk at fourteen [in 1934], because of havoc wreaked by the War of Resistance against Japan, it was not until my twenty-fifth year [in 1945], that I received my first master's kind permission to set out in search of spiritual instruction.[6]

Whereas the Indian began with a general statement about his tradition, both Chinese autobiographers mention their own acts—"I heard," "I resolved," "I left"—first and then immediately link the acting self with a human spiritual guide. The self-understandings of the individual are differently initiated: for the Indian, in the beginning was the particular character of his civilization; for the two Chinese autobiographers, in the beginning was the human act. For neither of them, as for the medieval European, in the beginning was the universally authoritative God.

For the two Chinese writers, one's meaningful life begins at a precisely definable age. It does not do so either for the medieval cleric or for the Indian holy man, for both of whom meaning begins outside of time. For the Neo-Confucian, meaningful life commences with an intellectual challenge. For the Buddhist, it begins with a spiritual permission. All three

Asian autobiographies considered here—Hindu, Neo-Confucian, and Buddhist—require a human spiritual guide, in the very first sentence, before the life of the author can begin to become meaningful.

These are not typical beginnings in either India or China. From the seventh to the twelfth centuries, there had developed in India an approximation to a native tradition of autobiographical writing, consisting of introductions or post-faces to texts glorifying rulers. A few poets would begin by identifying their own parentage and caste, and then proceed to their studies, and, in some cases, youthful follies, before entering into the main subject, the glorification of the king. The meaning of the poet's life is a little tributary to the great flow of the significance of the king; one ends by immersing oneself in the greatness of the other.

The Mughals, from the fourteenth to the eighteenth centuries, introduced a tradition that was originally alien to India, of autobiographies of rulers and officials, which, partly under Central Asian influence, has remained a part of the Islamic, rather than Hindu, tradition and was written in either Turki or Persian. An Islamic ruler's life starts to be significant when he becomes a ruler, as in the first sentence of Jahāngīr's *Memoirs:* "By the boundless favour of Allah, . . . I ascended the royal throne in the capital of Agra, in the 38th year of my age." Bābur began exactly the same way: "In the name of God, the Merciful, the Compassionate.—In the month of Ramzān of the year 899 (June 1494) and in the twelfth year of my age, I became ruler in the country of Farghāna." It is at the precise moment when Allah, calendar, country, and crown come together that the human meaning of an Islamic ruler begins. God is always invoked as the authorizing principle, not, in the manner of the medieval Christian, as the recipient of a personal confession. From this institutionalized starting point, the Islamic ruler may move through his life (composed of battles, hunts, gifts, punishments, and natural curiosities) like a leisurely river, as does Jahāngīr, or, in the case of Bābur, who had much trouble before he became established, events may come in energetic spurts, interspersed with intrusions of varying geographical environments and exhaustive lists of relatives of important people.

The only premodern autobiography "in one of India's own vernaculars," written in 1641 by Banārasīdāsa, a Jain poet, did not set a pattern. Only in 1832, when Raja Rammohun Roy wrote an autobiographical letter to an English friend at the latter's request, did an explosion of autobiographical creativity occur in India, influenced by European models and written mostly in English.[7] In line with this heavily Westernized tradition the apostle of Hinduism to the West, Paramahansa, identifies "the characteristic features of Indian culture" with a "Christ-like," that is an un-Indian, sage.

In China—where there have been, in various forms, many traditional autobiographical texts preceding any Western or other influences—not everyone commences with exposure to an intellectual influence. Kao's Buddhist contemporary Te-ch'ing (1546–1623) "begins with the usual account of family and origin, but he keeps that part to a minimum and proceeds to his first spiritual crisis, which occurred in his seventh year."[8] The dominant tradition of the Confucian scholar autobiographer, initiated by Ssu-ma Ch'ien in the second century B.C., from which Kao diverged, was to start "with a genealogy of his family, tracing it back . . . to the golden ages of the legendary past." Ssu-ma Ch'ien, however, places an encounter of his family line with authority itself at the beginning of his life story: "In ancient times [an ancestor] was ordered to take charge of the affairs of heaven, while [another ancestor] took charge of those of earth."[9]

From these commands by an unnamed ultimate authority—apparently neither human nor divine, since both men and gods have names, perhaps moral nature itself—Ssu-ma Ch'ien derives his hereditary *obligation* to be the Grand Historian. From the same source he draws the tremendous *authority* of the Chinese scholar: "to take charge of the affairs of heaven and of earth." And the obligation is indistinguishable from the authority, in contrast to the Christian tradition, which assigns the obligation to man and the authority to God. Encounters with authority thus occur at the beginnings of the meaning system of their own personal lives for both Ssu-ma Ch'ien and Kao P'an-lung. But the authority is never clearly divine, and for the Neo-Confucian it becomes purely human and draws its power solely from the spontaneous respect granted to subtlety of understanding.

A type of Islamic autobiography—that of the scholar, usually a lawyer or a physician—that has been prominent from the tenth century on typically either contains close to its beginning some variation of the formula: "I studied with X, the reader of Quran," or lists series of teachers with whom one has studied—as many as possible, as in one fifteenth-century case which named 1,200 in almost 80 locations—immediately after the date of birth (if any) and parentage.[10] The tenth-century physician, ar-Razi, after invoking Allah, at once identifies with a reinterpreted Socrates. Ibn al-Haitham, at the turn of the tenth and eleventh centuries, cites Galen, the Greek physician, immediately after describing the religious doubts of his own youth, and then declares that to him "exactly the same happened."[11]

In contrast, the prototypical European scholar, Abelard, mentions only those teachers he had fought against and vanquished in public debate, and he cites the ancient philosophers and poets only after he has established his own identity.

Against the notion of *beginning in the mind of the teacher*, the medieval European responds in the words of Bernard of Clairvaux: "Begin by considering yourself—no, rather, end by that. . . . For you, you are the first; you are also the last.[12]

III

Autobiographies are crucial documents for a civilization-analytic approach to the self.[13] If nature and society may be regarded as the key images in the psychoanalytic and the sociopsychological conceptualizations of the self, historicity, comparativity, and textuality are the identifying characteristics of the civilization-analytic perception of selfhood.

Historicity here refers to the analytical strategy of viewing the individual self as part of long-term processes of formation and dissolution of collectively created types of selfhood (each with its own symbolic form and dynamic thrust, both in individual lives and as a historical force) and of the encounters, conflicts, and intermixtures between them.

The conviction on which this investigation is based is that the historical formations of self-understanding are best grasped by immersing oneself—both as the experiencer and as the observer—in the most deeply personal and that one's grasp of the shared historical formation is most precisely illuminated by comparing what individuals have revealed of their self-experience with other such statements, earlier, contemporary, and later, from their own civilizational tradition, and by contrasting it with, in some significant respect, comparable cases from other civilizational traditions. *Comparison* is essential for a clear understanding of what a symbolic design, explicitly or implicitly, contains—and what it misses, which is also a part of its definition.

By *textuality* is meant that the story of the self—as distinguished from the life of the organism—must be told by means of the symbolic structures and the directions of signifying movement, which the individual draws from one or another tradition and re-creates for self-comprehension.

A text is a fully developed, sufficient-by-itself symbolic form for capturing the meaning of a particular range of experience. It is not an abstract dimension of experience, a code for guiding certain aspects of it, or a schematic, conversational, or conventional generalization about it, but a "living" effort at a total grasp of that range of experience. The conception allows us to view documents as differing in degrees of textuality.

The creation of the text, even when identifiable individuals produce texts about their consciousness of their own selves, is neither a purely individual nor an entirely conscious act. Even if it is taken for granted that a text is usually a part of a literary tradition (or a point of encounter—or of mutual offense—of several literary traditions), the pressures upon the text exerted, intentionally or unintentionally, by religious and other cultural movements and changing or unchanging power conditions must be considered if the goal is to explain how the text has acquired its distinctive characteristics. But, even more deeply, a text is drawn toward its uniqueness by the basic stance toward life of its author (or authors)—an underlying "my secret to myself," in the words of Saint Bernard—which, in the logic of the psyche, precedes ideological commitment and the choice of political action and decides what kind of a human being one will be within one's ideological commitments and political actions. Without this quality, a text wilts. Without some sense of this quality in the text, its interpretation fails.

The autobiographical text in the strict sense differs from other literary texts, which always retain an autobiographical aspect, not in that the former necessarily provides more informative content or more truthful documentation than the latter, but that it constitutes a firmer, more unconditional (private or public) commitment to a particular way of comprehending oneself. "Fictionalized autobiography" or "autobiographical fiction," in contrast, leave open the possibility of an escape from a binding commitment into a conditional perhaps so-perhaps not so statement, one of several possible statements, by which the author's identity is not responsibly bound.

But precisely because autobiography—particularly autobiography intended for publication—is so firmly committed to a particular mode of self-comprehension, it may be less revealing of those aspects of one's experience of oneself to which one is either less committed or which cannot be firmly grasped, than does fiction, poetry, the visual arts, and music (or even the unintentionally autobiographical strata of religious, philosophical, or scientific thought, legal arguments, and political oratory.)

A text is addressed to an audience, or at least an audience is allowed to have access to it, and therefore it implies a mode of sociability, an attitude toward a set of human beings and a practice of social relations, which is not entirely separable from the self-comprehension of the author of the text. Whereas a literary scholar may be allowed to dwell in the illusion that texts beget texts, for a civilization analyst textuality is, in part, a construction of the experience of sociability. A cultural analysis of the self, even of the individual self in the privacy of one's own mind, requires a *history of sociability* of a people or rather, by now, of several peoples.

The history of sociability can be defined broadly as a reconstruction of changes in the fundamental character of social life and in the basic types of social relations and their cultural meanings. Or it can be conceived narrowly as the reconstitution of changes in the structures, cultural meanings, and psychological experiences of those types of voluntary adult social relations in which some combination of spontaneity, intimacy or respect, mutual enjoyment, and self-revelation (or at least most of these) is expected. To the extent that any social relationship acquires a measure of these qualities, it would then belong to the history of sociability in the narrower sense.

In English and in French, sociability carries the connotations of "civilized sociability" and, unless otherwise qualified, tends to refer to the patterns of association evolved in the seventeenth- and eighteenth-century

French salon and the eighteenth-century English coffeehouse. But what is English or French sociability is precisely what Russian sociability is not.[14]

What is "sociable" in a particular sociocultural setting can only be understood by contrasting it to what is regarded, in that setting, as the opposite of the sociable or as lacking most painfully in it. *Maps of sociability*—which here are considered or implicitly referred to only to the extent to which they enter into the self-comprehensions of the autobiographers—are descriptions of the terrain of socioemotional experience, its boundaries, qualities of actual and imagined interaction with significant participants, and the points of danger in the communities of participation of their authors. An adequate mapping of the sociocultural and psychocultural patterns of sociability should indicate the basic thrusts, the vital metaphors, the underlying tonalities, and the fundamental categories of organization of the social life of an individual, a community, or a civilization in a particular phase of its historical trajectory.

However conceived, the history of sociability (as well as the history of selfhood) constitutes itself as a symphony—or, sometimes, cacophony—of histories. Different groups within a society, and even more so within a civilization, have different histories, which are perhaps only describable in languages of different tonalities. (Conceivably even the "history"—the story of the structural connections and the meanings of its existence over time—of a single continuous group cannot be adequately understood unless it has been described in all the alternative languages of description available to us.) The history of ideas *about* sociability is distinguishable from the history of the *experiences* of sociability, with the socially recognizable rituals of sociability constituting a bridge between ideas and experiences—occasionally so weak and broken down, or so burdened with tollgates and customs agencies, as to become a barrier to communication. And then there are the different realms of experience, the objective world of events, the inner world of moods, sensibilities, dreams, and fears. But the supreme significance of sociability for a symbolic analyst is that experiences of sociability can be read as emblems of the deeper modes of relatedness to what individuals may only darkly sense as existence itself.

Civilizations are, among other things, collections of linked forms of individual existences. Each new form of individual existence, if it becomes visible, if it expresses or establishes some linkage with or resonance to, major elements of the tradition of that civilization, and if it passes the tests of critical evaluation by later generations, enriches and expands the meaning of the civilization within which it arises. Individual existences acquire much of their form from the civilizational designs (including alien ones) among which they are experienced, but civilizations acquire (and constantly reacquire or change) their designs from the forms into which individuals organize their experiences.

If sufficient numbers and distributions of significant autobiographies existed, the overall form (or family of forms) of a civilization could perhaps be reconstructed from a civilization-analytic study of the autobiographical corpus alone. This remains a task for the future development of both the writing of autobiographies and their study in a comparative civilizational perspective. Even on a more limited scale, autobiographies provide the most reliable measure of crucial changes in the human experience of civilizations. Whereas the empirical evidence, as a sampling of the phenomenal world, is forever incomplete, the fundamental structural principles of its organization can be identified even from fragmentary evidence, provided that this evidence is of central importance both (a) for the analytical issue raised and (b) in the sociohistorical setting studied.

Clues to the structures and directions around which particular self-comprehensions are draped are frequently given in (or close to) the beginnings and endings of autobiographical writings. One must read the whole if one wants to understand what connects the beginning with the end. But a close scrutiny of the structures and emotional tonalities of beginnings and endings—the boundary system of personal meanings—is essential.

The beginning of an autobiography reveals assumptions about *what must exist (or occur) before the life of an individual can begin to change into a meaningful story.* An autobiographical ending suggests *into what an individual has been transformed by his passage through the machinery of his life,* what his life signifies to him at the point when he is ready to leave it, as a finished (but perhaps, in later autobiographies, revisable) text, to others.

IV

Abelard, writing *The Story of His Misfortunes* only two decades after Guibert, begins with his intention to console a human friend:

> There are times when example is better than precept for stirring or soothing human passions; and so I propose to follow up the words of consolation I gave you in person with the history of my own misfortunes, hoping thereby to give you comfort in absence.

First a principle of human relations is formulated; only then, guided by this principle, does the acting self appear ("I propose"). The acting self is at once given a sociobiological grounding: "I owe my volatile temperament to my native soil and ancestry and also my natural ability for learning."[15]

Guibert started with his own, but universally obligatory religious act. With Abelard, the starting point becomes secular and voluntary: what must exist before an individual's life can become meaningful is his particular intention in the world and his particular place in nature, and, in the hierarchy of priorities, *intention comes before nature.* The individual must perform an act of his own consciousness before his life can begin to have a describable meaning.

The shape of Abelard's life is no longer the medieval circle *from God to God,* but an upward line from *nature to reason*—traversed at an early age, since Abelard is as powerfully "rational" as a young student as he will ever be. The "modern" (and in some respects "classical") line is then broken, in the traditional manner of the Augustinian Christian,—by a fall into sin, followed by moral regeneration and a determined movement toward God. Only after passing through this crisis is one fully adult. At the end, Abelard, teaching submission to God, is himself as magisterial as ever. He enunciates, he explains what the Absolute demands of everyone:

> Let us then take heart from these proofs and examples, and bear our wrongs the more cheerfully the more we know they are undeserved. Let us not doubt that if they add nothing to our merit, at least they contribute to the expiation of our sins. And since everything is managed by divine ordinance, each one of the faithful, when it comes to the test, must take comfort at least from the knowledge that God's supreme goodness allows nothing to be done outside his plan, and whatever is started wrongly, he himself brings it to the best conclusion. Hence in all things it is right to say to him, "Thy will be done". . . . Farewell.[16]

The autobiography moves from a human principle to a divine principle, but it is addressed not to God (who already knows) but to a person (who needs to be helped by knowledge).

The first half of Abelard's story, with its assertions (from the very beginning) of independent reason, conscience, and (in his late thirties) human love—and of the feudal need for other people in order to fight with them and to master them one after another—seems "modern" (or at least Faustian). In the second half the medieval scheme is reasserted and only God—or rather obedience to God—becomes essential once again. The friend whom Abelard wants to console remains, for the Gothic man, nameless, perhaps a poetic abstraction on the level of the mythology of courtly love. Heloise, who is real, and the source of Abelard's happiness and misery, must hear of his autobiography, by chance, from others.

Among the autobiographers, the closest to a feminine counterpart of Abelard is perhaps Margery Kempe, the fifteenth-century Englishwoman of the entrepreneurial class. An uneducated woman (her autobiography is written for her by a priest, "after the information of this creature"), a visionary and pilgrim to the Holy Land, she proceeds willfully through all her acts, both profane (in the early part of her life) and religious (in the latter part), in utter disregard for the guidance of masculine authorities, both husband and priest, yet always with "full plenteous and abundant tears of high devotion, with great sobbings after the bliss of Heaven. . . ."[17] She begins not with her intentions (women autobiographers rarely do) but, in contrast to Abelard, immediately in nature: "When this creature was twenty years of age, or some deal more, she was married to a worshipful burgess (of Lynne) and was with child within a short time, as nature would."

Beginning in nature carries a different meaning to the laywoman of the bourgeoisie (fruitfulness of the body) than it did to the male clerical scholar of noble descent (inheritance of mental capacity and of character). She is then vividly reminded by the devils, on somatically appropriate occasions, of her sinfulness:

> And when she was at any time sick or dis-eased, the devil said in her mind that she should be damned because she was not shriven (confessed) of that default. . . . she saw. . . . devils opening their mouths all inflamed with burning waves of fire, . . . pulling her and hauling her, night and day. . . .[18]

Then comes a saving vision of Christ, several backslidings (inspired by pride and lust) followed by failures in the world, and a final conversion to a life of chastity, thrice-daily confessions, and religious pilgrimages. But in going on these pilgrimages, she is so far from humbly accepting the leadership of her spiritual guides (as a good Christian woman should have) that, upon return, she has to try hard to persuade them to accept her back into their fold.

> . . . . your confessor hath forsaken you, because ye went over the sea, and would tell him no word thereof. Ye took leave to bring your daughter to the sea side; ye asked no leave any further. There was no friend ye had that knew of your counsel; therefore I suppose ye will find but little friendship when ye come there!. . . . When she was come home to Lynne, she made obedience to her confessor. He gave her sharp words, for she . . . had taken upon herself such a journey without his knowledge. Therefore he was moved the more against her, but Our Lord helped her so that she had as good love of him, and of other friends after, as she had before, worshipped be God. Amen.[19]

Friendship, for a woman in this pre-Renaissance, bourgeois environment, was contingent upon her acceptance (or appearance of acceptance) of male guidance.

In her (or her priest's) interpretation, Margery Kempe is but a battleground between God and the devil. But there is in her story an individual willfulness, in the end accepted even by the authorities, that distinguishes her from what we might conceive of as the strictly "Medieval"—or, to borrow from the history of art styles, Romanesque—woman. (There were similarly willful women among the saints of the Catholic church from at least the thirteenth century on.[20] These women can be viewed as tending toward the Gothic type of self-comprehension, of which, among the autobiographers, Abelard is the only full-fledged representative.) In the idea, however, that there is internal development in a person's life and that this development begins solely from a sense of sin and willing acceptance of God's punishment for it, Margery Kempe—like Abelard—is still close to the medieval type of self-comprehension.

No approximation to the Gothic type of man, with his upward line of spiritual development, his passion and his guilt, and his sense of the supremacy of the individual based on his reason and his conviction alone, is to be found in the autobiographies of Abelard's Islamic contemporaries and status equals, Usāma and Umāra, a literate feudal knight and a businessman-courtier-poet. (Umāra begins his autobiography by envisioning the question: ". . . who are you? And to which nest are you going home to rest?"—referring, in the manner of a Hellenic poet-autobiographer, to his homeland.)[21] A type of man comparable to Abelard does not exist at any time in Islamic autobiography, which is also virtually devoid of women.

The Western autobiographer never goes home at the end in a secular, purely wordly, and objective sense. He rises to God, or concludes with his own chosen mission or insight, or is interrupted (as also happens to the independent man of action, such as the Islamic ruler, in other autobiographical traditions) in midpassage. Religious autobiographers—and some secular ones, who are primarily men and women of thought and not, or not only, of action—tend to frame their life within a "meaningful beginning" and a "proper conclusion." For the man of independent action, there is no proper conclusion; he is merely interrupted in midstride. His life is forever incomplete, and there is as much still to be done as he has already accomplished. A "proper conclusion" to his life story, in which the meaning of his life is definitively summarized or encapsulated so that the author can, in good conscience, part with it—seems to be an unfailing indication of the presence of the man of thought inside the man of action. Death before concluding is essential to the man of action (and to the eighteenth- and nineteenth-century "man of feeling"), accidental—and contrary to the logic of his life—to the man of thought.

The conclusion of going home is rare in any autobiographical tradition, but, among non-Westerners and twentieth-century Jews, approximations of it do occur. In the main thrust of the West, *You Can't Go Home Again;* the takeoff has torn you away from your natural roots.

V

Since Abelard, a secular origin of the self becomes a structural characteristic of Western autobiographies outside of the continuing tradition of medieval self-comprehensions. But the desire, which Abelard expresses, to help, with his self-revelation, another person, disappears from the points of origin of Renaissance autobiographies, in which the act of self-description no longer needs either a religious or an emotional justification, and which are addressed not to an *intimately known person* who suffers, but to the *general public* of cultured humanity who read books and admire the works of art and science and impressive individual deeds of whatever kind.

The "self" is a communicative message. Changes in the addressee to whom one speaks about oneself are therefore as important in the history of self-comprehensions—and in a properly conceived psychology of the self— as are changes in the metaphors one uses to describe oneself. Can people who report about their selves to psychoanalysts have the same kinds of selves as do people who open up only to their friends of a lifetime? Do individuals who reveal their selves by explicit verbal statements compose their beings into the same modes of selfhood as do people who express their selves only through their actions or the movements of their bodies or by their silent noncomplicities with the secret-police interrogator?

The Renaissance culture is a fusion, not always harmonious, of bourgeois craftsmanship and aristocratic pride, merging in the supreme ideal of artistic excellence. This ideal was later reduced, in the aristocratic culture of seventeenth-century France, to the aspiration of an otherwise unproductive individual making of his visible person a coolly admirable work of art, an ideal taken over, in a literary form, by the nineteenth-century dandy.[22] But in the Renaissance, one had to *produce* tangible achievements to be adjudged worthy of recognition.

Benvenuto Cellini in 1558 begins:

> All men of whatever quality they be, who have done anything of excellence, or which may properly resemble excellence, ought, if they are persons of truth and honesty, to describe their life with their own hand. . . .[23]

Cellini declares an obligation to mankind to report truthfully on one's achievements; a sophisticated sense that achievements may either substantively be or only perceptually resemble that which is worth talking about (although he can make the distinction, it does not matter to the Renaissance man so long as resemblance to the real thing is sufficiently "proper"), and that it is with their own hands, in the manner of the literate craftsman that people grasp the truth and reveal it to others.

Cellini establishes a universal purely human norm obligatory for all before he can start, in accordance with that general norm, to glorify himself. The traditional Chinese and especially Japanese autobiographer tends to be more modest. The early Islamic autobiographer, who is not always above praising himself, does so either in order to celebrate the glory of Allah who has showered such gifts on him or by simply declaring, with the tenth-century geographer al-Mukaddasi, his own quantitative inexhaustibility: "No single library, great or small, have I left unused, no theological direction which I have not studied, no pious man with whom I have not associated, no preacher whom I have not heard until I have discovered what to learn I had come." al-Mukaddasi absorbs everything worth doing in the world (which for him is identical with the world of Islam) into what he has done. The Renaissance self-glorifier is both more sober in his factuality of statement and more universalistic in his principled insistence that *not merely I, but all men who have done as much* are in duty bound to speak of themselves with the same pride with which I am reporting my achievements. The achievements might, for the Renaissance man, include murder.

Renaissance autobiographers report what their religious tradition would regard as serious moral transgressions or deficiencies, whereas al-Mukaddasi declares he has done everything that travelers have to do, "except for the craft of begging and heavy sins."[24] The Westerner is, throughout the history of his autobiography, more inclined than all other traditional autobiographers, except the Chinese during a short period in the sixteenth and seventeenth centuries,[25] to reveal his moral deficiencies. The secular Westerner is so inclined even more than the religious Westerner, who frequently contents himself with a generalized declaration of sinfulness. (Cellini, to be sure, is as proud of his crimes as he is of everything else pertaining to himself.) But nowhere other than in Renaissance Italy can a craftsman, whose prestige derives from the material objects he has produced, at least partly with his own hands, pronounce the proud declarations of Cellini.

Cellini is confident of the excellence not only of his works but also of himself. But the excellence of his self begins from his understanding of the discipline of work from which all human values arise, the differences of quality among these values, and the moral obligation of workmen to be "persons of truth and honesty." The presence in society of an ethic of honorable workmanship is the precondition for the transformation of his life into a significant story. To practice this ethic of workmanship is the chief obligation one owes to other people. The Renaissance autobiographer is not in need of other people except as a public watching him perform (and as utilitarian patrons and allies in what has come to be known, since his time, as "mercantile friendships"—prudently calculated bourgeois relationships).[26] The theatricality of self-revelation becomes more explicit in the seventeenth and eighteenth centuries. For the self-presentations of the Renaissance man, the theatrical audience already exists, but he himself is not yet a theatrical actor; he is still primarily a man who defines himself by his substantive achievements. Women perhaps do not participate in the Renaissance design of selfhood to the same degree as men. In any case, the major sixteenth-century woman autobiographer is Saint Teresa of Jesus, a Spanish nun. Her self-comprehension lies entirely outside of the Renaissance scheme of things.

Cellini's contemporary Girolamo Cardano, at the beginning of *The Book of My Life,* raises questions about the kind of pride Cellini exhibits:

". . . . knowing well that no accomplishment of mortal man is perfect. . . ."
But he also begins with the obligation to truth, not the *personal* "truth and honesty" of Cellini, but *scientifically demonstrable* truth:

> . . . none, of all the ends which man may attain, seems more pleasing, none more worthy than recognition of the truth . . . No word . . . has been added to give savor over vainglory, or for the sake of mere embellishment; rather, as far as possible, mere experiences were collected, events of which my pupils, especially Ercole Visconte, Paulo Eufomia, and Rudolpho Selvatico had some knowledge, or in which they took part.[27]

This is clearly a different conception of what in one's life is worth telling to others: the great deeds, "anything of excellence," in one case, "mere experiences" conceived as objectively demonstrable, consensually verifiable facts in the other. But both Cellini and Cardano begin with a purely secular obligation to tell the truth about their own actions and experiences in the world to a generalized audience *interested not in them as persons but in the events and characteristics of their lives.*

Cellini's autobiography breaks off suddenly with the departure of a duke, the sudden death of a Cardinal, and yet another voyage: "I allowed several days to elapse, until I thought their tears were dried, and then I betook myself to Pisa."[28]. The ending, for the Renaissance man, is merely an accidental interruption of *any* sequence of remarkable acts.

Cardano, in his epilogue, describes himself as he had always been: "a teller of the truth, an upright man, and indebted for my powers to a divine spirit," a man in whom secular and religious motives are inextricably intertwined: "one who has grown old in the love of truth, with which the love of God, the hope of immortal life, the possession of so much distinction and the advantage of wisdom are closely joined. . . ."[29] But God has now been allocated his sphere and human reason its own, and in the last paragraph human reason is given three times as much space as God. The Renaissance scientist both begins and concludes with the truth he can empirically grasp. For Cellini *his own actions* defined the initial as well as the final frontiers of his being. Cardano remains, both at the beginning and at the end, circumscribed by *his own reason.* The meanings of one's life are contained, for the Renaissance man, within these limits. God is no longer the addressee of autobiographical speaking either at the beginning or at the end of one's describable life. Religious themes, instead of providing a clearly defined *ultimate frame* of one's life, as they did for the medieval man, are now structurally *contained within* a frame of secular beginnings and secular endings. Religion ceases to be the totality and becomes a part. At most, religion is so intertwined with the secular as to become a supplementary source of heating for the worldly life: God "sides with those who have true wisdom," says Cardano, subsuming God to rational activity.

The Renaissance man is distinguished, on the one hand, from the medieval man and, on the other, from the Puritan by the absence of an overall symbolic direction, the sense of moving, through the events of one's life, from an origin to a destination. There is, in typical Renaissance auto-biographies, neither the religious story of a fall into sin and spiritual regeneration, nor the psychological story of moral development (or of identity crisis and reconstruction). In Renaissance self-descriptions, men move with Cellini from event to event or with Cardano from theme to theme, but the events constitute a Technicolored film of actions and not a trajectory of internal change, and the themes are placed, side by side, in a filing cabinet of classified memories.[30] Each action, from the creation of works of art to criminal assaults, and each theme, from medical research to encounters with guardian angels, exists on the same level of energetic experience in Cellini, or of the dispassionate dissecting table of Cardano. The Renaissance man moves through a series of temporary centers *in social action,* but *within the subjectivity of his self* he remains uncentered. (Only Cardano has a sense of a vague, undefinable "essence"—a power of his own nature that is there when needed, but which he cannot control by his will—within his self.) If anyone in sixteenth-century Italy had the subtlety of the Chinese, the Renaissance man could describe himself, as the master of ironic psychology, his contemporary Wang Chi (1498–1583) did: "A mere masked rider in a ceremonial procession, where the sleek horses seem most dazzling."[31] A self that sought, by revealing itself, to help another, as Abelard did, could not look like this; a helping intention requires a story with a dramatic design, and perhaps it helps a self acquire such a design.

We leave the Renaissance with a memory of Cellini the *bourgeois prince* as an excellent work of art of his own making, content with the perfection of whatever acts he performs, not altogether unlike John Fitzgerald Kennedy; and Cardano the *bourgeois practitioner* as a careful, calculating, conscientious agent/observer of his own purposes, observing himself while acting, not yet disciplined by the Reformation, not yet capable of resisting the temptation of gambling, but already thrown on his own:

> I prefer solitude to companions, since there are so few who are trustworthy, and almost none truly learned. . . . I question whether we should allow anyone to waste our time. The wasting of time is an abomination.

And: ". . . . I am never more with those I love than when I am alone."[32]

Max Weber's observations about the origins of the inwardly lonely individual in the Protestant ethic need to be revised by taking Cardano, the Renaissance Catholic and a staunch anti-Protestant, into account.

But we cannot allow ourselves to forget Leonardo da Vinci's note to himself:

Movement will cease before we are weary
of being useful
Movement will fail sooner than usefulness.
Death sooner than weariness. I am never weary of being
                                        useful,
. . .   is a motto for carnival.[33]

The sense of ironic distance from the fundamentals of one's own way of life has never wholly departed from the self-consciousness of the bourgeois man.

VI

The secular framing of autobiography is retained by the Puritan divine Richard Baxter. But, in contrast to Renaissance autobiographies, Baxter's is a *religious story* that is told *within the secular frame.* Baxter begins with the social location of his parents, but he at once comes to the critical point: "We lived in a country that had but little preaching at all. In the village where I was born there was four readers successively in six years time, ignorant men, and two of them immoral in their lives, who were all my schoolmasters."[34] Baxter concludes with his arrest and trial in a secular court, but what brings him to court is his religious activity. The world, for the moderate Puritan, *contains* his religious efforts, as it does not for the medieval man. The world contains, however, in the manner of an empirically respected but spiritually empty frame into which religious efforts are to be poured. The world as Cellini's *full frame* of experiences becomes Baxter's *empty frame* for spiritual efforts.

But neither does the moderate Puritan rise from nature to God, as the Gothic man did; his pilgrimage is all circumscribed by society. The Puritan establishes the sociological framing of man, a literary form suggesting that man neither emerges from nature, as in the Gothic scheme of consciousness, nor arises from his own self-sufficient activity, as the Renaissance man tended to think of himself, but rather begins and ends his existence in the world as a product—and perhaps a victim—of society. This *sociologization of the world of man* corresponds to, and perhaps arises from, the Puritan acceptance of the social world (the world of production, government, and the family) as the primary sphere of religious obligation.

John Bunyan represents a radical version of the Puritan self-comprehension. The story of the meaning of his life is prefaced with a reference to an external interference with the performance of his religious task. Although he later wrote a detailed *Relation* of his imprisonment, in the preface to his autobiography Bunyan handles this interruption in such a way that all its characteristics and agents disappear, and only the spiritual mission that has been interrupted is left.

> Children, Grace be with you, Amen. I being taken from you in presence, and so tied up, that I cannot perform that duty that from God doth lie upon us, to you-ward, for your further edifying and building up in Faith and Holiness, &c., yet that you may see my Soul hath fatherly care and desire after your spiritual and everlasting welfare; I now once again. . . . do look yet after you all, greatly longing to see your safe arrival into THE desired haven.[35]

The world, for the radical Puritan, is not a durable frame, which needs to be understood in its own objective character, but an insubstantial occasion for conscious existence and spiritual exercises; and beyond the community of true believers it is altogether worthless.

Bunyan's actual self-description begins with God and social background bundled into one sentence:

> In this my relation of the merciful working of God upon my Soul, it will not be amiss, if in the first place, I do, in a few words, give you a hint of my pedigree, and manner of bringing up, that thereby the goodness and bounty of God towards me, may be the more advanced and magnified before the sons of men.[36]

The lowly social setting of Bunyan's family and his own early sinfulness, which then follow, are worth noting only as a means for glorifying God, who has lifted him up. The "fearful dreams, . . . terrific with dreadful visions," "even in my childhood," connect the radical Puritan to the medieval Catholic.[37] Childhood dreams of religious terror appear, in autobiographies, to be largely a Christian specialty. But these dreams are not as frequent in Puritan autobiographies as some might have expected.

At the end of Bunyan's autobiography is a final, aggressively introspective account of the basic qualities of his religious experience: his sin and God's grace, his dryness of spirit and "joy, that is the sweetest that is mixt with mourning over Christ. . . ." *Grace* concludes, in a bookkeeper's way, with a list of "seven abominations in my heart" by which he is "afflicted and oppressed," and seven good results that his awareness of these abominations produces in him: abhorrence of the self; distrust of one's spontaneous emotions and of one's "inherent righteousness," and a sense of the absolute need for sober, disciplined reliance on God and on Christ's help. When everything is said and done, the radical Protestant is left with a sense, not of an impending return to God, but of the necessity for further efforts in this world (as his secular descendants will later say in concluding their scientific reports: further research is needed).

6. They show me the need I have to watch and be sober;

7. And provoke me to look to God thorow Christ to help me, and carry me thorow the world. *Amen.*[38]

Even for Bunyan, the world contains his spiritual efforts; his self-description moves from "Children" to "through the world." But, for the radical Puritan, *everything* between the first and the last word is "duty from God," "my Soul," "merciful working of God upon my Soul." Bunyan's sense of the world (in contrast to Baxter's) is thin; it is merely a place in which to be religiously active (as it will later become merely a place in which to be scientifically active). But it is still *in the world* that Bunyan, like Baxter, experiences his religious selfhood. If God is mentioned at the beginning or the ending of a Puritan autobiography, it tends to be not God alone, but associated with social institutions, with one's own followers, or (as for Thomas Shepard, one of the first settlers in the new American colonies), with one's wife and child.

What sets Baxter apart from the Renaissance man is not only the centrality of a this-worldly religion in his self-comprehension but also a clear sense of the direction of spiritual development and of the method for pursuing it:

> . . . . I could never from my first studies endure confusion. . . . I never thought I understood anything till I could anatomise it and see the parts distinctly, and the conjunction of the parts as they make up the whole. Distinction and method. . . . But. . . . the soul is in too dark and passionate a plight at first to keep an exact account of the order of its own operations. . . .[39]

Baxter employs the *scientific method* for giving an "exact account" of the "dark and passionate plight" of the soul. By these urgently needed "soul-experiments"—which are no longer the "mere experiences" described by the Renaissance man—the moderate Puritan seeks to understand the "order" of the "operations" of the soul, and thus—through a rational analysis of the passionate depths of his natural condition—to attain a mature spiritual consciousness. The attainment of spiritual adulthood and then acting as it demands in this world constitutes the direction of development of the Puritan self. But the soul-experiments must never end.

The Renaissance man also employed a scientific method for self-understanding, or at least Cardano did. Yet Cardano not only discerned by his scientific method a different pattern of selfhood, he also had a different conception of science, as it might be applied to self-comprehension:

> . . . . even as a net consists of meshes, all things in the life of man consist of trifles repeated and massed together now in one figure now in another like cloud formations. Not only through the very smallest circumstances are our affairs increased, but these small circumstances

ought gradually to be analyzed into their infinitely minute components.[46]

Where the Puritan envisioned passionate chaos rising with a powerful thrust toward an understanding of its ultimate spiritual orderliness, the Renaissance man saw only constantly shifting cloud formations, all equally consisting of assemblies of trifles that could always be dissected into their minutest components. Where the Puritan minister, in the seventeenth century, had attained a conception of science as an *analysis* of dynamic processes of a universal character, the Renaissance physician, in the sixteenth century, still thought of science as a *description* of entities in particular collections.

To understand the man we need to know the conception of science held by a modern European who is reporting to us about himself. (Until Harriet Martineau in the nineteenth century, we need not know the conception of science held by a woman autobiographer to understand her self.) In principle, the conquest of science for the task of self-understanding is accomplished by the Renaissance man and the Puritan. What the future requires is an improvement of that science, but the principle has been established. But whereas Cardano clearly reports *to us,* Baxter does not; his autobiography seems to be addressed to the sectarian community of his fellow-believers and potential converts, not to the general public.

The Puritans believed that everyone should not only keep examining his own spiritual life in his diary or a religious account book but also give public testimonies of one's spiritual experience, especially upon conversion, to the whole community of believers in common (instead of confessing to the priest in the privacy of the confessional, in the earlier Catholic manner, or revealing one's symptoms to the psychoanalyst in the privacy of his medical practice, later on). Puritanism may have made people more isolated in their social relations (everyone's own individual calling mattered most in the practical, everyday life), but it also made people more interested in each other's inner, spiritual experiences. The notion of the morally obligatory public testimony, not before a spiritual leader, but before the whole community as one's witnesses and judges, of a personal experience—the duty to the mutual revelation of inwardness—becomes the most significant single impetus to the explosion of Western autobiography after the Protestant Reformation. Women also participate in this explosion, but in no other tradition do the self-descriptions of women seem to differ less from those of men than among English Puritans. Puritan women present themselves largely as narrower, less elaborate versions of their men.

Close to the beginning of his autobiography, Baxter gives a clue to the sociability of the Puritan:

. . . . though the town was full of temptation. . . . , it pleased God not only to keep me from them, but also to give me one intimate companion, who was the greatest help to my seriousness in religion that ever I had before, and was a daily watchman over my soul. We walked together, we read together, we prayed together, and when we could we lay together. . . . He was the first that ever I heard pray *ex tempore* (out of the pulpit), and that taught me so to pray. And his charity and liberality were equal to his zeal, so that God made him a great means of my good, who had more knowledge than he, but a colder heart.

Yet before we had been two years acquainted he fell once and a second time by the power of temptation into a degree of drunkenness, which so terrified him upon the review. . . . that he was near to despair, and went to good ministers with sad confessions. And when I had left the house and his company, he fell into it again so oft that at last his conscience could have no relief or ease but in changing his judgment and disowning the teachers and doctrines which had restrained him. . . . And the last I heard of him was that he was grown a fuddler and railer at strict men. . . .[41]

The importance of friendship with an equal is coupled in the Puritan's experience with the most profound sense of the fragile character of human sociability. A man can be of "the greatest help" to another at a critical moment of his religious development, but one cannot expect him to endure in his strength and purity of spirit and to continue to be there when one needs him. The "soul friendships" of medieval clerics seem to have been more durable, emotionally effusive, literary—but mainly wanted for self-understanding, not needed to attain religious "seriousness."[42]

Another version of friendship, which was later to be called "romantic friendship," and defined by an eighteenth-century writer (Harriet Bowdler) as "a union of souls, a marriage of hearts, a harmony of design and affection, which being entered into by mutual consent, groweth into the purest kindness and most enduring love," had emerged, on the basis of classical examples, among sixteenth-century aristocrats (Montaigne).[43] Under the impact of Puritanism, romantic friendship becomes, until the end of the eighteenth century, mainly a prerogative of middle-class women, but the autobiographies register, until Rousseau, hardly any trace of it.

The symbolic designs of selfhood both influence and are influenced by the experiences of social interaction of their authors. But a design of selfhood incorporates, or is influenced by, a variety of other elements in addition to social experience. The self has to do not only with society but also (and in some traditions primarily) with moral order and with nature—or, more precisely, with the idea or image of them. The "self," like the "person," is a category derived not from the roles we play in relation to others, but from the cultural traditions of which we partake. A design of selfhood contains and projects forms of sociability (derived in part from social experience, and in part from that in his intellectual history which the author of the design, consciously or unconsciously, affirms or rejects) as one of its essential elements.

Baxter may represent the *early modern* stage of Christian self-comprehension. In addition to giving a secular framing to religious experience, the modern type of Christian self-comprehension (which is neither exclusively Protestant nor characteristic of all Protestants) begins to replace the medieval religious form of movement through one's life as a sequence of *sin and moral regeneration* with a more continuous effort at *clarification of faith and its practical implications against continued uncertainty*, the doubt at the basis of all faith. In this endeavor, adult conversion (or "engagement," or "commitment") becomes central but does not, without further continuous effort, provide sufficient understanding of the direction of one's life. One cannot say, with Cardinal Newman: "From the time that I became a Catholic, *of course* I have no further history of my religious opinions to narrate." (My italics.) A twentieth-century Catholic cannot say this; to him Cardinal Newman, a hero of intellectual nineteenth-century Catholicism, might well appear a bourgeois escapist like Norman Vincent Peale: "I have had no variations to record, and have had no anxiety of heart whatever. I have been in perfect peace and contentment; I never have had one doubt."[44]

With the decline of the fear of hell, the sense of sin also declines. When people run out of sin to fall into they fall into uncertainty. In some recent autobiographies of intensely religious Americans, the medieval pattern of a fall into sin, followed by moral regeneration, is entirely replaced by a *fall into uncertainty* (about the self) *followed by a reconstruction of identity*. Robert A. Raines begins in an encounter group:

> At one point in the conversation a middle-aged psychiatric social worker who was a member of the group looked at me and said, "Bob, I can't tell whether you're for real." Someone else nodded and said, "You seem to smile the same way at everybody. Do you really feel that good all the time?". . . . I felt a sore spot begin moving in me. . . . I've been living that question for nine years. It has taken me nine years to suffer, choose, and struggle my way through a painful transition, to a new place of integrity and wholeness.[45]

Where sin was, in religious autobiographies, uncertainty now is; returning to God means a reconstruction of identity in the middle of one's adulthood, in the process of which one inevitably discards one's wife, who inescapably becomes liberated and acquires a Ph.D. in counseling. This form of religious selfhood, whatever one's religion, seems to arise from a peculiarly American encounter of polite Protestantism with humanistic psychology.

VII

In the second half of the tenth century, a Japanese woman known today only as "the mother of Michitsuna" started describing herself:

"These times have passed, and there was one who drifted uncertainly through them, scarcely knowing where she was." After reviewing twenty years of marriage, she stopped in the middle of a sentence: ". . . I thought of how quickly the years had gone by, each with the same unsatisfied longing. The old, inexhaustible sadness came back. . . ."[46]

This woman of a thousand years ago lived within a repetitive sequence of vanishing times; traveled from her own uncertainty to her own unsatisfied longing without ever having been moved by a decisiveness of her own; had "doubts about the reliability of human affection"; remained, in her own story, nameless. But the various passing moments of her life, occurring as if they had accidentally floated by, are all accented by poems presumed to be spontaneously written on elegant paper.

Seven hundred years later, Matsuo Bashō begins the same specifically Japanese type of autobiographical text, a "poetic diary," in almost the same modality of drifting through time: "The passing days and months are eternal travellers in time. . . . There came a day when the clouds drifting along the wind aroused a wanderlust in me, and I set off on a journey to roam along the seashores." Bashō concludes with a sad departure for yet another journey, in quite a different tonality from the energetic departure with which the European, Goethe, ended his autobiography about a century and a half later:

> And now, though I have not yet recovered fully from the fatigue of my journey, . . . I shall set off once more in a boat. . . .
>
> > Sadly, I part from you;
> > Like a clam torn from its shell,
> > I go, and autumn too.[47]

At the point of beginning of its self-interpretation, a Japanese self looks like a drifting cloud and at the end it dissolves in sadness, whether one stays put, as the courtly woman of the tenth century, or departs, as the seventeenth-century poet, "a restless priest of relatively humble origins."[48]

Tokugawa Japan, only forty years after Bashō, produced a very different self-description, a full-length autobiography by a high official, Arai Hakuseki, in which everything is action and responsibility soberly set forth. The official's autobiography begins with memories of the sobriety and self-restraint of his samurai father:

> . . . . my father, in his seventy-fifth year, was on the point of death with typhoid fever. . . . Afterward my mother asked him why, during his illness, he had always turned away in bed from people and said nothing. He replied: "My headache was very severe, but as I had never betrayed suffering to others, I thought it undesirable to depart from my rule."

Hakuseki concludes with the final assertion of responsible officialhood: his own resignation of office at the death of the Shōgun, an explanation of his position within the division of labor at the top of the administrative structure, an effort to restore the reputation of another high official currently under abuse, and a precise official signature:

> I, Chikugo-no-kami Minamoto Kimmi of the Lower Fifth Rank Second Grade, close this account at about the middle of July 1716.[49]

Two types of self-comprehension existed in Tokugawa Japan: one in which the natural self is sensed as *an indeterminately moving cloud* (a sense that can be traced back continuously at least to the tenth century), the other in which the consciously chosen public self is expressed through the operations, prescribed in ritual and in philosophy, of the *responsible official*. (So far as self-descriptions are concerned, the latter modality seems more recent.) The first talks to her or his self and perhaps a few friends; the second (always a male) gives an official report to posterity. Recent analyses of the Japanese psyche suggest that whereas these two designs of being human may have different histories, the natural self now exists as the fluid inner content within the firm outer shell of the responsible official.

VIII

Chinese autobiography emerges with Ssu-ma Ch'ien, 145–90? B.C., who began at a point where the family line arises from the realm of the legendary:

> In ancient times in the reign of Chuan Hsü, the *Nan-cheng* Chung was ordered to take charge of the affairs of heaven, while the *Pei-cheng* Li took charge of those of earth. . . . During the Hsia and Shang dynasties the same Chung and Li families continued generation after generation to manage the affairs of heaven and earth. . . . In the time of King Hsüan of the Chou [827–781 B.C.] the family lost its position and became the Ssu-ma family. The Ssu-ma family had for generations had charge of the historical records of the Chou.[50]

This hereditary family responsibility becomes the personal identity of the Grand Historian. It is characteristic of the thrust of the generations in the life of the individual that Ssu-ma Ch'ien incorporates a lengthy philosophical text of his father in his own autobiography. The autobiography ends with a celebration of continuity and, implicitly, with a show of the form-giving power of the historian (who had been previously humiliated and punished by castration for an incautious political move):

> [For] a period of some one hundred years, the books that survived and records of past affairs were all without exception gathered together by The Grand Historian. The Grand Historians, father and son, each in turn held and carried on the position.

Ah, I remember that my ancestors once were in charge of these affairs and won fame in the time of T'ang and Yü, and in the Chou they once again managed them. So the Ssu-ma family generation after generation has been the masters of astronomical affairs. Now it has come down to me. This I remember with awe! I remember with awe!

In the end, there is a tremendous assertion of the masterful I, surpassing anything that a Western man (or a Japanese) would say of himself:

> I have sought out and gathered together the ancient traditions of the empire which were scattered and lost; of the great deeds of kings I have searched the beginnings and examined the ends; I have seen their times of prosperity and observed their decline. . . . *I made* the ten "Chronological Tables." Of the changes in rites and music, the improvements and revisions of the pitch pipes and calendar, military power, mountains and rivers, spirits and gods, the relationships between heaven and man, and the faulty economic practices that were handed down and reformed age by age, *I have made* the eight "Treatises." . . . . of them *I made* the thirty "Hereditary Houses." . . . . of such men *I made* the seventy "Memoirs." (My italics)

And yet what the masterful I has declared he has done is nothing but his mode of participation in his family tradition. The I is not detachable from a continuous generational project: "It is the work of one family, designed to supplement the various interpretations of the Six Classics and to put into order the miscellaneous sayings of the Hundred Schools."[51]

A difference between Chinese and Japanese self-comprehensions can be brought out by a comparison of the autobiography of Arai Hakuseki with that of the Chinese official Kao P'an-lung, who finished his autobiography, characteristically entitled "Recollections of the Toils of Learning," in 1614.[52] It begins—untypically for the Chinese—with a reference not to his family line, but to an encounter, at the age of twenty-five, with two scholars who were discussing learning. Kao immediately, and decisively, "resolved to pursue the quest of sagehood." The Japanese official also seeks virtue through Confucian scholarship, but in his autobiography he speaks mainly of his actions in the sphere of administration. The Chinese autobiographer hardly refers to his official acts, but writes of the inner crises of his spiritual development, presenting a distinctive model of developmental psychology for adults.

Kao first experiences the crisis of *constriction* of his spiritual energies by what seems to be narrowly abstract intellectualism ("I was aware only of my vital forces being oppressed and my own person being bound."). He is saved by the discovery of body-mind identity: his mind then expands freely to fill the body. He then undergoes the crisis of *lack of clarity* of perception ("I have not yet perceived anything of the Way"), which is resolved by the recollection of integrity (doing away with what is false by listening with complete sincerity to what comes naturally to him). The final crisis comes from his perception of the *superficiality* of his understanding. Salvation from this crisis comes through passive mystical contemplation on a trip through the countryside of rivers and mountains, where he finally senses a complete merger with all things and cycles of change. Then his mind becomes "clear and peaceful." Further studies—in heterodox traditions, in Buddhism and Taoism—only confirm him in his Neo-Confucian enlightenment. In his later years Kao finally comes to "truly believe," one after another, four essential Confucian principles: the goodness of human nature; the spontaneity of nature that yet needs to be "cared for, watered and fostered" by men if it is to remain natural; the principle of "knowing the root"; and the principle of centrality and normality: "If there is only a slight amount of artifice or contrivance, it will not be ordinary or dependable."

It is Kao's spiritual development, not his official actions, that constitute the meaningful pattern of his life. Another autobiography of the same period, by the Buddhist monk Te-ch'ing is also conceived in this way, but the Buddhist's crises start with an exposure not to scholarship but to the mysteries of death and life, not at age twenty-five but at age seven, and his spiritual development ceases at the age of thirty, while the Confucian's— like the Puritan's—never ends.[53] No Confucian could declare confidently with the eleventh-century Arab scientist Avicenna (Ibn Sina): "By eighteen, I had acquired the knowledge of all sciences and have since then learned nothing new."[54]

Kao concludes not as the disciplined official, which is the proper way for a Japanese official to terminate his accounts, but as a still developing man in need of further efforts at self-perfection:

> The Sage cannot fathom the limits of Heaven and earth. How much less people like us? How can there be a limit [to our efforts]? We should honor human relations, speak with care, act diligently and be cautious unceasingly until the day of our death. In the foils of study the years mount up and the months accumulate with only more difficulties. And still there is nothing sufficient to bring the smile to the face of a wise man. For those who are deficient like me, they may find something useful in my account.[55]

Kao signs off, in a personally toned but nevertheless characteristically late-Confucian manner, with the *dream of the smile of the wise man*. As he began, Kao ends admiring the wisdom of other men. He returns, at a higher level of self-development, the task of his life accomplished, to the starting point that is proper to the secular intellectual. Within this cyclicality of intellectualism, he has progressed from overhearing *words* to the still unrealized possibility of receiving *smiles*. Between the human word and the human smile lies the universe of experience, the Confucian equivalent of the Puritan "sociologization of the world."

As Ssu-ma Ch'ien began and ended with the *family line*, so does Kao P'an-lung, seventeen centuries later, begin and end with *human sages*. The circular form persists, but the familiar rigidity is replaced by the possibility of choice of intellectual "role models." Whether within the natural family line or the voluntary chain of scholarship, the same conception of the task of life is evident: strenuous intellectual effort aimed at ordering "the affairs of heaven and earth" (Ssu-ma Ch'ien), at putting oneself at one "with the Great Transformation until there was no differentiation between Heaven and man, exterior and interior" (Kao P'an-lung). Under the influence of Buddhism and Taoism, a contemplative attitude toward the universe replaced, in the Neo-Confucian, the managerial attitude of the old Confucian, but the goal of *ordering* man and the universe in a single coherent scheme by human understanding remains. However, the four "true believings" of Kao displace the four "makings" of Ssu-ma Ch'ien. The Neo-Confucian has a less tough self-confidence in his mastery.

Why is friendship, which is persistently celebrated by the Chinese poet, never central to the self-comprehensions of the Confucian autobiographer (almost always a man), even though he both read and wrote this poetry?[56] Perhaps because self-comprehension was conceived as a primarily ethical task, and the deep feelings that were allowed in friendship flowed outside of the ethical seriousness of continuing one's tradition and of spiritual development within it. The meaning of one's life is locked up within this seriousness. Whatever allows for a liberation from this seriousness does not belong to the meaning of one's life.

IX

The Renaissance autobiographer was usually a member of the higher bourgeoisie—an independent professional of note engaged in the practice of arts or sciences for sale to his clients, and usually sponsored, to a greater or lesser extent, by the upper classes. Upper-class sponsorship of the bourgeois autobiographer disappeared in mid-seventeenth-century England, where it was replaced by encounters with a religious revolutionary elite (and where the autobiographer was, in any case, more a member of a religious movement than of a social class). The eighteenth-century continental European autobiographer still depended, with very few exceptions, on upper-class sponsorship at some time during his life, but his cultural aspirations, under the influence both of Protestantism and of the Enlightenment, became more independent of the aristocracy than they were in the Renaissance. Outside of Benjamin Franklin in the United States (and the earlier cases of Margery Kempe and a few European Jews, where, again, religion was more important than social class in shaping self-comprehensions), it is only in the nineteenth century that the wholly independent bourgeoisie furnished its own autobiographers. They can therefore, more than earlier autobiographers, be presumed to express some approximation to a "purely" bourgeois point of view. But this "point" not only stretches from the liberal to the romantic (and beyond), but also changes over time (and persists even while the bourgeoisie, in its classical form, comes close to disappearing).

The self-comprehensions of distinguishable individuals are influenced, but not determined, by their social positions, and the primary problem, even for the social scientist, is not to account for the specificity of these comprehensions, but to describe them adequately. Indeed the most urgent need of sociology at present is to acquire a capacity for an adequate description of the symbolic structures of individual and collective experience that is *sensitive enough to register their constantly ongoing changes, interactions, and conflicts.*[57] Only a sufficient understanding of the processes of symbolization in history—and in comparative perspective—can provide, or serve as the necessary basis for providing, their explanation. The social conditions in which individuals and groups conduct their existences only soften or harden, fracture or promote encounters between, the symbolic forms that they elaborate for comprehending themselves; social conditions—as well as intellectual histories—provide much raw material for the shaping of such symbolic forms; but social conditions do not determine the overall character and the inner energy of a fully elaborated symbolic design.

Both Rousseau and John Stuart Mill, like Abelard many centuries earlier, begin their autobiographies, in the hallowed European manner, by declaring their intentions. Mill even shares with Abelard the intention, by the disclosure of his self, to help others. But here the similarities end.

Rousseau, the Romantic, in the very first line, asserts himself as an individual agency: "*I have resolved. . . .*", a beginning in which one hears echos of Guibert's: "*I confess. . . .*" Mill, the liberal, starts with the burden of the impersonality of a generalizing scholar: "*It seems proper . . .*"—not so differently from Abelard's: "*There are times. . . .*"[58] The intention of Rousseau in speaking about himself is to reveal his uniqueness. It is his moral duty and high enterprise to tell the truth, not about his acts, but about his feelings. Revealing the uniqueness of the feelings of a single individual, who is extraordinary only in his honesty, is so important to others that they must *all* listen. This peculiar idea looks like a fusion, on the one hand, of the public testimonials of the Puritans—who laicized Saint Augustine—and, on the other hand, of grand theater. (Both of these models were unavailable to secular autobiographical writings in non-Western societies, until they could be translated in the twentieth century, from Western languages.)

The theatrical staging of self-revelation may be characteristic of one type of *eighteenth-century*, rather than of specifically *Romantic*, self-comprehension: Casanova, the Sensualist, shares this characteristic with Rousseau. But the Sensualist's audience is attending a comedy, Casanova conceiving his autobiography as a "most worthy subject for laughter";[59] the Romantic's audience is witnessing a tragedy. Casanova's public is a well-bred one, seeking above all to be amused; Rousseau's public is, at the beginning, humanity as a whole, needing to be shaken up whether it wants it or not. The Sensualist-Romantic distinction overrides what is frequently assumed to be a correlation between comedy and democracy, tragedy and aristocracy.

But for the eighteenth-century Romantic, the theater was the form of his reporting about himself to his audience, not the form of his life; and for both the Romantic and the Sensualist, it was a *theater of their own, entirely human, making*. In contrast, with a greater depth of vision, the quintessential European, Goethe, perceives aspects of a puppet show in his life itself. A gift of a puppet theater—the last gift of his grandmother—is mentioned early in his autobiography. Goethe's most important work is described in that imagery: "The significant puppet-show fable of the latter [*Faust*] resounded and vibrated manytoned within me."[60]

Goethe's preface explicitly states the view of one's life as a *plaything of time* and this view is illuminated at both ends of the autobiographical text.

> . . . . the century . . . sweeps both the willing and the unwilling along with it, determining and forming them, so that it can truthfully be said that any man, had he been born a mere ten years earlier or later, might, as far as his own formation and his outward achievements are concerned, have become an entirely different person.

The beginning is an astrologically controlled performance of nature, within which the individual is embedded:

> On the 28th of August, 1749, at midday, as the clock struck twelve, I came into the world, at Frankfort-on-the Main. My horoscope was propitious: the sun stood in the sign of Virgin, and had culminated for the day; Jupiter and Venus looked on him with a friendly eye, and Mercury not adversely; while Saturn and Mars kept themselves indifferent; the moon alone, just full, exerted the power of her planetary hour. She opposed herself, therefore, to my birth, which could not be accomplished until this hour was passed.

The conclusion is a departure, at which the eternally youthful Goethe is moved deeply enough to become an actor declaiming from his own play, *Egmont*:

> Child! child! no more! The coursers of time, lashed, as it were, by invisible spirits, hurry on the light car of our destiny; and all that we can do is in cool self-possession to hold the reins with a firm hand, and to guide the wheels, now to the left, now to the right . . . whither it is

hurrying, who can tell? and who, indeed, can remember whence he came?[61]

Goethe had begun in his natural embeddedness, within a universal mechanism governing everyone (his equivalent of our beliefs in the character-shaping power of the family drama); he concludes carried by the mysterious energies of his individual destiny toward his creative tasks. His life moves from universal determinism to a particular determination, from mechanism to energy, from childhood to youth. But both at the beginning and at the end the key image is *time*, which first determines in a generally knowable manner, and then drives toward the uniquely unknown. The conscious individual, for Goethe, in all his experiences and hopes—ceaseless striving and "cool self-possession"—is a puppet moved by partly knowable, partly mysterious time. Where for Rousseau and for Casanova theater was a form of sociability, for Goethe, an individual by cosmic necessity, it was the manner in which the universe treated man, a mystery of nature.

With Goethe, Western self-comprehensions cease to be located in either God-related (medieval) time or the individual's purely biographical (Renaissance) time defined by his own actions and become embedded in *historical time*, in the transformations of society and culture in which the individual participates. The individual is made not by his biological heritage or group identifications, nor by his intentions or his individual achievements, but by an interaction of cosmic determination and the inexorable, but open-ended historical transformations of social reality.

Henry Adams, less than a century later, and on the American east coast, locates himself even more exclusively in historical time. But he is no longer attuned to historical change and time has ceased, for him, to be open-ended. Natural vitality is diminished, the sense of mystery within the puppetry of one's life disappears. One becomes a late Roman intellectual. And the individual's "Ego" turns out to be merely a "manikin" around which his educational experiences—"the toilet of education"—are to be draped. The core of the self must be presented *as if it had been alive*, if it is to serve adequately in the education of others.

> The manikin . . . has the same value as any other geometrical figure of three or more dimensions, which is used for the study of relations. For that purpose, . . . it must have the air of reality; must be taken for real; must be treated as though it had life. Who knows? Perhaps it had![62]

The author hopes he may have been alive at the center of his describable being—a concern that becomes central only in the self-descriptions of the upper and middle classes in the nineteenth century who felt alienated from history.

Adams' contemporary Booker T. Washington, a representative of the rising underclass (or quasi-caste), moves through historical change in the opposite direction from that of the son and grandson of presidents, knowing not when he was born (an uncertainty shared by nineteenth-century American Negro slaves with several twentieth-century African political leaders, Oginga Odinga as well as Kwame Nkrumah), Booker Washington concludes with a reception for the president of the United States in the educational institution he has himself founded, the Tuskegee Institute.[63] He has arrived, in perfect tune with what he regards as the historical process of reconciliation of the races and the inevitable recognition of individual merit. But to whom does the future of the sense of time belong? For a powerful current of Western consciousness, it has belonged to Rousseau's *subjective time*. It is in reaction against a surfeit of subjective times that the twentieth century will once again initiate a search for timeless forms of self-comprehension, a family of "mythological consciousnesses" transcending both history and the ecstatic vivisections of purely individual subjectivity (Mircea Eliade).

There is a deceptive similarity between the Romantic and the Sensualist which, if looked closely into, helps reveal the fundamental difference between these two eighteenth-century modes of self-comprehension. Like Rousseau, Casanova defines his mode of being by his ability to feel ("I know that I have existed . . . because I have felt"; "I have all my life acted more from the force of feeling than from my reflections").[64] But the Romantic analyzes his feelings and their stormy contradictions, the intense sufferings that they cause him, and the exorbitant costs of living by his emotions, and he unfolds a wide and volatile range of feelings. For the Sensualist, his feelings are like the other utensils he employs to the practical purposes of his life: the same feelings, within a narrow range, get used again and again, from adolescence into old age, without change, without analytical dissection, without one emotion ever challenging or clashing with another, but with much cleverness in fitting the details of the employment of the generally available feelings to the particularities of the situation in which they are to be used. What Casanova describes of his life consists not of feelings, but of acts expressing high craftsmanship in pleasure seeking. In his self-definition, in theory, Casanova is thus, on the surface, close to Rousseau; in his self-description, in practice, he is, in somewhat greater depth, not far from Cellini. Casanova reveals himself as a belated Renaissance adventurer, with only his body as a tool for practicing his art; he appears only to himself, in a comedy of his making, as a sensitive rationalist.

No one could be more dissimilar from the eighteenth-century continental libertine than the nineteenth-century English liberal of nonconformist Protestant origins. John Stuart Mill's starting intention is first to be useful to those concerned with the improvement of education, and second to:

> . . . make acknowledgment of the debts which my intellectual and
> moral development owes to other persons; some of them of recog-
> nized eminence, others less known than they deserve to be, and the
> one to whom most of all is due, one whom the world had no opportu-
> nity of knowing,—[65]

his wife. It is worth noting that the paradigmatic liberal, the defender of
individual rights, locates himself at once within a bond of gratitude—
declares himself *bound* by the most voluntary of emotional ties—to others.

Whereas the liberal, at the starting point of his selfhood, places his
voluntary, but durable, boundedness to others, the libertine, Casanova,
had announced his *freedom:*

> I begin by declaring to my reader that, by everything good or bad
> that I have done throughout my life, I am sure that I have earned
> merit or incurred guilt, and that hence I must consider myself a free
> agent.[66]

Whereas the secular liberal had begun with his intention to be *useful to
others,* the libertine, practicing an inverse utilitarianism, seeks out what
might be *useful to him,* and (at the start of a career in seductions) finds it in
religion: "I am not only a monotheist but a Christian whose faith is
strengthened by philosophy, which has never injured anything. . . . Despair
kills; prayer dissipates it; and after praying man trusts and acts." Whereas
the liberal could recognize what others had contributed to his development, the libertine is of his own making, a self-producing artifact,
obligated by itself to be in love with itself: "I have rejoiced in my ability to
be my own pupil, and in my duty to love my teacher."[67]

The eroticization of the self by the self—man playing God loving Himself—is saved from Satanism only by the clear perception of the Sensualist
that he is god only in a comedy. But he has to attract the love of as many
others as he can to keep being the *god* of self-love, even in a comedy.
(Indeed it is only a god in a comedy who needs to measure his own vitality
by the numbers of adherents he attracts.) The need of the rootless Sensualist, floating through society as the winds of fortune move him, to love
himself, with an ever-fresh awareness of the sensation of this love, makes
him a perpetually avid consumer of others loving him. In Casanova's view,
it has been uniformly pleasant for all women he has seduced to have served
as the means of convincing him that he loved himself sufficiently. Of "human dignity" there cannot be much in a comedy anyway.

In explaining their intentions, both Rousseau and Mill reveal their
fundamental assumptions about the sources of their being. The eighteenth-century Romantic presents himself as a unique product of nature,
the nineteenth-century liberal as the product of an unusual, but potentially
universalizable education. Neither is a self-producing artifact. The Romantic speaks of what he *is* as nature made him; the liberal speaks of what he

has become by social shaping: "my intellectual and moral development," which "owes to other persons. . . ." (There is also a secular Catholic tradition of autobiography as "ethical and intellectual development"—Vico, Croce—but it is propelled mainly by a struggle with texts, essentially an overcoming of antiquarianism by the spirit of scholarship.) In contrast to the Puritan, there is no consciously chosen, self-directed development during the adulthood of the Romantic, only, on the one hand, Rousseau's "succession of feelings"—not conscious choices or strenuous efforts— "which marked the development of my being," and, on the other hand, changes in his relationship to society.[68] The "nature" of his emotions always remains pure, crystal clear to himself, and their expression utterly spontaneous, but he first flounders in a corrupt society (which corrupts his actions as well), then speaks powerfully in efforts to reform it, and then withdraws from it again in apparent defeat.

The nineteenth-century Romantic (from *Die Nachtwache des Bonaventura* in 1804 on) replaced the childlike sincerity thrust of the relationship to society with an adult multitude of masks, which, in their artificiality, become the only means of communication through which the no longer tangible "nature," the "nothingness," of the self can be expressed. The —quite appropriately—anonymous author of *Die Nachtwache* wrote: "It is indeed terribly lonely in the ego, when I clasp you tight, you masks, and I try to look at myself—everything echoing sound without the disappeared note— nowhere substance, and yet I see—that must be the Nothing that I see!— Away, away from the I—only dance on, you masks!"[69] Later on, masks are found particularly prominent in the autobiographies of twentieth-century American blacks:

"Malcolm X moves from one mask to another. . . . He is variously known as Malcolm, Malcolm Little, Homeboy, Detroit Red, a prison number, even Satan, until he reaches the identification of Brother which to him is not a mask, but himself. . . . Both in black autobiography and fiction the final discarding of masks is a character's primary goal because such an act is a demonstration of selfhood and freedom. . . . When the appeal is not answered, as it usually is not, something curious, in the Lewis Carroll sense, happens to the heroes of black autobiography; they disappear.[70]

The eighteenth-century Romantic felt himself identical with his nature, which society could not understand; the nineteenth-century Romantic sought to make himself understood by himself through the intense language of artificial ecstasies—or experimental epiphanies—which he presented to society. (From the latter perspective, the eighteenth-century Romantic could also be interpreted as having done this, by donning the supremely crafted mask of total masklessness, but he was not conscious of doing it, as the nineteenth-century Romantic, particularly in Germany, was.) Tnis change is best revealed, however, in literary and theoretical, rather than autobiographical writings, if, for a nineteenth-century Romantic—and his heirs—they can be distinguished as separate genres. (The present tendency to interpret everything as autobiographical is an expression of a late-Romantic attitude.) Out of these masks, the defense mechanisms of the psychoanalysts evolved. But a "defense mechanism" captures only one function of the mask. The Romantic's mask is both a "defense mechanism" and an "analysis"—a perhaps more wholesome condition that must disintegrate, or prove impossible to sustain, for psychoanalysis to become necessary.

The eighteenth-century Romantic could only reveal the unmanageable vicissitudes of "the history of my soul." The English liberal had inherited from the Puritan the directionality of "intellectual and moral development" (the priority of the "intellectual" is not accidental) as the symbolic shape of his life and secularized it. But there is a price to be paid for the single-minded pursuit of rationality, responsibility, and self-control, a price of which the liberal was fully conscious as in Mill's depression and Charles Darwin's: "I have attempted to write the following account of myself, as if I were a dead man in another world looking back at my own life," his horror at having lost, through a surfeit of science, his capacity to respond to poetry and music: "My mind seems to have become a kind of machine for grinding general laws out of large collections of facts. . . . This curious and lamentable loss of the higher aesthetic tastes. . . ."[71]

How different is this from the pleasure in self-description of the eighteenth century, more conservative Englishman: "*My own amusement* is my motive and will be my reward," begins Edward Gibbon, immediately after referring to "the completion of a toilsome and successful work" and an expression of commitment to "truth, naked unblushing truth. . . ." (My italics).[72] Benjamin Franklin, Weber's prototype of the secularized Puritan, mentions "pleasure," as no one else does, in the very first line of his autobiography and concludes its first paragraph: ". . . . in many Cases it would not be quite absurd if a Man were to thank God for his Vanity among other Comforts of Life."[73] The Anglo-French hedonism of the eighteenth century made it possible for the highly disciplined worker to indulge himself in the story of his self-disciplining, as the nineteenth-century man no longer can.

Gibbon was writing primarily for himself, then for a few friends, and even less so perhaps, for "the public eye."[74] Both Rousseau and Mill address their autobiographies to potentially universal audiences. Rousseau speaks to humanity as a whole that is expected to respond emotionally as one does to a theatrical performance: "let the numberless legions of my fellow man gather around me, and hear my confessions. Let them groan at my depravities, and blush for my misdeeds."[75] For the Romantic, universal humanity consists of the *audience for the sacred theater of his soul.* (We note here that whereas Nietzsche's experience of the self, revealed in the philosophical texts which constitute fragments of perhaps the greatest autobiography since Saint Augustine, is quite different from Rousseau's, Nietzsche's *conception of his audience* and of his relationship to his audience is of the same structural type as Rousseau's: for Nietzsche too, universal humanity consists of the audience for the sacred theater of his soul.)

In contrast to the Romantic, the liberal speaks to the reader who is soberly interested in the subject under discussion, whoever he may be: "The reader whom these things do not interest, has only himself to blame if he reads further, and I do not desire any other indulgence from him than that of bearing in mind, that for him these pages were not written."[76] For the liberal, universal humanity appears as a *public debating society consisting of reasonable men*. Not only the addressee to whom one speaks but also the image of the addressee one has influences not only the manner of self-presentation but the very character of what is conceived of as essential to the self. For the liberal, the self is what it is appropriate to tell about oneself to a rational debating society. For the Romantic, the self is what demands to be displayed—or dramatically sacrificed—to a world felt to be a sacred theater of the soul. And for a type of twentieth-century man, the self is what standardized psychological tests allow for.

Neither Rousseau nor Mill addresses their autobiographies, to any extent, to those who have been (and, in Mill's case, remain) closest to him. This has much to do with their conceptions of sociability. Both separate the public and the private spheres of sociability quite sharply, but in wholly different ways. The liberal identifies himself strongly and clearly with various public causes, but *nothing* of his most important adult relationships, at the center of which is his egalitarian marriage, is revealed to others, except their public aspects (e.g., joint publications). The Romantic avoids, with horror, any public cause and organized group ("My mortal hatred for everything that went by the name of party, faction or cabal kept me free and independent, without any bonds but the affections of my heart").[77] But he uncovers what he regards as *all* of his experience of intimate sociability.

The core of intimate sociability, for the Romantic, consists of an unfulfilled search for ecstatic fusion: "for intimate companionship . . . only two souls in the same breast could have sufficed. Failing that, I always felt a void." The fusion sought, however, is not mutual (as was its equivalent in Mill's marriage), but achievable only through total absorption of the other into the God-like self: "the single idea that I was not everything to her caused her to be almost nothing to me."[78] The exorbitant ideal of total intimacy translates into repetitive cycles of exhilaration and collapse, impetuosity and annihilation. The liberal's autobiography must be addressed to the general public since he does not speak in public of what is firmly private. The Romantic's autobiography has to be addressed to an audience of strangers since he cannot sustain his friendships long enough to speak of friendship to his friends.

We must point to the presence (quite possibly, a *necessary* presence), in the autobiographies of the Romantic and the liberal, of elements of the opposite type. For the Romantic's self-comprehension, it is important to know oneself to be both the free citizen of a democracy and a self-supporting craftsman, proud in his independence and in his refusal of the king's pension. The liberal falls, at the age of twenty, into a severe depression when he tries to imagine the fulfillment of his rationalistic program of social reform and is saved from his depression only by Romantic poetry, the thought of his father's death, and his love for Harriet Taylor. His liberal elements give firmness to the volatile self-comprehension of the Romantic; his Romantic elements inject emotional vitality into the liberal's organization of the self that is otherwise so prudential, so restrained, that Mill could declare in *On Liberty,* "That so few now dare to be eccentric marks the *chief* danger of the time." (My italics.)[79]

There were women liberals in nineteenth-century England, and it is curious that whereas Mill's life evinces a secular, and almost closed, circularity (from books, etc. to books and an intellectual family), the pattern of an individual's life as a rigorously progressive development is found, more clearly than in any man's, in *Harriet Martineau's Autobiography.* This autobiography is conceived of as a secular last confession of a dying woman of a Huguenot background, who has "from my youth upwards . . . felt that it was one of the duties of my life to write my autobiography." She was nursed by "a Methodist or melancholy Calvinist of some sort," and her childhood was filled with a fear of nature, of people, and of her own body.

> Milk has radically disagreed with me . . . till I was old enough to have tea at breakfast, I went on having a horrid lump at my throat for hours of every morning, and the most terrific oppressions at night. Sometimes the dim light of the windows in the night seemed to advance till it pressed upon my eyeballs, and then the windows would seem to recede to an infinite distance. If I laid my hand under my head on the pillow, the hand seemed to vanish almost to a point, while the head grew as big as a mountain. Sometimes I was panic struck at the head of the stairs. . . . The starlight sky was the worst; it was always coming down, to stifle and crush me, and rest upon my head. . . . To the best of my belief, the first person I was ever not afraid of was Aunt Kentish, who won my heart and my confidence when I was sixteen.

From vivid childhood horrors, adulthood is an abstracted liberation through secular reason. When Martineau thinks she is dying, she soberly concludes:

> I need not say that one's interests in regard to one's race, and to human life in the abstract, deepen in proportion to the withdrawal of one's own personal implication with them. Judging by my own experience, one's hopes rise, and one's fears decline as one recedes from the action and personal solicitude which are necessary in the midst of life,

but which have a more or less blinding and perturbing influence on one's perception and judgment. . . .

When our race is trained in the morality which belongs to [scientifically] ascertained truth, all "fear and trembling" will be left to children; and man will have risen to a capacity for higher work than saving themselves,—to that of "working out" the welfare of their race, not in "fear and trembling," but with serene hope and joyful assurance.[80]

More remained in the twentieth century of Mill's narrow cyclicality than of Martineau's rigid progressiveness. But in taking up the terrors of childhood (where the radical Puritan had left them) as the starting point of her self-comprehension Harriet Martineau is a pioneer of a twentieth-century Western sensibility.

In the conclusion of Rousseau's *Confessions,* the audience, which initially was to have encompassed the whole of humanity, contracts (one hopes not in anticipation of the ultimate destination of Romanticism) to a group of five aristocrats in a salon soon to fall to the French Revolution, and Rousseau, like an actor after a performance, peeps through the curtain to observe its effects:

> Thus I concluded my reading, and everyone was silent. Mme d'Egmont was the only person who seemed moved. She trembled visibly but quickly controlled herself, and remained quiet, as did the rest of the company. Such was the advantage I derived from my reading and my declaration.[81]

In Rousseau's last autobiographical text, *Reveries of the Solitary Walker,* the scene changes to a setting without physical qualities, an interior state of mind, and the actor is no longer conscious of being observed by anyone but himself. Rousseau still intends, as at the beginning; he no longer feels in the present moment, as throughout most of the *Confessions,* but remembers, in gratitude, a woman, long dead, he had met fifty years earlier.

> Today, Palm Sunday, it is exactly fifty years since I met Madame de Warens. . . . There is not a day when I do not remember with joy and living emotion that one short time in my life when I was myself, completely myself, unmixed and unimpeded, and when I can genuinely claim to have lived. . . . Were it not for that short but precious moment, I should perhaps have remained uncertain about my true nature. . . . helped by her teaching and example, I succeeded in imparting to my still simple and naive soul the form which best suited it and which it has retained ever since. . . . I resolved to employ my leisure hours in making myself able if possible one day to repay the best of women for all the help she had given me.[82]

Rousseau concludes, as John Stuart Mill later began, with gratitude to a woman he loved, by whom his soul (Rousseau) or intellectual and moral development (Mill) had been shaped, single-handedly (Rousseau), more than by anyone else (Mill).

Rousseau's autobiography emerges as the first consistently psychological framing of self-interpretation of an individual's life in the history of the West: a psychological state (proud individual intention) at the beginning, a psychological state (a humbly grateful remembrance) at the end. The two states may represent the stance toward life of an adult and an old man. The two conclusions contain an implicit theory of psychological development in late adulthood. But the essential point is that, with Rousseau, the *sociological framing* of the Puritan is replaced by the *psychological framing* of the Romantic. The primary sphere of religious action is relocated from the social world to the secularized interior. (The Japanese poetic diarist of the tenth century has anticipated, in a more passive tonality, the psychological framing of the meaning of one's life.)

To some degree, George Sand stands to Rousseau as Harriet Martineau stands to John Stuart Mill. Whereas Rousseau started with his nature and with mankind and concluded in humble gratitude to a woman he had loved fifty years ago, Sand begins with her husband and her class origins and ends by asserting "my own will," "my own instincts," "my own nature." To the extent that Rousseau and Sand may be regarded as paradigmatic, the male Romantic moves through his life in the opposite direction from the female Romantic: *from himself to the other* in the first case, *from the other to herself* in the second. But the other is only remembered, and herself only declared.

Mill concludes with his current works, and in the company of his daughter:

> . . . . various articles in periodicals . . . speeches on public occasions . . . with some additions by my daughter and myself . . . commenced preparations of matter for future books, of which there will be time to speak more particularly if I live to finish them.[83]

The Romantic speaks theatrically, seeking to excite the emotional resonance of strangers (or to revive his own feelings), the liberal sets forth the facts of his life soberly, dispassionately, in the manner initiated by Cardano.

Whatever the current misinterpretations of liberalism, it was a liberal—and a left liberal at that—who invented the affirmation of family relations as the proper conclusion of the account of the meaning of one's life. This type of conclusion remains uncommon in autobiographical writings throughout the world. Not even the completely traditional Jewish mother, Glückel, was able to come out of the machinery of her life as a person for whom children, in conjunction with one's work, are entirely sufficient. Nor will they be for the completely modern (or "post-modern") Anne Roiphe, even though she concludes in the twentieth century, like Mill, but far more anxiously, with children and books.

The proper conclusion of the liberal contrasts sharply with the accidental ending of the libertine. Casanova concluded his *Memoirs* by tying together the themes of religion (as a framework for his calendar), the theater, and sensuous enjoyment: "At the beginning of Lent she left with the whole troupe, and three years later I saw her in Padua, where I resumed my acquaintance with her daughter on far more tender terms."[84]

Casanova's end, like Cellini's, is merely an interruption of activities. But Cellini, the Renaissance man, knew that the end was the end, and Gibbon, in some respects an autumnal Renaissance man himself, knew that "the abbreviation of time and the failure of hope, will always tinge with a browner shade the evening of life"[85]—while the Sensualist disappears from sight hoping for the perpetual renewal of his circle of pleasure, a circle of the processes of nature in which the daughters, in due course, replace their mothers, with himself alone as its eternal, immovable center.

X

We have to return to the seventeenth century to trace the outlines of another history of selfhood that intersects with the mainstream of Western selfhood only in the nineteenth century and until then is usually ignored in efforts at historical reconstructions of Western selfhood. Six years after Baxter finished his autobiography, the Jewish housewife and businesswoman Glückel of Hameln began writing hers.

The beginning of her story is her emotion of pain arising from the loss of her husband, and the audience to which it is addressed is her children. "In my great grief, and for my heart's ease I begin this book. . . . I began writing it, my dear children, in the hope of distracting my soul from the burdens laid upon it. . . ." Then, before telling anything about herself, she gives religious and moral advice to her children:

> . . . to serve God from your heart, . . . not giving out to people that you
> are one thing while, God forbid, in your heart you are another . . . put
> aside a fixed time for study of the Torah, as best you know how. . . .
> Above all, my children, be honest in money matters, with both Jews
> and Gentiles. . . . The first question put to a man in the next world is,
> whether he was faithful in his business dealings.[86]

As Mary Mason has shown, European women have tended, in their autobiographical writings, to identify their selves by a relationship to others—God, a husband, or a community, whereas European men have concentrated on their own relatively isolated individualities.[87] But what Mason takes as the general male pattern is evident in Europe only since the Renaissance, if one disregards Abelard in his youth, and it does not hold for the English liberal John Stuart Mill, who describes himself as fused in one spiritual enterprise with his wife.

Nor do all women describe their identities only in relation to others: Georgia O'Keeffe, in the twentieth century, does not.[88] And already in the nineteenth century, George Sand, while devoting great attention to her social engagements, nevertheless concluded most emphatically:

> I have told or given some inkling of everything that has come into my life *of my own will,* everything drawn thereto by *my own instincts.* I have told how I have borne whatever was inherent *in my own nature. . . .* As for those mortal sorrows which *other natures* caused to weight upon me, they are the story of the secret martyrdom to which we all submit, either in public or in private, and which we must suffer in silence. (My italics.) [89]

Glückel of Hameln, two centuries earlier, may have represented the *historical* feminine pattern of linking one's self with one's husband and children. What seem to be characteristic features of the *Jewish* tradition of self-comprehension in Glückel's autobiography is the intimacy with pain, which is evident in choosing it as the starting point of the story of one's life, on the one hand, and the immediate entry into religious and business responsibilities, between which no distinction is made, on the other.

Nothing, however, in the Jewish tradition suggests that one should begin one's meaningful existence by *asking* for pain, as some Christian mystics—for example, Mother Julian of Norwich in the fourteenth century—do in order to identify, by reexperiencing them, with the sufferings of Christ: "These revelations were shown to a simple and uneducated creature on the eighth of May 1373. Some time earlier she has asked three gifts from God: (i) to understand his passion; (ii) to suffer physically while still a young woman of thirty; and (iii) to have as God's gift three wounds." (The wounds meant are not *stigmata,* but "the wound of true contrition, the wound of genuine compassion, and the wound of sincere longing for God.")[90] To the Jew, acceptance of inevitable pain may be a religious duty, but to actively seek suffering as an expression of a readiness for love and a precondition for the blissful immersion in it (which is celebrated at the end of Julian's *Revelations of Divine Love*) tastes of either heresy or perversion.

A Russian peasant might understand the intimacy with pain (Maxim Gorky indeed starts his autobiography with his father's death and Pitirim Sorokin begins his with the death of his mother).[91] A somewhat secularized Puritan, the man of Weber's Protestant ethic, might respond to the fusion of religious principle and business ethics. But a Puritan woman would be hard put to accept the renunciation of her own moral development for the sake of a familial responsibility, or to seem fairly relaxed about it:

> No, dear children, I am a sinner. . . . God grant that I may find the means and occasions for repentance. But, alas, the care of providing

for my orphaned children and the ways of the world, have kept me far from that state.[92]

There is no inner development in Glückel's adult life, which, except for her close involvement in the affairs of an extended family and religious community, and for her preoccupation with practical matters, looks much like Cellini's meandering from one act to another. But it is a series of maneuverings in the world with a transcendental end in sight.

Glückel's autobiography concludes with the story of a miraculous event:

> In the month of Nisan, 5479/1719/, a woman was kneeling by the bank of the Moselle, washing her dishes. It was about ten o'clock at night, and of a sudden it became as light as day, and the woman looked in the Heavens, and the Heavens were opened, . . . and sparks flew therefrom; and then the Heavens closed, . . . and all was dark again. God grant that it be for our good![93]

Glückel's selfhood—and in this she is paradigmatic for the traditional Jew—is located between suffering and a possible sign of the coming of the Messiah.

A hundred years later, in the autobiography of Solomon Maimon, the shape of movement of a Jewish selfhood has changed. It still begins with a story of suffering by his grandfather, who had been a leaseholder "of certain villages in the estates of Prince Radzivil," responsible for a bridge:

> Traffic was heavy and the bridges in bad repair, so that it not infrequently happened that they broke down just as some Polish nobleman with his rich entourage was passing, and horse and rider would be plunged into the swamp. The wretched leaseholder was then dragged to the bridge, where he was laid down and flogged till the demands of vengeance seemed satisfied.[94]

This sort of beginning is sometimes found in the autobiographies of black Americans:

> When my mother was pregnant with me, she told me later, a party of hooded Ku Klux Klan riders galloped up to our home in Omaha, Nebraska, one night. Surrounding the house brandishing their shot-guns and rifles, they shouted for my father to come out. . . . Still shouting threats, the Klansmen finally spurred their horses and gal-loped around the house, shattering every window with their gun butts. Then they rode off into the night, their torches flaring, as suddenly as they had come.—[95]

This is what must exist for the life of Malcolm X to begin to acquire its significance, but his story ends with his willingness to die in order "to destroy the racist cancer" in America, whereas Maimon concluded with the author becoming a correspondent of Kant and the co-editor of a journal of empirical psychology.

Heinrich Heine, in the nineteenth century, belonged to a type of Western European Jew who did not begin with pain, but with literature and political history.

> I will tell thee the fairy-tale of my life. . . . The last moonbeams of the eighteenth and the first red dawn of the nineteenth century played about my cradle.
> My mother tells how, during her pregnancy, she saw an apple hanging in someone else's garden but forebore to take it that her child might not be a thief.[96]

Whereas pain has to be learned later in the course of his life, the meaning of this life commences, as it did for Glückel, with the moral theme entering into the mother-child relationship. Close to the end of Heine's life (and of the collection of *Heinrich Heine's Memoirs* edited for him by Gustav Karpeles) is a solution to the dilemma of the converted nineteenth-century German Jew:

> I have never spoken with due respect of the Master or of his work, the Jews, and this too was because of my Hellenic temperament which was repelled by Jewish asceticism. My preference for Hellas has since declined. I see now that the Greeks were only beautiful youths, but that the Jews have ever been men, strong, invincible men, not only in old days, but even to this day, in spite of eighteen centuries of persecution and misery; I have learned to judge them better, and except that any pride of birth were a foolish contradiction in the champions of the Revolution and their democratic principles, the present writer might take pride in the fact that his ancestors belonged to the House of Israel, and that he is a descendant of those martyrs, who have given the world a God and a morality, and have fought and suffered on every battlefield of thought.[97]

The nineteenth century has injected into the self-comprehensions of European Jews both world-historical leadership (that is, Hegel) and a significant experience of nature (that is, Rousseau), sometimes in the same person. The rise of a powerful social movement—Socialism—in which neither ethnicity nor religion nor race nor sex should have mattered—has facilitated the former development, and in general would tend to suppress the latter. Only Rosa Luxemburg could write, on the one hand:

> . . . I sit tall in the saddle. No one has yet laid me low, and I would be curious to know the one who can do it. . . . my watchword—"Here I stand, I can't do otherwise!" . . . . A leader in the grand style. . . . holds fast to his tactics in spite of all "disappointments" and, for the rest, calmly allows history to bring its work to maturity.

On the other hand:

> I am at home wherever in the world there are clouds, birds and human
> tears. . . . I feel so much more at home. . . . in the meadows when the
> grass is humming with bees, than at one of our party congresses.[98]

But there is nothing specifically Jewish here.

What is specifically Jewish in twentieth-century Jewish autobiographies
is the conception of the course of life as either a *staying put against great odds:*
"My parents were Jews, and I have remained a Jew myself," writes Sigmund Freud on the first page (as who but a Jew would need to say?); or a
return to the historical home: "I am describing the life of a young Jew whose
path took him from the Berlin of his childhood and youth to Jerusalem and
Israel," writes Gershom Scholem also on the first page.[99]

American Jews hardly ever begin their autobiographies in either of
those two ways. We do get a sense of the portable home in some dissolving
American neighborhood, to which one returns in his middle age both
homesick and enraged, as in Alfred Kazin's *A Walker in the City.* And considerable importance, in the autobiographies of twentieth-century American Jews, must be given to the exaggeration of a general American strain in
the Norman Mailer beginning:

> Like many another vain, empty, and bullying body of our time, I
> have been running for President these last ten years in the privacy of
> my mind, and it occurs to me that I am less close now than when I
> began. . . . The sour truth is that I am imprisoned with a perception
> which will settle for nothing less than making a revolution in the con-
> sciousness of our time.

To the exorbitant desire corresponds, perhaps by a law of nature—or
at least of Durkheim's *anomie*—cosmic disgust:

> . . . in recovering the past I am chasing after the future, so that the
> past, the net of the namegiving surface-perceiving past, is my future
> again, and I go out into the past, into the trail of the cold eye of past
> relationship, the eye of my I at home in the object-filled chaos of any
> ego I choose . . . Or worst of all am I?—and the cry which is without
> sound shrieks in my eyes—am I already on the way out? . . . with only
> the toilet of Time, oldest hag of them all, to spin me away into the
> spiral of star-lit empty waters.[100]

In the autobiographies of younger Jews, or perhaps specifically American Jews, an ambiguous note creeps into the theme of returning home.
Sigmund Diamond, in a recent autobiographical text, finds himself rooted
in four historical settings—Germany, Russia, the United States, and Israel—and yet not fully belonging to either of them. His text is virtually a

reversal of direction of movement in Maimon's life. Diamond begins as a professor of history and sociology at Columbia University going off on an "unwanted pilgrimage" to the "birthplace of my mother and father" and he concludes:

> Tonight I read what I had written in this journal about the museum in Tallinn: among the pieces of debris, now under glass, left at the death camp at Klooga, Estonia, is the identification card of Shepsul Proschow of Vilnius, born 1912, murdered at Klooga with his wife and children. I remember; Shepsul is the Yiddish word for sheep. What will separate the setting from the suffering? *El Moleh Rachamim* (Lord God, full of mercy). . . . [101]

Something about the nature of the audience for self-revelation by a contemporary Jewish writer is revealed by Diamond's motto, which comes from a letter by Heinrich Heine to Goethe: "There are a hundred reasons why I should send Your Excellency my poems. I will name only one: I love you." It is as if the relationship of a Jew to a Gentile interposes itself into the most intimate relationship of a Jew to Jewish history, and he has to use the language of the former to describe the latter. (But some version of the translated experience has become, in the twentieth century, almost inevitable for intellectuals.)

Here, toward the end (for the time being), as at the beginning (Glückel), children reemerge, but in a historically problematic manner, no longer taken-as-given (by trustworthy biocultural maternity): "They share with me certain empty spaces where a sense of who they are and who they were and where they came from is thin, slippery and just possibly inadequate. . . . In their universalism will the furnishings of their souls look like Olympic stadiums?"[102] Anne Roiphe frames her autobiography by providing ambivalent responses to the Congregational Church in Washington, Connecticut—its white architectural purity at the beginning, a book sale at the end. At this Congregational Church sale, to Roiphe a symbol of the *secular* life, to which she comes with her husband and children, she buys books by Jewish authors. "Maybe we can be of both Jewish and secular worlds. . . . I hold on to my books. I belong to them and nothing will part us again."[103]

We need to keep the continuous existence of the Jewish pattern of selfhood and the directions of its change in mind as we watch, in Christian and de-Christianized Europe, the unfolding of the rich profusion of bourgeois types of selfhood and their assorted breakdowns and alleged dissolutions.

XI

We now interrupt these historical sequences to consider the autobiographies of several nineteenth-century reformers from outside the Western stream of autobiographical writing. This is not to suggest, as some authorities have done, that the history of written self-revelation begins, outside of the West, only in the nineteenth century or arises only under the impact of Western influences. Although the numbers of extant autobiographies from each non-Western tradition are smaller than the ones from Europe, three still living non-Western traditions of autobiographical writing—the Chinese,[104] the Japanese,[105] and the Islamic[106]—have histories at least a thousand years old, as does India, where, however, autobiography has a discontinuous, fractured history in several languages.[107]

Judging by the numbers provided by the experts on the particular traditions, based on varying but relatively strict definitions of autobiography, the Islamic corpus of autobiographical writing appears to be the most numerous, followed by the Chinese, the Indian (particularly if writings by Indian Moslems are excluded), and the Japanese, in that order. But both China and Japan are rich in autobiographical writings in a wider sense, such as self-eulogies in China and poetic diaries in Japan. If this is taken into account, East Asia before the eighteenth century rivals the West in the range and depth of attention to individual self-understanding, and is radically surpassed in numbers only since the Puritan revolution, more precisely after 1648.

China has the longest continuous tradition of autobiographical writing in one language in the world, more than two thousand years old. Bauer finds traces of autobiographical writing first in Ch'ü Yüan, the legendary Chinese dissident, a "Promethean" and "Romantic" figure, in the fourth century B.C. But it is Ssu-ma Ch'ien, the founder of Chinese historiography (145–90? B.C.), who wrote "the first autobiography of China."[108] It is characteristic of the Chinese civilization that a dissident minister-poet and a secular historian, both Confucian scholars deeply rooted in their native traditions, were first.[109]

Whereas the Chinese appear to have generated an autobiographical tradition entirely out of their own native soil, Islamic autobiography originates in a tremendous confluence of civilizations, empires, religious movements, and oral literatures of preliterate chiefdoms. The beginning of Islamic autobiography can be sought in Burzōē, a sixth-century Persian, who, at the order of a Sassanid king, translated an Indian epic. Burzōē introduced the work with a description of his spiritual quest, strongly flavored by Hindu and Buddhist themes and images, concluding, in direct opposition to the absolute certitude of the typical Islamic autobiographer, in the position of an unfulfilled searcher for truth. (To add to the strangeness of the case, the autobiography has been rewritten by a Moslem writer who translated it into Arabic two hundred years later and may have added his own spiritual anxieties to it.) With his inclination toward Indian spiritualities, Burzōē anticipates Sufi mystical autobiography, which culminates with al-Ghazzālī in the late eleventh to the early twelfth centuries. But the Sufi course of spiritual development *from sectarian differences of opinion to troubled reflexivity to uncertainty to dogmatic truth* is closed precisely in the manner in which Burzōē's is not.[110]

In its cross-culturalness and the stance of the unfinished seeker after truth—characteristics that are not found at the beginning of any other autobiographical tradition—Burzōē differs from virtually the whole corpus of subsequent Islamic autobiography (he was not himself a Muslim), and in this respect the relationship of the initiator to the tradition that begins from him is far more discontinuous than the relationship of Ssu-ma Ch'ien to the rest of Chinese autobiography (or of Augustine to the Western).

Whereas India has influenced the mystical stream of Islamic autobiography, Greece has provided models—significantly reinterpreted by the latter—for Islamic scholar- and poet-autobiographers. The royal and aristocratic autobiographers have drawn upon Persian, pre-Islamic Arab, and central Asian Turkic traditions. The result of this immense confluence is a distinctive Islamic typology of forms of self-comprehension. The fundamental patterns of Islamic self-comprehension become established in the autobiographies of the tenth to the twelfth centuries, and then they do not change very much (except for a decline in the literary quality of the evidence) until they were exposed to Western influences in the nineteenth century. This is in striking contrast not only to the continuous self-transformations of the West precisely since the eleventh and twelfth centuries but also, to a lesser extent, to China, especially during the sixteenth and seventeenth centuries, and Japan, particularly during the Tokugawa era. The Islamic world has been more dependent on outside influences for changes in self-comprehensions than either China or Japan. But the modern Western autobiographical tradition also began, with Saint Augustine as its perpetual point of reference, in a confluence of Greek, Roman, Christian, and Manichaean influences. Augustine, however, adopted a more combative, analytical, and culture-critical stance than the founder of any other autobiographical tradition, and he differs from the Asian pioneers of autobiography in being located both at the "end" of one autobiographical tradition and the "beginning" of another.

In contrast to China from the beginning and the Islamic world from the tenth and eleventh centuries on, persons who were rooted in traditions native to India wrote subsidiary autobiographical texts only from the seventh to the twelfth centuries. From the fourteenth to the eighteenth centuries, the Islamic invaders of India wrote autobiographies of rulers and officials, initially produced under Central Asian influences, which remain a part of the Islamic, rather than the Hindu, tradition, and are written in either Turkic or Persian. One full-fledged native autobiography has come from the seventeenth century. When the great development of Indian autobiography occurred in the nineteenth and twentieth centuries, it was done mostly by individuals who were strongly influenced by Western traditions, though not to the point of ceasing to exhibit a powerful impact of their own heritage. But their specifically *autobiographical* heritage is, for the moment, not in evidence: by the beginning of the nineteenth century, the non-Western traditions of autobiography, with the possible exception of the Islamic, had become too weak to be revitalized.

The nineteenth century is an important benchmark in that Western and non-Western traditions of self-comprehension begin to encounter each other in considerable numbers in the experiences of selfhood of particular men, though hardly ever women. Some earlier non-Western autobiographies, such as the twelfth-century *Memoirs* of Usāma ibn-Munqidh, reported on encounters with individuals or groups from other civilizations.[111] But the self-comprehension of the autobiographer is not, until the nineteenth century, significantly shaped by such encounters, nor do they emerge either at the beginning or at the end of his interpretation of the significance of his life. Among Western autobiographers the intercivilizational encounter emerges to prominence only in the twentieth century. Westerners have tended to be more curious to understand non-Western cultures than non-Westerners, except for the Japanese since the middle of the nineteenth century, were to understand the West. But this Western curiosity has been largely limited to the *object itself* and did not extend to the point of significantly transforming the *self-conceptions* of the major autobiographers.

In non-Western parts of the world, the encounter with the West since the nineteenth century has affected the self-conceptions (or at least the self-presentations) even of the traditionalists. Dayanand Saraswati, an Indian nineteenth-century religious reformer, wrote the first version of his autobiography "in Hindi for *The Theosophist,* a monthly journal of the Theosophical Society of India, Adyar (Madras), at the instance of Col. H. S. Olcott," and it was first published in English.[112] An encounter with the West is the immediate stimulus for the writing of the autobiography of a man who seeks to revitalize Indian traditions against Western influences threatening to inundate its modernizing educated classes. For a world-renouncer, to publish an autobiography is an extraordinary novelty, unlikely to have developed out of Hinduism alone: "The very fact that a *sannyasi* writes about his life is a step against the established code of conduct that enjoins him not to talk, much less to write, about his pre-monastic life. It is understood that a *sannyasi,* who renounces this world, takes a new birth and the door on his past life is completely shut."[113]

Dayanand's autobiography, however, both begins and concludes in a manner one would expect from a traditional Hindu:

> I was born in an Audichya Brahmana family in the state of Morvi in Majokatha region of Kathiawad, South Gujarat, in *VS* 1881 (= AD 1824).

· ·

   May God, the Lord of Justice, the mightiest of all, the Lord of the
Universe, the Omnipresent, be the giver of happiness to us. Saluta-
tions to Brahma, the supreme Lord of infinite power, the great God,
whose true knowledge I have preached. I have spoken the truth. You
have, therefore, given protection to me, the truth Speaker. May you,
Lord, save us from three kinds of sufferings.[114]

The symbolic direction of Dayanand's life is clearly defined as a pilgrimage *from the family as its starting point to God as its destination.* But it is a
pilgrimage that contains nothing remotely resembling a Christian fall into
sin or Abelard's combative rationalism and dramatic love. Nor is there,
from the earliest years of childhood, any self-doubt, identity confusion, or
division of the soul. "In the careers of those Indian men of religion who
have written autobiographies there is no sudden change from a sinful life
to a virtuous one as in Saint Paul and Augustine."[115] Sacredness grabs a
traditional Hindu with the single-mindedness of a child; it rarely does so
for male Europeans (or Americans), who need a lot of adolescence before
they are ready to become adults. In the twentieth century, doubts and
unresolved uncertainties appear in some Indian religious autobiographies
(for example, Sadhu Santinatha's). But these are not elements of religious
lives in Hindu autobiographical writings of the traditional sort.
   What catches our attention in Dayanand's autobiography is that in the
very second sentence the author, who became a *sannyasi* at the age of
twelve, declares, as probably no Jewish or Christian religious leader could,
at any rate not in the nineteenth century, have said:

   I refrain from mentioning the name of the town of my birth, for if
   my father, mother, or any other relative happen to be alive at the
   moment, they might come to me and create obstructions in the work of
   reform I have undertaken. I do not want that any part of my energies,
   resources, etc., should be used up in moving with or attending to the
   needs of my parents or my relatives.[116]

On the one hand, the extreme obligation, which might threaten even a
religious mission, of "attending to the needs" not only of one's parents but
of all other relatives as well; on the other hand, the total justification of
complete severance of such ties, in order to perform the mission. At the
beginning of the system of significations of the life of the Indian world-
renouncer is both total embeddedness in and total separability from society. And society is represented by a family to a far greater extent than it
could be for a European. Indeed a European may be *born into a world,* not
into a family. Consider the beginning of the Trappist monk, Thomas Merton: ". . . . in a year of a great war . . . I came into the world . . . the prisoner
of my own violence and my own selfishness, in the image of the world into
which I was born." The world is the Western man's primary framework,
the family merely initiates him into the world; for the traditional Hindu,
the world *is* a family world.[117]

In between his origin in the imprisoning extended family and his transcendental destination, the Hindu world-renouncer travels, not only without a human attachment, but also without responding in any personal way, with any show of emotion, to the unique qualities of others—in contrast to the medieval European cleric, who continued to experience, while in the sacred service, human attachments, and who kept responding to others in deeply personal ways.

At the end of Dayanand's autobiography, in 1879—six years after the death of John Stuart Mill—Brahma is still, in European terms, entirely medieval: "the mightiest of all, the supreme Lord of infinite power," who gives protection in exact return to speaking the truth he demands. The autobiography is addressed to Brahma, but printed in a newspaper; its implicit audience is a traditional religious community that the author seeks to reform. The God, the conception of the community, and the manner of communication seem ages removed from their counterparts in Gandhi's autobiography, only fifty years later.

The first book-length autobiography by an Indian in English, written in 1854 by a Muslim, Lutfullah, and in all fundamental respects quite different from Dayanand's, begins with an ingratiating dedication to a Westerner: "With due respect I place before you my humble work . . . the unvarnished truths contained therein, if cleared of grammatical errors by your able pen and published under your auspices," etc. The Westerner is to correct the Indian's mistakes. Lutfullah begins the actual account of his life with his family line in history, but also with sociological observations—of a kind that do not appear in Indian autobiographies before the nineteenth century—on poverty and tensions with relatives. The "Pedigree of Lutfullah," listed immediately before the actual autobiography begins, commences with Adam and Seth, and reaches Shekh Lutfullah in the ninetieth generation. But the generations transmit to him no specific responsibility, as they did to Ssu-ma Ch'ien in China almost two millennia earlier.

Lutfullah concludes as a somewhat successful man, returning from a trip to England, remarried, after the death of his first wife, surrounded by children, and relying upon God.

> My domestic cares are now aggravated, my years advanced, and my income inadequate to cover the expenses of a large family. But I resign myself to the will of that Omniscient Being, whose omnipotent power first creates the food and then his creatures destined to live upon it. Amen![118]

The meaning of his rationally observed life is circumscribed by the frame *from eternal family line created by God to my own present-day family under God as its unbroken continuation.* A person's life is placed firmly in the world, which is permanently delimited by one's family ties and presided over by a non-participating nineteenth-century God whose outstanding characteristic is his rationality in first producing the material conditions (the food), then the consciousness (the creatures dependent upon it for survival): a God almost good enough to be a Marxist, a far cry from Dayanand's Brahma, defined by his own prerogatives of power and truth.

The next case is the autobiography of a Malayan interpreter and teacher, also a Muslim, Abdullah bin Abdul Kadir, finished in 1843. Again there is a clear sense of the symbolic direction of life. The autobiography begins:

> In the name of Allah the Merciful and the Compassionate!
> It happened that on about the twenty-second day of October 1840 a friend of mine, an Englishman of whom I was fond, urged me strongly to give an account of my history, and the events of my life. He suggested to me that I should write my autobiography in Malay.

Only then does Abdullah describe himself:

> I am indeed an ignorant man, lacking in wisdom and understanding.[119]

The hierarchy of importance, the initial framing of the significance of Abdullah's existence, could not be clearer: Allah, an Englishman, I. What is particularly striking is that the agency initiating the autobiographical act is not only external to the individual but also alien to his civilization as well. An alien invades your story as its initiating principle. The story is yours, but its telling is a submissive, not a self-assertive act.

Yet it is only by submitting to the invading alien and to his forms of expression that one can tell one's own story to the world at all. This dynamic operates in all nineteenth-century non-Western autobiographers, but works out with particular clarity in the first "autobiography" by an American Indian, Black Hawk, published in 1833. This autobiography—like most American Indian autobiographies that followed in the twentieth century—was written jointly by its subject and a white editor, who thus emerged as the form-giver to the raw materials of native experience. Like other nineteenth-century non-Western autobiographers, Black Hawk could begin telling his story only when his people were defeated by Westerners—in his case, when he himself was defeated in battle (and transformed by this defeat into an appropriate "hero" for an "autobiography").[120] The modern non-Western autobiography begins as a self-description of a member of a *defeated people*,—though the defeat is not at that time made into an explicit issue, as it will tend to become in the twentieth century. In the nineteenth century, non-Western writers take their defeat for granted, insisting that their conqueror is "friendly" and that they are genuinely "fond" of him.

"Friendship" was also what Black Hawk concluded with, or was made to conclude. How different from Avicenna who, in the eleventh century, had finished: ". . . . I fell very ill. I returned to Jurjan, and there made friends with Abū 'Ubaid al-Jūzjāni," a disciple who then continued his autobiography.[121] Friendship is possible with a student, who becomes one's equal by virtue of his own scholarship. But friendship with a conqueror? What friendship with Westerners means in the nineteenth century seems to be normal, reasonably polite social intercourse, with some show of interest by the more powerful in the less powerful (gratefully received by the latter). In the nineteenth century, one pretends that this is enough.

Abdullah's story differs from the long line of Arabic autobiographies reviewed by Franz Rosenthal in not being located chiefly within the traditional universe of the author. Abdullah's life is mainly a series of faces through which the West has presented itself to the nonoffice-holding Malayan intellectual of the first half of the nineteenth century: from the judicial torture by the Dutch to the upholding of individualistic responsibility under the law by the English. In contrast to Sukarno's autobiography written one hundred twenty years later, there is little in Abdullah's story on which a psychologist could exercise his analytical skills: the essence of the individual's life is the history of the cultural encounters of his people with the West, all the initiatives emanating from the latter.

The purely subjective provides the minor accents of the individual's life. The core of one's selfhood is the clash of two objectified entities: one's tradition and alien modernity. The clash defines where one's duty lies. One's dutiful public acts are no less close to the center of one's individual being than one's most intimate private sensations, and a good deal more important to report to one's countrymen. A psychology of the individual gets hold only of the means by which the essential historical condition finds an accidental individual expression: the position of the nineteenth-century European liberal, unaffected, on the one hand, by Romanticism, prior, on the other hand, to psychoanalysis.

Whereas the autobiography ends as it began, with Allah, just before he comes to the end, Abdullah lists a variety of purposes he had in writing it. Intentions, with which west Europeans used to *begin,* suggesting a conscious choice as the starting point of the meaning of their existence, here emerge *at the end,* as an unintended distillation from historically inflicted experience. They are all secular. Abdullah wants to be useful to his people, to teach them history, "industry and diligence," moral standards and rules of language: essentially what he perceives the West to stand for.[122] (In contrast to the earlier Europeans, the twentieth-century American Anne Roiphe also lists her intentions close to the conclusion, perhaps also suggesting that they are not conscious initial choices by an ultimately free agent, but unanticipated sedimentations from the experiences of someone who has been, in large part, a victim of unpredictable historical circumstances. But consider how different, how much more *personal,* more questioning, and simultaneously more universal and more particularistic are the intentions of the twentieth-century American woman than those of the nineteenth-century Malayan Arab, even in the concern that they both share, to a not incomparable degree, for "their people":

> Perhaps there is a kind of Reform Judaism that exists or can be created that would be: (1) Serious and genuinely intellectual. . . . (2) Political. . . ., that is to say in active opposition to human suffering of all kinds, in active relation to not just Soviet Jews but Cambodians, Afghans, blacks, and others. (3) A Judaism that creates a new emphasis on the heroic Judaic tradition and not the lachrymose one. It must not engender a sense of helplessness or victim mentality. (4) Liberal, tolerant, unafraid of or threatened by other Jews' ways of doing things or other people's. (5) Deeply tribal but without the exclusivity, the snobbism, the clannishness that deprives one of the outside world. . . . (6) Can there be a truly non-patriarchal Judaism?)[123]

Abdullah's outline for an unwritten second volume of the autobiography is even more secular and consists entirely of a sociological analysis of the various sources of corruption in the life of nineteenth-century Malaya: an arbitrary political culture, bad education, inhibition of initiative, fear of innovations, and the ignorance of one's language.[124] If Abdullah's plan for the second volume is taken into account, the apparently *circular scheme of his life (from Allah to Allah)* becomes, what in fact it was, *linear (from a traditionalist religious beginning to a modern secular ending, from Allah to cultural nationalism)*.

But the first autobiography by an ethnic Malayan, Mohamed Salleh bin Perang, written some seventy years later, is more traditionalist than Abdullah's and consists mainly of the enumeration of the offices held and tasks performed by the author, beginning: "I . . was born on the island of Singapore. . . . The first post I held. . .," and concluding with the traditionalist directive for life: "Never fear to do what is best and right for your raja. . . . The inevitable thing is death, but reputations, both good and bad, live on for ever in this world. Amen, oh Lord of the Worlds."[125]

The life of the Malayan official even at the beginning of the twentieth century is, as that of the Chinese scholar official at its best could not be, nothing but a movement from the merely factual birth to the religiously sanctioned service to the prince. *But the modernist came first, the traditionalist followed.* (As he does throughout the world.)

About a decade before the traditional Malayan official completed his autobiography, a modernizing Javanese princess, Raden Adjeng Kartini, wrote a series of letters to friends that, taken together, can be regarded as the equivalent of an autobiography—the first Indonesian autobiography of note. She speaks in an entirely different, more supple, more personal voice than anyone else among nineteenth-century non-Western (and more freshly, more innocently than most Western) autobiographers. The beginning and ending summarize the life space and direction of movement of a modernizing turn-of-the century woman of the privileged class:

I have been longing to make the acquaintance of a "modern girl," that proud, independent girl who has all my sympathy! She who, happy and self-reliant, lightly and alertly steps on her way through life, full of enthusiasm and warm feeling; working not only for her own well-being and happiness, but for the greater good of humanity as a whole. . . .

How delightful is the odor of the little fruit which is our true native perfume! I have put it away with the baby's frock, in a chest with other garments, so that they will be perfumed delicately. My treasure must smell sweet.[126]

From liberation through modernity and humanism to returning home through intimacy and nature. An expectable story? But who among Western women autobiographers has put it this way? (And, of course, no man has.) Kartini died suddenly at the age of twenty-five. Did the life form endure?

The next case to be considered is the autobiography of the nineteenth-century Japanese educator Yukichi Fukuzawa (who is said to have taken Benjamin Franklin as his model, but diverges from it sharply both at the beginning and at the end). Fukuzawa's autobiography is a firmly secular document, beginning with a precise, objective analysis of the position in Tokugawa social structure of both of his parents.

My father, Fukuzawa Hyakusuke, was a samurai belonging to the Okudaira Clan of Nakatsu of the island of Kyūshū. My mother, called O-Jun as her given name, was the eldest daughter of Hashimoto Hamaemon, another samurai of the same clan. In social order, my father was barely high enough to have a formal audience with the lord. He was a few ranks above the common soldier *(ashigaru)*, but he was of the lower order among the samurai. In today's society his position would probably correspond to *hanninkan,* the lowest rank of government officials.

In the end, Fukuzawa describes the hopes of his old age for his nation, which he sees to have made immense strides since the opening up to the West, but which he still judges to be insufficiently "civilized."

But I should like to put my further efforts toward elevating the moral standards of the men and women of my land to make them truly worthy of a civilized nation. Then I should like to encourage a religion—Buddhism or Christianity—to give peaceful influence on a large number of our people. And thirdly, I wish to have a large foundation created for the study of higher sciences in both physical and metaphysical fields.[127]

The combination of a firmly secular frame for the comprehension of one's own life and a strong assertion of individual independence with an ongoing participation in the stream of life of his people without a perma-

nent sense of alienation seems, in the nineteenth century, to be more characteristic of the Japanese than of other non-Western peoples. Fukuzawa's
opening to the moralizing influences of several religions, both Oriental and
Western, distinguishes him from his Western counterparts, who tended to
have a more rigid faith in science, or in *one* religion alone. He is writing for
his own nation, and the direction of his life is clearly defined as the movement *from imprisonment within a hierarchic traditional order of stratification and
clan embeddedness to liberation, by virtue of science and changed governmental
policy, in a modernizing society.*

But is Fukuzawa Japanese when he says, almost in the tones of Rousseau: ". . . I attached little value on any man or clan," ". . . helpless but
resolute, I took my stand alone. . . ."?[128] We might indeed connect him, in
the words of Ivan Morris, "with certain inner qualities, notably a strong
nonconformist nature, that are especially admired in Japan because they
tend to be so rare."[129] But in what sense is any autobiography representative
of a people? Presumably a person who writes an autobiography does so
because he perceives himself to possess some *significant uniqueness*, therefore to be *significantly different* from the people around him. If any autobiography is to be considered representative, it is representative not (or not
only) of the social group to which the author belongs but of a spiritual
community, or cultural type, that may partly overlap with his social group,
but which, in its most important qualities, may well extend beyond the
boundaries of particular time or space and express not a historically
specific culture, but a basic stance toward life for the emergence of which
history is perhaps but an auxiliary condition.

Finally an autobiography from eastern Europe. Jonas Basanavičius, a
physician and liberal patriarch of the Lithuanian national reawakening,
begins his first autobiography in 1888 not by declaring his intentions, as
many west Europeans do, and not by identifying his parentage, as Asian
autobiographers typically do, but by describing the landscape of the region
of his birth and its history, stretching back to the first and second centuries
A.D.[130] A twentieth-century Chinese autobiographer, Chiang Yee, also starts
his autobiography by evoking his historical landscape, but *only as refracted
through the works of poets and artists.*[131] The Lithuanian communes with nature
directly, from his own unmediated experience of nature—but of nature
containing the bones of remembered history rattling at its heart.

This *rootedness in a history-laden natural landscape* seems to be particularly characteristic of the east Europeans. Czesław Miłosz, who came from
the same area as Basanavičius, begins his autobiography, written some
seventy years later, in virtually the same way, though in a more evocative
tonality.[132] To be sure, the historical rootedness of the east Europeans is
revealed in only *some* autobiographies of the literati, whether of peasant or
aristocratic origins. Although in western Europe peasants do not write
autobiographies, there are a few east European autobiographies of peas-

ants who did not become literati, and they entirely lack the sense of historical rootedness. In the autobiographies of Polish and Lithuanian peasant immigrants to the United States, the self is locked in between the family lines of one's parents and either poverty or house-buying in America.[133]

An autobiography of an old peasant woman, Rožė Sabaliauskienė, recently published in Soviet Lithuania, begins with a description of the traditional cooperation of two villages in maintaining a ferryboat and in holding dances for the young. Parents and other relatives are introduced only in the second chapter, after a full account of the operations of the traditional community and a lyrical evocation of the river Merkys, beloved, as she says, by "birds, flowers, and trees." Sabaliauskienė concludes with the educational progress made since her youth: "Oh that this had happened to me! A pity—I was born too early."[134] There is some similarity between the east European peasant beginnings and the initial framings of African twentieth-century autobiographies analyzed by James Olney,[135] except that the lyrical note is perhaps more characteristic of the east Europeans and firm tribalism of the Africans.

Basanavičius concludes, like Mill, but more alone, with the works he is trying to complete.[136] Regardless of their very different starting points, there is, in the nineteenth century, a remarkable confluence of endings between, in the historical sequence of their writing, Abdullah, Mill, Basanavičius, and Fukuzawa. A similar kind of intercivilizational confluence would be difficult to demonstrate in twentieth-century autobiographies. The nineteenth-century liberal model of selfhood—and of a universally benevolent but emotionally restrained sociability—exerted a universalizing influence over the self-comprehensions of many individuals educated in the "modern" manner in various parts of the world, even though Alexander Herzen (the Russian, and therefore more communal, version of the Romantic liberal) retained his autonomy from this force as he did from all others.[137]

The non-Westerners of the nineteenth century generally present their selves as much more deeply interdependent with either a religious collectivity or a nation than do major Western autobiographers of the same period. All the non-Westerners seem to speak, in the nineteenth century, to their own people, rather than to universal humanity (except Kartini, who wrote most of her letters to a Western friend. Abdullah has been accused by later Malayan critics of having written for English readers—though he wrote in Malay; what he did was to identify himself, as a modernizer, with a Western standpoint). They are all, from their school years on, from their early teens, firmly committed to a particular direction for their lives. But the directions of their lives are all defined by their objectively visible actions, with little attention (Herzen again being an exception) to the kind of internal development so dear to the Puritan in the seventeenth century and the psychologist in the twentieth century. There is no excavation of the unconscious at all, and no autobiographer is faced with problems that he does not clearly understand or know solutions for.

<h1 style="text-align:center">XII</h1>

In the sophisticated culture of the twentieth-century West (actually from the second half of the nineteenth century on)—and for men more than for women—the idea of the self, insofar as it could not be reduced to objectively describable acts, has become the focus of questionable activity, a "scandal." The *littérateurs* took Dostoyevsky's discovery of the "mouse with a heightened consciousness"[138] to heart:

> What is known as *la vie intérieure* aroused the greatest disgust among Sartre's circle of friends, *les petits camarades;* the gardens where sensitive, refined souls cultivate their delicate secrets these folk regarded as stinking swamps, the background for constant discreet trafficking in betrayal, or the consummation of filthy narcissistic pleasures.
> In order to dissipate this dark miasmic atmosphere, they themselves had acquired the habit of exposing their lives, thoughts, and feelings in broad daylight.[139]

This contempt for the "inner self," with its connotations of some incommunicable Emersonian mystery at its core, went beyond the uncertainties about, contradictions within, and dissolutions of selfhood that are characteristic of earlier periods of psychocultural transition since the Middle Ages (Petrarch, Montaigne). The contempt for interiority seems to be a part of a larger process sometimes described (not quite correctly) as the "breakdown of the bourgeois personality." What has been breaking down, from the second half of the nineteenth century on, has been the self-confidence of the rationally organized self in its capacity to manage itself and the world in a responsible manner while simultaneously cultivating emotional and moral responsiveness in its subjective inwardness. It is not the personality of John Stuart Mill, but the confidence of this kind of personality in its self-sufficiency, that has been dissolving.

This confidence had been subverted, on the one hand, by such changes in the organization of society as a great expansion in economic and political bureaucracies and the rise of organized labor, by the development of colonial empires, with their self-evident exploitations and denials of justice administered by parts of the educated classes of the West, and later on by the emergence of full-fledged totalitarianism and its genocidal campaigns. On the other hand, the self-confidence of the "bourgeois man" has been undermined by the powerful intellectual analyses of Marx, Nietzsche, and Freud—each of whom, in his own way, tended to detract from the sense of self-sufficient mastery by the rationally organized individual. In addition (or as part of these trends), the rationally organized individual has been becoming increasingly aware of the emotional costs of his kind of rationalization of personality.

English middle-class liberal intellectuals of the early nineteenth century were already aware of these costs. Indeed the self-sufficiency of the bourgeois self has been challenged by Rousseau before it became dominant, and some sense of challenge to the possibility of rational self-sufficiency of the individual has been a part of the bourgeois self-comprehension from its very beginning: "the plenteous and abundant tears" of Margery Kempe, Leonardo da Vinci's irony, the threat of chaos on which the Puritan had built his control, Henry James' conception of his life as nothing but the transition from the experience of a social atmosphere both richly saturated and somehow intangible to its recollection in devotion.[140] The bourgeoisie always, in the depths of its self-consciousness, knew what it was beyond, or before, "being bourgeois," as other classes generally do not.

The discovery of the pettiness of the self by Dostoyevsky is partly derived from the pessimism about human nature of Russian orthodoxy and partly from the peculiarly stalemated quality of life in nineteenth-century Russian society. Sartre's rejection of interiority is closely connected with his perception of subjectivistic—perhaps especially Protestant—religiosity as a source of "mystifications" used by the "bourgeoisie" of his imagination to justify its dominant position in society. Neither Dostoyevsky nor Sartre—nor the culture of the bourgeoisie between Nietzsche and Sartre as a whole—can be understood without taking into account the widespread disillusionment with the exorbitance and collapsibility of Romantic selfhood.

All of these forces, acting both directly and through the great synthesizers of imaginative literature and a public political-literary discourse, have produced, since approximately the middle of the nineteenth century, a phenomenon among literary circles of Europe—but less so, and later, in the United States—that can most precisely be described as a *repulsion from the self*. The bland, aseptic treatment of the self in later American social psychology—after George Herbert Mead, but including Erving Goffman[141]—is perhaps a scientized, frequently mechanized form of such repulsion from the deep designs of subjectivity that have been central elements of self-comprehension in the West since as least Saint Augustine.

In writing autobiographies, people now—in the "post-bourgeois" but not quite a "post-Romantic" age—seek to identify that in their lives which will resist the corrosiveness of doubt in the validity of the statement of individual selfhood, in the worthwhileness of speaking about one's self in any but the documentary manner.

Many of the most prominent twentieth-century autobiographies have been written by people living outside their country of birth. But whether written by exiles or natives, these self-descriptions begin not with the natural circumstances (family, tribe, birth of the individual) or with any set of programmatic intentions (as many European autobiographies have in the past), but with an analysis, or evocation, of the fundamental features of experience in which the individual self is grounded.

This essential quality of a man might be a basic contradiction, or series of contradictions, that he experiences in himself; it might be a problem which he has been facing all his life for which he does not know the solution; it might be a lifelong seeking to immerse oneself in the depths of one's individuality which prove indistinguishable from the most universal in man; it might be a sense of the dissolution of this self in the memories of one's childhood.

The starting point is what one carries in oneself, what defines one as a distinctive human being, but of which one is not a master and which one has not chosen. The meaning of one's life begins with the discovery of the essential quality, or qualities, of the experience of oneself throughout one's lifetime. The beginning is not concentrated at a point in time or in intention, but extends through the life. *One always begins* discovering one's qualities, *one always begins* either in new settings or with a new poignancy, greater depth, or growing sense of loss. And the audience is, at least to a greater extent than in earlier times, oneself. What begins in our tradition as a confession to God becomes a surprise to the self.

Four distinctively twentieth-century beginnings are offered in the autobiographies of Nicholas Berdyaev, André Malraux, Carl Gustav Jung, and Rafael Alberti:

> Despite the Western element which is active in me, I belong to the Russian intelligentsia whose characteristic attitude is a perennial search for truth. . . . I am also conscious of being an aristocratic thinker who has come to acknowledge the truth of socialism.[142]
> "What has confession taught you about men?". . . . ". . . that *there's no such thing as a grown-up person*. . . ." . . . .To reflect upon life—life in relation to death—is perhaps no more than to intensify one's questioning.[143]
> My life is a story of the self-realization of the unconscious. . . . What we are to our inward vision, and what man appears to be *sub specie aeternitatis,* can only be expressed by way of myth. . . . The only question is whether what I tell is *my* fable, *my* truth.[144]
> . . . . there was a melancholy place, covered over with yellow and white Spanish broom, called The Lost Grove. . . . Everything there was like a memory: birds circling trees that had disappeared long ago. . . . Now as I retreat further and further into myself, becoming smaller and smaller, a distant point along the road that will eventually lead to that "gulf of shadows" which waits to close in upon me. I hear the muted sound of footsteps behind—the inexorable, advancing invasion of that remembered lost grove of my youth. . . . becoming totally transformed into the lost grove that lives and pulsates inside of me.[145]

The mid-twentieth-century European autobiographer lives at a conjunction in which the self begins where historical contradictions, insoluble ontological problems, universal myths, and private memories intersect. In the West of the twentieth century, selfhood begins whenever a life has discovered a *problematic quality,* simultaneously eternal and evanescent, in itself. And a twentieth-century conclusion, in the West, is the *moral or aesthetic attitude* toward life at which this problem has arrived. An encounter between different cultures or different historical epochs is an essential part of the situation in which this attitude toward life defines itself. In Western autobiographies before the twentieth century only Solomon Maimon, the eighteenth-century east European Jew, concluded in a manner to which an intercultural encounter was essential. In the nineteenth century the non-Western peoples pioneered in breaking out of provincial definitions of selfhood. Only now does the West begin to catch up.

An early twentieth-century conclusion, by Leon Trotsky, in the very pride of its progressivism, still points back to the nineteenth and even the eighteenth century:

> . . . . Rosa Luxemburg wrote to a woman friend from prison: ". . . . I do not demand that you write poetry as Goethe did, but his view of life, the universality of his interests, the inner harmony of the man, every one can create for himself or at least strive for." . . . . Proudhon wrote to a friend from prison: ". . . . Destiny—I laugh at it: and as for men, they are too ignorant, too enslaved for me to feel annoyed at them."[146]

The other four conclusions—by Czesław Miłosz, Carl Gustav Jung, Agehananda Bharati (born Leopold Fischer), and André Malraux—were written after World War II. The difference is quickly apparent.

> It may be that we Eastern Europeans have been given the lead in this search. By choosing, we had to give up some values for the sake of others, which is the essence of tragedy. Yet only such an experience can whet our understanding, so that we see an old truth in a new light: when ambition counsels us to lift ourselves above simple moral rules guarded by the poor in spirit, rather than to choose them as our compass needle amid the uncertainties of change, we stifle the only thing that can redeem our follies and mistakes: love.[147]
>
> When Lao-tzu says: "All are clear, I alone am clouded," he is expressing what I now feel in advanced old age. Lao-tzu is the example of a man with superior insight who has seen and experienced worth and worthlessness, and who at the end of his life desires to return into his own being, into the eternal unknowable meaning. . . . This is old age, and a limitation. Yet there is so much that fills me: plants, animals, clouds, day and night, and the eternal in man. The more uncertain I have felt about myself, the more there has grown up in me a feeling of kinship with all things. In fact it seems to me as if that alienation which has so long separated me from the world has become transferred into

my own inner world, and has revealed to me an unexpected unfamiliarity with myself.[148]
   I believe that cultural criticism is the only contribution we can
make to cultures not originally our own, or not our own by choice. . . .
The method tends to avoid the disastrous distinction between "out-
siders" and "insiders", for the fact that one contributes to a culture
makes one an "insider", and if cultural criticism is successful then the
critic becomes an "insider" by virtue of the value of his criticism; or to
be more exact, the distinction between "outsider" and "insider" becomes irrelevant.[149]
   I went back to Lascaux. . . . "Huts for the specialists?" "No, they
only come from time to time. They're for the *conscientious objectors*. The
conservation work has been entrusted to them." (My italics.)[150]

   At least some twentieth-century Europeans—the "conscientious objectors" to the limitations of modernity—conclude with a protective return to
the earliest sources of their culture.[151] Others end by committing themselves to critical responsibility for alien cultures. One orientation balances
the other and prevents it from spawning monstrous offspring. The self-
examination that reveals "an unexpected unfamiliarity with myself" proceeds together with the discovery of "the only thing that can redeem our
follies and mistakes: love." Individual efforts, taken together, compose
themselves into a system of coordinates. But the autobiographies suggesting this "system" have all been written by literary men of middle-class or (in
two cases) aristocratic backgrounds. Neither the autobiographies of states-
men or military officers, nor those of working-class men and women, exhibit any of these directions.[152] How central are these dimensions to the self-
consciousness of the age?
   Whereas the "higher consciousness" of their culture must have been at
least recognizable to most people in the cities of Renaissance Italy, and
whereas all classes of male Jews and of Puritans without sex distinction
must have understood something of the self-comprehensions of their most
literate elites, in the twentieth century the most profound autobiographers
may have become entirely detached from the self-perceptions of the great
majority of the people who are not habitual book readers. What is novel in
the self-comprehensions of this period is a recognizable, presumably a
historically significant, form. But to what beyond, or underneath, the
higher peaks of culture does it speak? Do the great autobiographers of the
twentieth-century West articulate, beyond their individualities, an emerging frame of self-comprehension that, in its most general characteristics,
speaks to what is crystallizing out of a great many self-uncertainties and
innumerable, to speak in the words of William James, "native hardnes[ses]"
which "must break down and liquefy" in a search of "salvation through self-
despair"?[153]
   The "mass culture" of the advanced industrial societies is not a reliable
gauge to what changes in self-comprehensions may or may not be occur-

ring in the "broader masses." In the first place, "popular culture" of this variety is produced not by but for the broader strata by commercial "culture producers" who, removed from their audiences but not expected to express their own selves, communicate only with their own image of the broader strata. Second, the fashions of mass culture change so rapidly, moving back and forth in unpredictable ways, as to raise doubts whether (beyond the omnipresence of certain basic motifs of true folk art, its sexual humor included) they reflect anything deeper than the necessity, in the mass media, constantly to sell easily perceivable appearances of novelty.

Third, and most important, the mass culture now being produced (to the extent that it does not rise, by its creative energies, above mass culture) lacks sufficiently powerful symbolic organization of its own contents to transmit to its recipients much more than merely the raw materials of experience, with which they are likely to be already, more or less, familiar. Mass culture takes hold of the various accumulations of experience, but neither adequately identifies nor effectively shapes the deeper symbolic patterns into which experience must be organized if it is to be adequate to the needs of human beings. (One cannot live inside a compost heap of experiences too long.)

Mass-produced culture (in contrast to folk art) is not culture in a historically valid sense. Culture consists not of the record of human experiences, whether "truly recorded" or "artificially constructed," but of the durable symbolic designs into which humanity has succeeded in organizing its experiences. Even more important, mass culture does not tell us precisely what we need to know: what sorts of deforming and reforming processes might be taking place in our societies and civilizations below our threshold of conscious perception. We have only "serious culture" to reveal to us even the cultural changes taking place in the broader strata of contemporary societies, and can only ask to what extent and in which aspects serious culture gives form to these broader changes. Serious culture, in present usage, includes conscientious efforts by people who are not professional culture producers to make sense of their experiences. It is ultimately this source of information—not only "high culture" in the traditional sense, and "mass culture" least of all—on which the culture analyst of the twentieth century (as of all other times) must rely.

One is tempted at this point to inquire what could be said about the state of the particular civilization in which these autobiographies have been engendered and, in general, what sort of relationship exists between individual autobiographies and the civilization in which their authors participated. This relationship may well have become looser now than it was in the past, so that making inferences from the individual text to the collective condition may have become a more complicated matter. In any case, the method adopted in this investigation precludes, particularly in the twentieth-century West, the use of autobiographies for diagnosing the state of a civilization. For that purpose, a wide range of autobiographies—both "traditional" and "novel"—would have to be analyzed. But, whereas we have pointed to the persistence of ancient patterns in autobiographical writings of the twentieth century, the main concern has been to identify, for each epoch, what was novel in the personal boundary systems of its designs of self-comprehension. The "current state" of Western civilization is composed not only of both ancient and novel cultural designs of various kinds (the comparative intensity and prevalence of which are not easily determinable), but also of their interactions, under varying social constraints, in shaping the acts of which the stream of everyday existence of a civilization largely consists. We have not addressed ourselves to these questions. We can, therefore, instead of providing a complete analysis, only seek to transmit the sense of what conducting one's life seriously in the current conjunction of Western civilization feels like to those autobiographers who seem to us to have made the most profound efforts, novel to this epoch, to come to grips with the problem of the meaning of their experiences.

In the twentieth century, individual experiences of sociability vary a great deal. What is common, more or less, to the six Europeans who have published their autobiographies since World War II is the experience of sociability as simultaneously a joint participation in historical processes (of political or cultural history) and a series of shared resistances against the oppressiveness, explosiveness, or diffusiveness inherent in these processes. Sociability is both historically involved and personally resonant, involved as tragedy and enlightenment, resonant as a touch of spirit indomitable in a world of human weakness and overbearing power. This twentieth-century European sociability is also discontinuous, "exiled": one is always torn away from one's own initial pattern by the unpredictable "historical developments" and by differences in subjective (emotional or ideological) reactions to them. In no way had history ever before invaded the very pattern of sociability—and of selfhood—of literate Europeans to the same extent, even at the height of the revolutionary wars of the eighteenth century. (Before the eighteenth century, history as a constructed process was essentially irrelevant to the basic structures of sociability and of self-comprehension of continental Europeans: it was not history, but legend, which provided even the concrete models of behavior.) And Americans, even in the twentieth century, with the exception of the Jews whose Jewishness has not been irreparably flattened by assimilation, have remained incapable of even understanding this sense of sociability and its effects on the comprehension of the self and its responsibilities.

A penumbra of lesser textualities surrounds the key paradigm of mid-twentieth-century Western self-understandings.[154] But among them emerges a possible short-term direction of change. Western European autobiographies suggest, in the stories of the transit over time of the selfhood of the author, an inversion of the nineteenth-century (or English) schema *from culture (books) to nature*—John Ruskin, Oscar Wilde[155]—in the twentieth century (or French) design *from nature (one's body) to culture (litera-ture engaged against ongoing processes of destruction of cities, languages, and values)*—Michael Leiris, André Malraux.[156] Books could be taken for granted as the reliable lineaments of existence in the nineteenth century; a recovery of the experience of nature was an achievement. Only one's own body can be taken for granted in much of contemporary European con-sciousness; books are fragile means by which to struggle against its mortal-ity and the universal processes of corruption, pollution, and despoliation.

In *The Armies of the Night,* characteristically subtitled "History as a Novel, the Novel as History" (the difference between "fact" and "imagina-tion" having now become unclear), Norman Mailer—speaking of himself in the third person, like Henry Adams and the first English autobiographer, the fifteenth-century housewife and visionary Margery Kempe—describes the structure of the self as a lively lizard within a socialized illusion, as a tiny bit of useless nature, in the deadness of the night flittering in and out of the shared social constructions of reality, as flesh still unliberated from Egypt and in subconscious need of it: "He had in fact learned to live in the sarcophagus of his image—at night, in his sleep, he might dart out, and paint improvements on the sarcophagus."[157]

Life as self-education has become a creeping adjustment to the per-petual entombment within one's own (individual and collective) gifts of creation. At the end of the *Bildungsroman,* in 1968, is the cold subconscious eye staring at itself as the prisoner of its own *Bild,* contributing by its dreamlike actions only to the further elaboration of the prison house of its own language (and of the languages of other strangers). The firmly em-placed, wholly external, entirely conscious, and thoroughly enjoyable Ren-aissance theater, completely of one's own making (not the whole of the Renaissance, but certainly a major thrust of it), has become a system of incarceration, unceasingly developing by itself, to which the individual, in his moments of liberating escape from his own consciousness, merely con-tributes marginal decorations of doubtful value. It is surely significant that a man as theatrical as Norman Mailer experiences himself as the worm's-eye view of the theatrical conception of the self which Cellini, more than four hundred years earlier, so unself-consciously celebrated. The same sensibility of a theatrical worm—but less advanced in that one satisfies oneself with the cleverness of his perception of his mere-worminess—speaks through Erving Goffman's *The Presentation of Self in Everyday Life* and the pop-sophisticated journalism of Tom Wolfe.

The writer imprisons himself in his own developing language. For Piri Thomas, life in the streets constitutes itself as a perpetually repetitive circle from which there is no escape. Walking in the streets of Harlem, observing "an unreal scene of frightened silence at 2 A.M.," watching "the junkies' faces, taut, like waiting was the worst thing in the world" in the beginning;

streets, noises, and "His eyes closed and the needle still in his arm . . . like a
lover who has loved and cannot find the way to withdraw" at the end. Only
Thomas' father, who beats him at the beginning, is not there at the end.
Except for the eventual disappearance of his natural progenitor, the slum
dweller is locked in within a system for which there is no progress.[158] In the
most advanced industrial societies, circular schemes of self-comprehension
gain new strength. But the circle, which was once the design for a return to
a God, is now the form of infinite depletion.

On the whole, twentieth-century American autobiographies appear to
be less important than the European in a history-of-consciousness perspective. One finds less compelling novelty in the American cases, especially
among white Protestants and Catholics (though possibly a greater closeness
to the actual experience of the "man in the street"). No single twentieth-
century American autobiography has attained the stature of Henry Adams'
Education. In Europe, the twentieth century probably surpasses the
nineteenth in the originality and vitality of autobiographical writing.

One may possibly seek to account for the comparative dearth of
significant autobiography written by twentieth-century Americans by the
effects of democracy on the psyche identified by Alexis de Tocqueville
("there prevails among those"—democratic—"populations a small, distress-
ing motion, a sort of incessant jostling of men, which annoys and disturbs
the mind without exciting or elevating it"); by the strong tendency among
the educated to reverse the Protestant abolition of "spiritual guidance,
casuistry, and the cure of soul," by restoring all of these practices in the
form of protracted psychoanalysis (which either precludes the need to
confess to the general public or inclines toward confessing in the manner
approved by the psychoanalyst); or by an excessive preoccupation with the
current-events orientation of the mass, especially the electronic, media and
by a trivialization of language associated with it.[159]

Perhaps the metaphysical concepts that are essential for autobiographical writing—"beginning" and "ending," "essence of experience" and
"significant movement"—have become too nebulous in the consciousness
of what some have called a post-modern, or late-modern, culture to sustain
coherent devotions to self-revelation, in a text built to endure, as contrasted
to accidental illustrations of vanished selfhoods, failed faiths, and fragments of shipwrecked dreams. (Or, worse still, a lifelong preoccupation
with the insufficiencies of one's parents, suggestive only of the lack of an
adequate conception of one's own adulthood.)

XIII

The twentieth-century autobiographies so far reviewed are all written
by males. Against them, we can observe a distinctively feminine starting
point of Georgia O'Keeffe and Simone de Beauvoir:

My first memory is of the brightness of light. . . . I was sitting among pillows on a quilt on the ground. . . . Aunt Winnie's dress was thin white material, a little blue flower and a sprig of green patterned over it. The bodice was close-fitting with long tight sleeves, the skirt straight and plain in front and very full and puffed and ruffled at the back—a long dress touching the ground all around, even trailing a little extra long at the back.[160]

In the family photographs. . . . can be seen ladies in long dresses and ostrich-feather hats and gentlemen wearing boaters and panamas, all smiling at a baby: they are my parents, my grandfather, uncles, aunts; and the baby is me. . . . I retain only one confused impression from my earliest years: it is all red, and black, and warm.[161]

Not all women writers of autobiography—not even a majority—start in this mode. But it seems to be the case that only middle-class Western women born around the beginning of the twentieth century frame the meaning of their existence within an initial perception, both sensuous and precise, of a dressed-up world, *a world in which clothing presents itself first,* to be followed by the smiles and the people and the words inhabiting it. A world in which "sensuous stuff," sharply perceived and immortalized in the self, is the beginning—or preconditon—of humanity.

The world of these two twentieth-century women begins with the earliest memories of childhood; for the late thirteenth- early fourteenth century Japanese Lady Nijō—that is, the lady from the Second Avenue, otherwise nameless—the world began with being noticed by the Retired Emperor whose concubine she was to become. But we find the same sensuous evocation of clothing, this time her own:

I recall wearing a layered gown shaded from light pink to dark red, with outer gowns of deep purple and light green and a red formal jacket. My undergown was a two-layered small-sleeved brocade patterned with plum blossoms and vines, and embroidered with bamboo fences and plum trees.[162]

In the two unmistakably twentieth-century autobiographies of women previously cited, the author ends either by feeling deceived by life and defeated by death at the age of fifty-four, or by learning new creative skills at an age close to ninety.

I loathe my appearance now. . . . Either I shall see Sartre dead, or I shall die before him. It is appalling not to be there to console someone for the pain you cause by leaving him. It is appalling that he should abandon you and then not speak to you again. . . . The promises have been kept. And yet, turning an incredulous gaze toward that young and credulous girl, I realize with stupor how much I was gypped.[163]

A young potter came to the Ranch and as I watched him work with the clay I saw that he could make it speak. . . . I hadn't thought much about pottery but now I thought that maybe I could make a pot, too—maybe a beautiful pot. . . . I rolled the clay and coiled it—rolled it and coiled it. I tried to smooth it and I made very bad pots. . . . He helped me with this and that. I finally have several pots that are not too bad, but I cannot yet make the clay speak—so I must keep on.[164]

Western women in the twentieth-century autobiographies that we have reviewed conclude by *aging concretely in their appearances, their intimate relationships, and their work.* They do not find themselves, in the end, with a general, abstractly identifiable principle of relatedness to humanity, history, or the inner self, as the major male autobiographers of the twentieth-century West tend to do (and as Harriet Martineau did a century earlier). Whereas male autobiographers end up declaring the individual moral or aesthetic stance toward life at which they have arrived during their lives, some of the most distinctively twentieth-century women autobiographers conclude by the ever-continuing discovery of themselves, in the company of men, aging naturally in disappointment or in increasing productivity.

Other autobiographical patterns have been worked out by twentieth-century women, such as that of the world citizen:

They say that at eighty you remember your childhood best. Perhaps, in a way, that is true of me. But is is not myself as a little girl in Rome, New York, that I recall most vividly; it is my other "childhoods," when I was reborn in the wonder and newness of strange, far places. Sometimes it seems to me as if I have had true reincarnations within one long lifetime.

. . . .

Ten dollars? That's what it takes to start a man or woman reading in India. . . . The taxi driver's two dollars added to the collection of nickels from a bunch of Chicago schoolchildren who opened their sticky hands to release them into mine, to a five-dollar check from a retired schoolmarm in Utah, and on the other side of the world a human being learned to read.[165]

Or the pattern of the rejector of patterns, who yet survives: a shapeless life that merely quiets down, meandering from repulsion against civilized ugliness to the trivial tranquility of still comparatively natural events. From:

Only the number 19 bus to Cambridge Circus past Soho porn houses, girl's gray breast calling from photo behind glass, fellow in a booth selling tickets,—

To:

The people next door talking about the spaghetti they had for dinner. Just sounds floating by. One of the children had two helpings. There is success in the sound of it.[166]

But these patterns do not distinguish between men and women—or identify distinctively feminine elements of self-comprehension—as sharply and as paradigmatically as do Simone de Beauvoir and Georgia O'Keeffe. And we are primarily concerned not with what is statistically representative, but what is uniquely characteristic of an epoch, a group, a human type (and what, in comparison to the past, is novel in this uniqueness).

XIV

In the twentieth century, whatever its actual political and economic circumstances, each stream of humanity feels free to insist on being itself. Our minds no longer spontaneously incline to identify a civilizational variant with the universally significant.

For individuals who write autobiographies, this reversal of the nineteenth-century tendency toward hegemonic universalization usually entails experiencing intercultural and intercivilizational encounters in their own societal and individual ways, with their own beginnings and their own endings. Autobiographical texts reflect the dismantling of one cross-civilizational consensus of the illuminated after another.

Whereas there remain both traditional and nineteenth-century Westernizing men among the non-Western autobiographers of the twentieth century, the basic thrust is toward a more egalitarian encounter between civilizations. The specificity of the native tradition asserts itself in the way in which it responds, usually, to the West, hardly ever to any other civilization not one's own.

In the sense that *people respond, beyond their own native tradition, almost only to the West,* in its several versions, the West retains, in the experiences of selfhood by non-Westerners, a centrality among strangers. But there is an increasing diversity in responding to this centrality, and in this diversity both individual peculiarity and the particular historico-cultural climate of each civilization, region, and nationality asserts itself.

But also the material conditions. It is only in twentieth-century autobiographies that one's own experience of *unmitigated hunger*—and the garbage dump as a metaphor of fulfillment—become the starting point, as they do for the Moroccan writer Mohamed Choukri:

> One day when the hunger had grown too strong, I went out to Ain Ketïouat to look in the garbage dump for bones and ends of dry bread. I found another boy there before me. He was barefoot and his clothes were in shreds. His scalp was covered with ring worms, his arms and legs scarred with sores.
>
> The garbage in the middle of town is a lot better than it is here, he said. Nazarene garbage is the best.

And at the end, returning from a prostitute, at the age of twenty, the author begins to learn how to write. He visits the nameless grave of his little brother, killed by his father in a fit of anger, when the sick child had called for bread, of which there was none. "My little brother never had a chance to sin. All he did was to live his illness. . . . And I, what shall I become? A devil, most likely."[167]

There is not necessarily more hunger in the twentieth century than in the past, but the hungry (or the formerly hungry) have entered, as form-giving agents, into the history of consciousness. Hunger, for the first time, has become the beginning (and its memory the end) of all meanings that a literate man may expect to encounter in a human existence. Hunger, prostitution, writing, and death: stages on the life's way.

The individual begins with the consciousness of the raw needs of *his* own body; he graduates to the sad recall of the death of *another*. This is all there is to the meaning of his voyage through the spaces of his life. But he does not live alone, and certainly not in the moral world of the nineteenth-century European, circumscribed by his own intentions.

The experience—transformed into a myth—of *alien power* as the starting point of one's own first tribal and then individual self-comprehension is also a distinctively twentieth-century phenomenon (if one disregards the somewhat different case of Solomon Maimon):

> Among the Luo of Central Nyanza, the forecasters had said of the White people "If you touch them the skin will remain in your hand because they are very soft. But they will come with thunderstorms and they will burn the people." . . . When these people first came (the story goes), the elders had warned that we should never, never try to fight them because their weapons were better than ours.

Oginga Odinga ends as a former minister of the independent state of Kenya, now in opposition to the entrenched nationalist elite that has emerged from the struggle for freedom:

> We are struggling to prevent Kenyans in black skins with vested interests from ruling as successors to the administrators of colonial days. . . . our cause is the cause of the people of Kenya and so must triumph, however long and hard the struggle.[168]

From a passive experience of alien power to an active struggle against the corruptions of one's own: what better describes the life story of a conscientious participant in a successful movement of national liberation?

Deprivation and the West may have intruded more deeply into the very roots of the meaning of their lives for the African than for any other twentieth-century autobiographer. There is a similar variant—yet differing in tone and in the conclusion in some Chinese autobiographies, in which the meaning of life begins with the experience of an individual or collective beating—whether by one's own or by aliens—and concludes with a sense of delivery through concerted social action. Hsieh Ping-ying begins:

Earlier in the day I had been severely beaten by my mother with a stick, and even now there were distinctive marks on all parts of my back.

And concludes:

.... I could hear labourers ... singing aloud. ... This is their song, this is their groan and their war-cry. It will awaken mankind.[169]

Li Tsung-jen begins:

I was a boy when a series of severe national crises occurred at the end of the Ch'ing dynasty. China had been repeatedly defeated in foreign wars and was relegated almost to the position of a common colony.
During this critical period the Manchu rulers became more vicious than ever.

And concludes:

More than two thousand years ago our ancient sages preached the ideal of a cosmopolitanism which they called the Great Harmony. I have an unshaken faith that a modern counterpart of this ancient Chinese ideal will ultimately prevail in the form of a world union of democratic-socialism in which all peoples will be equal and no national boundaries will exist.[170]

This pattern of moving *from a dispassionate description of a humiliating attack to a serene confidence in a secular salvation*—within which both men and women, both Communists like Hsieh and nationalists like Li, can locate themselves—does not describe all twentieth-century Chinese autobiographies, certainly not those of the Catholic, John C. H. Wu, or of the Buddhist, Chen-hua. The latter concludes with his "final wish" to "realize the perfect and unequalled enlightenment" by "studying Buddhism."[171] From the 1930s on, and especially from the 1940s to the 1970s, in many instances the secular-salvation pattern may not have been spontaneously chosen, but suggested, or even imposed, by political pressures. The last emperor of China, Aisin-Gioro Pu Yi, describes such pressures in his autobiography *From Emperor to Citizen*.[172] But the best-known Indian or Indonesian autobiographies do not exhibit such a pattern at all. The pattern is only approached by a few Africans, and it is hardly imaginable in the twentieth-century West since World War II.

Chinese autobiographies of the twentieth century appear more like collective productions than Western or even Indian autobiographies. Not only is individuality less pronounced, but no modern Chinese autobiography stands out by its literary effectiveness or as a paradigmatic cultural document much above the others. Mothers assume a position of greater importance in modern Chinese autobiographies than they do in Western autobiographies (or even in Indian ones, where the father tends to loom larger). One twentieth-century Chinese autobiographer, Sheng-Cheng, begins with his mother speaking about her own family background and concludes it, after his participation in the Chinese revolution of 1911, with his mother giving him moral advice about the brotherhood of all men (and citing ancient poetry[173]). Sheng-Cheng's autobiography is organized around an interwoven analogy between family relations and the contemporary history of China: his grandmother represents the last Empress and tyrannical tradition, he himself and his older brother stand for modernity and revolution, the others waver. This close interpenetration and symbolic equivalence of family relations and national historical change—particularly the symbolism of the grandmother (rather than a paternal figure) as the dominating upholder of an oppressive ritualistic tradition—seems more characteristic of Chinese than of any other twentieth-century autobiographies. As there is some tendency in India to identify the family with the world, so there is some tendency in China to identify the family with history. Neither tendency is universal in the two civilizational traditions, but neither appears to be as strong in autobiographical writings anywhere else.

Whatever the reason—a common Indo-European background and linguistic similarities resulting from it, or the more recent (since the eighteenth century) greater closeness of historical immersion—Indian autobiographical responses to the West are generally conceived in a more intimate mode than the Chinese. However, the intimately understood West has tended to be limited, for Indian autobiographers, largely to England. Even though one is a religious and the other a secular activist, Gandhi and Nehru share their starting point in psychologically observed relationships within a history-soaked family line. Nehru even begins, in the very first sentence, with an objective psychological observation about himself: "An only son of prosperous parents is apt to be spoiled, especially so in India." An observation about himself is simultaneously an observation about India; objectivity is also criticism, and indulgence goes together with loneliness. "And so in the midst of that big family I felt rather lonely and was left a great deal to my own fancies and solitary games."[174] For Nehru, the system of meanings of an individual's existence begins with a critical psychological self- and culture-analysis of an ultimately lonely, but not socially isolated or historically rootless, individual.

Both psychological analysis and history separate Gandhi and Nehru from the nineteenth-century Indian, Dayanand, and they share historical family lines, but not their psychological analyses, with twentieth-century Chinese male autobiographers of gentry origins. Both Gandhi and Nehru describe themselves as engaged in a *continuous intrapsychic struggle,* as twentieth-century Chinese autobiographers generally do not, within a mass movement, in an East-West encounter. Gandhi's life incorporates the religious pattern (more characteristic of medieval Christian than of traditional Hindu autobiographers) of falling into corruption and moral regeneration; Nehru's does not. Gandhi, at his loneliest, sustains a sense of spiritual kinship with the Indian masses. Nehru in the end writes perhaps the most moving dissection of the spirit of a man not lost between, but strongly attached to, two civilizations:

> . . . . I often wonder if I represent anyone at all. . . . I have become a queer mixture of both the East and the West, out of place everywhere, at home nowhere. Perhaps my thoughts and approach to life are more akin to what is called Western than Eastern, but India clings to me, as she does to all her children, in innumerable ways; and behind me lie, somewhere in the subconscious, racial memories of a hundred, or whatever the number may be, generations of Brahmans. I cannot get rid of either that past inheritance or my recent acquisitions. They are both part of me, and, though they help me in both the East and the West, they also create in me a feeling of spiritual loneliness not only in public activities but in life itself.[175]

Who else but a high-caste Indian can, in an encounter between "East" and "West," experience his self as being simultaneously, and equally, a full-bodied heir of Mill and Rousseau *and* the firm possessor of the racial memories of a hundred proud generations of his own high culture? Who can be perfectly intimate with the rich diversity of Western civilization and yet not overdo his identification with one part of it? Something of this sort, with Christ replacing Mill and Rousseau, is evident in Gandhi as well. If Nehru (after having expressed his disagreement with Gandhi) concluded with "the last words of the great Socrates," Gandhi speaks at the end with what is at least in part the voice of Christ: "So long as man does not of his own free will put himself last among his fellow creatures, there is no salvation for him."[176]

Formally, the framework of Gandhi's life, although far richer in its contents, is similar to Dayanand's: from family to God. And Nehru's is analogous: from family to Socrates (but, equally, also to the battle for national independence). In autobiographies written by Indians since the attainment of India's independence, grand religious or national pursuits have, by and large, ceased to provide the guiding form for the self-comprehension of particular individuals.

Nirad Chaudhuri's beginning is traditional European: a very firm individual intention. The particular intention is not what one finds among West European autobiographers, but still less is it traditionally Indian: to come to grips with the whole history of his civilization. (Of all civilizations, India has been least concerned with history.) This theme is the constant framework of Chaudhuri's life: as he begins with it, so he returns to it in the end, as the medieval Christian to his God. But there is also a movement toward a nonreligious (perhaps Romantic in inspiration) transcendence of the permanent historic-civilizational framework.

Whereas the significance of Chaudhuri's life, on the one hand, coincides with the history of his civilization (as it might also for a scholarly Chinese), it is, on the other hand, independent of it (and opposed to the direction of its development during Chaudhuri's own life)—a formulation one rarely finds anywhere else in autobiographical writings, except for some east Europeans.

> . . . . my personal development has in no wise been typical of a modern Indian of the twentieth century. It is certainly exceptional, and may even be unique.
> During the years of my education I was becoming a stranger to my environment and organizing my intellectual and moral life along an independent nexus; in the next ten years I was oppressed by a feeling of antagonism to the environment; and in the last phase I became hostile to it. . . . The process was simply this: that while I was being carried along by the momentum of our history, most of my countrymen were being dragged backwards by its inertia.[177]

The discovery of *personal independence from the history of one's civilization* (and from environmental determinism, with which the actual description of the events of his life begins) opens up, for the secular critic, a "liberation from a nightmare" and a *reconciliation with the universe:*

> For long years I thought that the best which that thinking reed, man, could do was to go on maintaining an unyielding defiance to the universe. I subscribed to a creed of intellectual Prometheanism. . . . But in the last five or six years, . . . I have come to see that I and the universe are inseparable, because I am only a particle of the universe and remain so in every manifestation of my existence—intellectual, moral, and spiritual, as well as physical. . . . I have found that to sit by the rivers of Babylon is not necessarily to weep in Hebraic sorrow. Today, borne on a great flood of faith, hope, and joy in the midst of infinite degradation, I feel I shall be content to be nothing for ever after death in the ecstacy of having lived and been alive for a moment.[178]

At almost the same time as Chaudhuri, an Untouchable, Hazari, was writing his autobiography. There is no history of Hazari's civilization—or even family history—at the beginning, only one's own village, district, mother, father, the death in childhood of eight siblings (who are all "lost" not by both parents but by the mother alone), and the eternal principle of Karma:

> The death of these children was the reason for my father taking a second wife living under the same roof . . . behind his action lay the

idea of Karma . . . for every Hindu must have a male child to leave in the world . . . my father's second marriage . . . was to fulfill his duty towards his parents and his community. . . .

The mother "loses," the father "takes." And the significance of an individual's life begins in the eternal repetitions of the sociocosmic cycle defined by the village way of life and the religious tradition.

At the end, still a young man, he attains a sort of liberation by converting to Islam (yet "I could never be a devout and orthodox disciple of Islam, and this knowledge only increased a consciousness of guilt from which there seemed no escape"); is both charmed and disturbed by the beauty of the dancing girls of Lucknow ("In the houses of dancing girls, new poets and philosophers were born, and the rich youth of Lucknow explored the depths of degradation and learned to wear a mask of civilization"); and departs, under the sponsorship of an Englishman, to Europe (concerned in advance about the "loose morality" of European women, "as they had no family ties or family code").

> Already I felt that I was part of a new world, encircled by the mighty ocean which knew no creed or caste, and as I gazed towards the wide horizon, I prayed that one day I might find that peace of soul which I had never known but always sought.[179]

The outcaste moves *from a cosmic cycle to an anxious liberation*—a quite different pattern from what we find in the twentieth-century autobiographies of working-class Chinese. It is entirely different, too, from the self-assurance and cultural steadiness of the nineteenth-century Indian Muslim Lutfullah.

An exceptional case among Indian autobiographers, a tribeswoman, Sita Rathnamal, employs a symbolic design that might have been generally characteristic of members of tribal societies if they had been spontaneously writing autobiographical texts. She begins so immersed in nature as to be inaudible among its more powerful noises (much as Georg Simmel has argued we become inaudible to ourselves and to each other in the metropolis).

> The south-west monsoon was filling the mountain streams and turning them into torrents when I was born. . . . The rain made so loud a noise on the thatch of the hut that my first cries in this world were not heard above it. It is like that in the forest where men and women and their children are, as other animals, dwarfed by the trees and the mountains . . . The lives of my parents and our tribe were dependent on the gods of nature. . . .

She ends her autobiographical account by coming home to her South Indian village from the big city, Madras:

 . . . . perhaps we do travel a full circle: the simple wheel of life. . . .
How many generations, I wondered, had climbed this same path? The
memory of the tribe is lost in antiquity. . . . Yet their spirit lingered and
I felt again a oneness with them and with my father.[180]

What is possible even for a twentieth-century Indian (though not for
all Indians)—"the simple wheel of life"—has *never* been possible for the
Western autobiographer. A Westerner is born to be exiled from his natural
home. His community of origin ceases to exist with his coming of age. If he
wants his natural home, he has to reconstruct it; he needs to reinvent his
community of origin. Only a Westerner could have said: "Much art is
required to prevent man in society from being altogether artificial."

The autobiography of the Indian tribeswoman needs only to be compared with that of the Swedish actress Viveca Lindfors to sense the fundamental differences in the uses to which cyclical forms of self-
comprehension can be put in diverse twentieth-century settings. Lindfors
begins with an image in which her theatrical role in a show coincides with
her sense of selfhood after the breakdown of her fourth marriage: " 'It is
about a woman removing her mask,'. . . . The mask torn off the
imposter. . . . In my life I am finally accepting the 'unmasking' as a daily
routine as essential as brushing my teeth."

She had herself "created," not her self but two "perfect images" for
herself: one the wife-mother-friend, the other the actress-lover-
breadwinner. These masks proved not only contradictory in their demands
but also false to her true self, and now she is paying the price: they "left me,
the real woman, neglected, frustrated, ambivalent, and incapable of open
and lasting intimacy." But only by paying this price does she discover her
own true selfhood.

One's beginning is not in the past but in the present moment and it
coincides with the understanding of the genuine self. Lindfors both begins
and ends with the state of her mind after her fourth divorce. Where there
was once, in the dominant Western tradition, the objectively predestined
movement from God to God, there is now the subjectively circular framing
of the meaning of one's existence *from one's own mind to one's own mind.* But
for the Swedish actress, this frame, in addition to one of the most recent
events of her life, also contains one of its earliest memories. The memory is
that of a persistent flower of her "childhood country. . . ., far away from
where I live today": "The stepmother violet seems to survive in spite of the
wind and the heat of the sun and the burning salt of the sea. It even
spreads itself all over the world. Forever, it seems."[181]

The cycles of contemporary losses are balanced by the tough fragility
of childhood memories, from which hope arises. Yet the childhood hope
does not lead back home, but to a spreading of the self disillusioned of its
personal masks all over the world. The circularity of one's life is one's own
circularity, its expansiveness is one's own expansiveness. Nevertheless, the

northern European delineates herself at least partly by her memories of nature (even though a "stepmother" nature), and comes back, in the very end, even while declaring her universality, to those memories, as other European—and especially American—autobiographers do not.

Could either a Chinese or an Indian in the twentieth century—or a European at any time—have brought forth an autobiography in which the events of an action-packed life are stretched out, from sensuous love to the anticipation of a public death, within the framework of *unmitigated self-enjoyment, but self-enjoyment with a sense of complete fusion with his people enjoying him,* as has Indonesia's most famous autobiographer, who began: "The simplest way to describe Sukarno is to say that he is a great lover. He loves his country, he loves his people, he loves women, he loves art, and, best of all, he loves himself," differing from the classical Euro-American narcissist—a Rousseau or a Casanova—in the security of both self-perception and community immersion, in his genuine heroism and utterly untroubled orality, and in the innocence of his magniloquence, and concluded:

> I do not wish all my titles on my tombstone so that it reads: 'Here lies His Most Exalted Excellency, the Honorable Doctor Ingenieur Hadji Raden Sukarno, the First President of the Republic of Indonesia, Commander-in-Chief of the Armed Forces, Great Leader of the Revolution, Prime Minister, Mandatory of MPRS, Chairman of the Supreme Advisory Council, Peperti Chief War Administrator, Highest Leader of the National Front, Commander of the State Police' and so on. . . . When I die, bury Bapak in accordance with the Islamic religion, and on a plain little stone write simply: Here lies Bung Karno, the mouthpiece of the Indonesian people.[182]

One of the most recent non-Western autobiographies seems to raise questions about the hypothesis of increasing differentiation in the responses of non-Westerners to the West. Rato Khyongla Nawang Losang, a twentieth-century reincarnation of a famous Tibetan lama, has escaped from Chinese Communist control and ends up in America:

> In mid-1968, I returned to New York. . . . With the help of friends I found an apartment and a job at B. Altman & Co. as a stockroom clerk, which I thoroughly enjoyed. For the first time I could go to a job, do whatever I was told, and come home at the end of the day with no further responsibility. . . . It seems to me that there is a particular sympathy and similarity between Americans and Tibetans. Both are open, friendly, fun-loving, eager to learn and to try new experiences. . . . Now, far from my origins, I try to continue the teachings I have lived from my childhood. I think there is a place for them in my Western world and perhaps, slowly, this will prove to be true.[183]

What many Westerners view as the burden of a routine job can appear to a Tibetan lama as a liberation from his far more heavily structured responsibilities. He probably misperceives Americans in finding them similar to

Tibetans. He finally identifies with "my Western world," but within this West of his he seeks to live by the teachings of his Tibetan religion. To a Buddhist, the change from one world to another does not matter. What matters are his teachings, which do not depend on any world. In his efforts to show convergences between Tibetans and Americans, Losang succeeds in demonstrating the surviving specificity of a Buddhist response to the West.

The distinctiveness of the Tibetan's conclusion is evident when it is compared with that of the Filipino writer Carlos Bulosan, who also came, three decades earlier, to live in the United States. Bulosan concludes thinking of his *brothers* concretely, sensually:

> I wanted to shout good-bye to the Filipino pea pickers in the fields who stopped working when the bus came into view. . . . One of them, who looked like my brother Amado, took off his hat. The wind played in his hair. There was a sweet fragrance in the air.

In a similar way he identifies fully with the good American *earth*, citing his own experiences but not his ideological abstractions, as the Tibetan had done:

> . . . . the American earth was like a huge heart unfolding warmly to receive me. I felt it spreading through my being, warming me with its glowing reality. . . . . my faith in America was something that grew out of the sacrifices and loneliness of my friends, of my brothers in America and my family in the Philippines—something that grew out of our desire to know America, and to become a part of her great tradition, and to contribute something toward her final fulfillment.[184]

You end as a man who, in exile, has reconstituted primordial fraternity and regained the earth.

Whatever Bulosan's political radicalism, the connectedness with brothers in the womb of the maternal earth would appeal as the end of all wisdom—the only nondeforming condition of existence—to many European Catholics of peasant origin. (Not because they are Catholics but because Catholicism has destroyed peasant culture less than any other Western religion.) One does not find any of it in the conclusions of Protestant autobiographies. In the Russian conception of fraternity, attachment to nature tends to disappear. And if a Jewish autobiographer concludes with brothers, they are the dead ones, only to be remembered. "What will *separate* the setting from the suffering?" (My italics).

The peasant wants exactly the opposite. But where the post-classical, secular Western spirit of *analyzing, even if the demonstrable truth kill us, and full speed ahead* is active, even the descendants of peasants have to learn about brotherhood and the earth from books of poetry and ethnography; or from the dead phosphorescence of their own lived-in mistakes.

XV

It seems unlikely that the nineteenth-century tendency toward hegemony of one Western (or any other) mode of self-comprehension—which was not absolute even then—could reassert itself, in the foreseeable future, in the non-Western parts of the world (or, for that matter, in the West). Short of a nuclear catastrophe, which would terminate our story anyway, no single model of being human seems likely to gain the imperial supremacy in the world comparable to that which Western liberalism exercised in the nineteenth century.

Even if industrialization should become worldwide, there is little reason so far to assume that it will homogenize individual self-comprehensions, blotting the effects (apparently more powerful on subjective self-perceptions than anywhere else) of local civilizational traditions, the most popular of which seem likely only to be revitalized by the impact of the forces of modernization rather than extinguished. (The "smaller" traditions might have a more problematic future.)

Tendencies toward universalization and toward particularization in self-comprehensions are likely to keep asserting themselves either concurrently or in phase cycles of temporary partial domination of one, followed by equally temporary partial dominance of the other. Political powerlessness does not necessarily preclude—and may, in a highly conscious people not wholly devoid of passion, even enhance—a steady development of the powers of discovery of one's own inner particularity, a cultivation of selfhood that is impermeable to tyranny, and its expression in the nuances of the significant buried in the mountains of the prescribed.

The mystery of the individual's experience of the depths and the nuances of his own being—and the courage to stand by one's own depths and one's own nuances—is likely to remain not wholly extinguishable so long as people continue to write about themselves in their natural languages.

Only an artificial language, and only if it acquires a hegemony over the totality of our imagination, seems capable of destroying us as individuals and as details of humanity signifying, by their own existences and expressions, their solidarity with each other.

XVI

We need to uncover the trajectories of the self-comprehensions of the various streams of humanity if we are to locate our own selfhoods where they belong, to identify the beginnings and endings of our constituent parts, *our own* histories of boundaries and encounters (and those of future generations).

An archeology of selfhood is perhaps not yet possible for any non-Western region and it remains unwritten for many constituent parts of Western civilization. It remains a pressing task for us to accomplish. I propose the creation of a network of cooperating scholars to reconstruct the historical trajectories of self-comprehension for the particular nations, linguistic groups and social classes, and cultural regions of the world as a preliminary to fundamental comparative studies in a cross-civilizational perspective.

This need has not disappeared in a society in which one of the youngest autobiographers begins the account of his life with a college commencement:

> *June, 1969:*. . . . The night before, someone had taken white paint and painted "Commence what?"—

then imagines his own commencement address:

> . . . . here you are at the ridiculous age of twenty-one, with virtually no real skill except as conversationalists. . . . Being a good conversationalist is really what a liberal arts education is all about.

Mark Vonnegut lived his youth entirely in the disorderliness of the immediate present and he finds a stable voice only in the end, writing as a recovered schizophrenic to a friend suffering from that condition:

> The important thing to keep in mind is that others have gone through and come out in good shape.[185]

Whether he knew it or not, Vonnegut's conclusion is Abelard's starting point:

> . . . . . and so I propose to follow up the words of consolation I gave you in person with the history of my own misfortunes, hoping thereby to give you comfort in absence.[186]

Is it too much to suggest that the forgetfulness of the symbolic frameworks for self-comprehension of which an essential part of the history of human culture consists has contributed to the psychic breakdown of the young American autobiographer? Does the spontaneous recovery of Abelard's starting point in a secularized guise give him a selfhood—perhaps even a history of selfhood and a map of sociability—to be trusted?

Notes

1. John F. Benton, ed., *Self and Society: The Memoirs of Abbot Guibert of Nogent* (New York: Harper & Row, 1970), pp. 35, 228.

2. *The Confessions of St. Augustine* (New York: New American Library, 1963), pp. 17, 350.

3. Thomas Merton, *The Seven Storey Mountain* (New York: Harcourt, Brace and Company, 1948), pp. 3, 422–23.

4. Paramahansa Yogananda, *Autobiography of a Yogi* (Los Angeles: Self-Realization Fellowship, 1971), p. 3.

5. Rodney L. Taylor, "The Centered Self: Religious Autobiography in the Neo-Confucian Tradition," *History of Religions* 17 (1978): 266–81, quote from p. 276.

6. Chen-hua, "Random Talks About My Mendicant Life," *Chinese Sociology and Anthropology* 13 (Fall 1980): 5–110; 13 (Summer 1981): 3–113; and 14 (Spring 1982): 3–90; quote from the first installment, p. 5.

7. R. C. P. Sinha, *The Indian Autobiographies in English* (New Delhi: S. Chand & Company Ltd., 1978): 26, 41, 46–48. See also Judith Walsh, *Growing Up in British India* (New York: Holmes & Meier, 1982). Jahāngīr's quote is from *The Tūzuk-i-Jahāngīri or Memoirs of Jahāngīr* (Delhi: Munshiram Manoharlal, 1968), p. 1; Bābur's from *Bābur-nāma (Memoirs of Bābur)*, vol. 1 and vol. 2 (combined) (New Delhi: Oriental Books Reprint Corporation, 1970), p. 1.

8. Pei-yi Wu, "The Spiritual Autobiography of Te-ch'ing," in Wm. Theodore de Bary and the Conference on Seventeenth-Century Chinese Thought, *The Unfolding of Neo-Confucianism* (New York: Columbia University Press, 1975), pp. 67–92, quote from p. 68.

9. Burton Watson, *Ssu-ma Ch'ien, Grand Historian of China* (New York: Columbia University Press, 1958), p. 42.

10. In contrast to the tendency of Islamic scholars to mention many teachers, the theory of Sufi mysticism contends that "only a specific and lasting relationship with one single master can initiate a novice properly into the Path of Truth." Shelomo D. Goitein, "Formal Friendship in the Medieval Near East," *Proceedings of the American Philosophical Society* 115 (December, 1971): 486. The effect on the experience of selfhood is, on the one hand, a *concentration* of the substance of this experience and, on the other hand, the *effacement of the separateness* of the individuality of the disciple who speaks from the master who remains silent, "as when Jalāl ad-Dīn Rūmī, the greatest mystical poet writing in the Persian language, concluded his poems not with his own pen name, but with that of his master" (ibid). The Islamic scholar neither concentrates his own substance as much nor effaces his individuality as fully as the mystic. And the Western mystic, Heinrich Seuse, "makes his beginning," in the eighteenth year of his life, through his own ecstasy, without any spiritual guidance by a master. Heinrich Seuse, *Deutsche mystische Schriften* (Düsseldorf: Patmos-Verlag, 1966), p. 18.

11. On Islamic scholars' autobiographies, see Georg Misch, *Geschichte der Autobiographie. Dritter Band: Das Mittelalter. Zweiter Teil: Hochmittelalter im Anfang. Zweite Hälfte.* (Frankfurt am Main: Verlag G. Schulte-Bulmke, 1962), pp. 962–1006. In addition to modern Western and Islamic autobiography, Misch also describes Egyptian, Assyrian, Greco-Roman, and Byzantine autobiographical traditions. These are not considered in the present investigation of *living* autobiographical traditions. In line with the general tendency of Western writings on autobiography, both historical and critical, Misch ignores Chinese, Indian, and Japanese autobiographical traditions.

12. Colin Morris, *The Discovery of the Individual 1050–1200* (New York: Harper & Row, 1972), p. 66.

13. On earlier approaches to selfhood in the civilization-analytical tradition, see Benjamin Nelson, "Self-Images and Systems of Spiritual Direction in the History of European Civilization," in Samuel Z. Klausner, ed., *The Quest for Self-Control: Classical Philosophies and Scientific Research* (New York: Free Press, 1965), pp. 49–103; Vytautas Kavolis, "Logics of Selfhood: Civilizational Structures for Individual Identities," in *Identity and Authority: Explorations in the Theory of Society*, ed. Roland Robertson and Burkart Holzner, (Oxford: Basil Blackwell, 1980), pp. 40–60, 268–71, 284–87. Also relevant: Vytautas Kavolis, "Structure and Energy: Toward a Civilization-Analytic Perspective," *Comparative Civilizations Review* no. 1 (Winter 1979): 21–41, and "Romanticism and Taoism: The Planes of Cultural Organization," *Comparative Civilizations Review* no. 5 (Fall 1980): 1–32.

14. Whereas for the Russian the opposite of sociability is "strong individual friendship," the Indian considers sociability to be opposed to formless, morally uninformed

"gregariousness." Nicolas Berdyaev, *Dream and Reality* (New York: Collier Books, 1962), pp. 267–68; Nirad C. Chaudhuri, *The Autobiography of an Unknown Indian* (Berkeley: University of California Press, 1968), p. 383. The question remains to what extent the two authors describe their own personal conceptions of sociability and to what extent they are shared in their societies (or at least in their more educated classes). The Indian's notion of sociability corresponds to the Englishman's and is probably derived from it. The Russian's conception of sociability may have originated in German Romanticism.

15. *The Letters of Abelard and Heloise* (Harmondsworth: Penguin Books, 1974), p. 57.

16. Ibid., pp. 105–6.

17. Margery Kempe, *The Book of Margery Kempe* (New York: Devin-Adair, 1949), p. 5.

18. Ibid., pp. 1–2.

19. Ibid., pp. 226–27.

20. Elizabeth Petroff, "The Paradox of Sanctity: Lives of Italian Women Saints, 1200–1400," in *Life Histories as Civilizational Texts*, ed. Edmund Leites, International Society for the Comparative Study of Civilizations (U.S.) Occasional Papers, No. 1 (1977), pp. 4–24.

21. Misch, *Geschichte der Autobiographie*, p. 956.

22. Domna C. Stanton, *The Aristocrat as Art: A Study of the Honnête Homme and the Dandy in Seventeenth- and Nineteenth-Century French Literature* (New York: Columbia University Press, 1980).

23. Benvenuto Cellini, *The Autobiography of Benvenuto Cellini* (New York: Bantam Books, 1956), p. 1.

24. al-Mukaddasi's quotes are from Misch, *Geschichte der Autobiographie*, p. 919.

25. Pei-yi Wu, "Self-Examination and Confessions of Sins in Traditional China," *Harvard Journal of Asiatic Studies* 39 (June 1979): 5–38.

26. "The conception of 'friendship' was itself corrupted by self-interest; as a Florentine merchant remarked, 'It is good to have friends of all kinds, but not useless men.'" William J. Bouwsma, "Anxiety and the Formation of Early Modern Culture," in Barbara C. Malament, ed., *After the Reformation: Essays in Honor of J. H. Hexter* (Manchester: Manchester University Press, 1980), p. 227. The Near Eastern Judeo-Arabic tradition of commercial friendship, well-documented for the tenth through the thirteenth centuries, seems to have been simultaneously more formalized in the manner of its establishment and dissolution and more emotional in its substantive content than European "mercantile friendships." In the Near East, a man could address a letter to what was objectively his "legal and business representative" by a directive on the reverse side: "Carry this letter to my intimate friend, the friend of my soul," his friendship being so well known that he did not have to tell the name of his friend to the carrier of the message. Goitein, "Formal Friendships," pp. 487–88. There is no evidence in Renaissance autobiographies written by bourgeois authors of the aristocratic ideal of the exalted self-sacrificing friendship on the model of Shakespeare's *Merchant of Venice*. Thus it may be possible to explain the decline of this ideal by social-class dynamics alone. Protestantism may have contributed only a specific emotional tonality of rejection—and a rigorous formulation of an alternative ideal.

27. Jerome Cardan [Girolamo Cardano], *The Book of My Life* (New York: E. P. Dutton, 1930), p. XVII.

28. Cellini, *The Autobiography*, p. 308.

29. Cardano, *The Book*, pp. 291, 290.

30. The twelfth-century Arab autobiographer Usāma ibn-Munqidh combines both methods of description. In the first part (begun in his sixties), he tells stories of the events of his life in battle and at court. The second part (written when he was close to ninety) consists largely of a classification of over one hundred types of activities and qualities of character appropriate to a warrior nobility (including a section on the courage of women in battle), which he has observed and lists one after another. The first approach is reminiscent of Cellini, though a different social setting is described by a more heroic man and the events are not

arranged in a rigorously temporal sequence, but presented as scattered retrievals from memory. (In this respect, Usāma is close to a late twentieth-century sense of flowing with one's memories, without imposing on them an "artificial," calendar-dictated pattern.) The second approach is similar to Cardano's, except that, in the case of the Arab warrior-gentleman, there is nothing remotely resembling a systematic analysis of his own character (and certainly no mention of any weakness of character in him). Nevertheless, the comparison suggests that an atomizing dissection of the life stream into its components can arise in a classically educated aristocracy as well as in a science-practicing bourgeoisie and that it is therefore not to be identified as a "bourgeois" trait. Gustave E. von Grunebaum considers "the atomizing outlook . . . on people and things" to be a general characteristic of the Arab tradition, which has "prevented for the most part the drawing of fully individualized portraits in poetical form." *Medieval Islam: A Study in Cultural Orientation*, 2d ed. [Chicago: The University of Chicago Press, 1961), p. 266. If anything is characteristic of bourgeois—as contrasted to aristocratic— self-comprehensions, it would seem to be *efforts to attain a greater unity of self-interpretation out of a greater awareness of variety, inconsistency, and change in self-experience.* The presence of these qualities sets the Renaissance man apart from the Arab nobleman. But in both of these historical types of self-comprehension, no psychological, moral, or intellectual movement from a point of origin to a point of destination is to be found in spite of a great deal of physical mobility. An Islamic mystic, on the other hand, could conceive of his life as a directional movement: "You wish to know . . . how I have dared to climb from the low level of traditional belief to the topmost summit of assurance." *The Confessions of Al Ghazzali* (London: John Murray, 1909), p. 11.

31. Quoted from Pei-yi-Wu, "Self-Eulogy: An Autobiographical Mode in Traditional Chinese Literature," presented before the University Seminar on Traditional China, Columbia University, November 20, 1973, p. 18.

32. Cardano, *The Book*, pp. 72, 281.

33. Leonardo da Vinci, *The Notebooks of Leonardo da Vinci*, (ed.) Pamela Taylor (New York: The New American Library, 1960), p. 190.

34. Richard Baxter, *The Autobiography of Richard Baxter* (London: J. M. Dent & Sons, 1931), p. 3.

35. John Bunyan, *Grace Abounding to the Chief of Sinners* (Oxford: At the Clarendon Press, 1962), p. 1.

36. Ibid., p. 5.

37. Ibid., p. 6.

38. Ibid., pp. 102–3.

39. Baxter, *The Autobiography*, p. 19.

40. Cardano, *The Book*, p. 195.

41. Baxter, *The Autobiography*, pp. 7–8.

42. Colin Morris, *The Discovery of the Individual.*

43. Quoted from Lillian Faderman, *Surpassing the Love of Men: Romantic Friendship and Love Between Women from the Renaissance to the Present* (New York: William Morrow, 1981), p. 68. On the tendency of Puritans to distrust human friendship, see Benjamin Nelson, *The Idea of Usury: From Tribal Brotherhood to Universal Otherhood*, 2d ed. (Chicago: The University of Chicago Press, 1969), pp. 142–64. Puritans did, however, allow, as did John Winthrop in New England, for the possibility, as well as political necessity, of an emotionally subdued " 'friendship and affection' among those charged with the governing and the guiding of men." Wilson Carey McWilliams, *The Idea of Fraternity in America* (Berkeley: University of California Press, 1973), p. 136. While friendship was known to be fragile, it was regarded by the Puritans as suspicious only when it became emotionally intense and thus either diverted men from the tasks of constructing God's kingdom on earth or stood in danger of acquiring (or merely suggested) erotic qualities, all of which should have been contained entirely within marriage. The Puritan distrust of friendship, especially "excessive" friendship, is in its fundamental logic

quite different from the calculated utilitarianism of "mercantile friendships," which go back, in the modern European experience, at least to the Renaissance, even though many Puritans were members of the mercantile class.

44. John Henry Cardinal Newman, *Apologia Pro Vita Sua, Being a History of his Religious Opinions* (London: Longmans, Green, and Co., 1905), p. 238.

45. Robert A. Raines, *Going Home* (San Francisco: Harper & Row, 1979), pp. 3, 6.

46. *The Gossamer Years (Kagerō Nikki). The Diary of a Noblewoman of Heian Japan* (Tokyo: Charles E. Tuttle, 1964), pp. 33, 167.

47. Bashō, *A Haiku Journey* (Tokyo: Kodansha International Ltd., 1974), pp. 27, 66.

48. Earl Miner, tr., *Japanese Poetic Diaries* (Berkeley: University of California Press, 1969), p. 40.

49. Joyce Ackroyd, trans., *Told Round a Brushwood Fire: The Autobiography of Arai Hakuseki* (Princeton: Princeton University Press, 1979), pp. 35, 277.

50. Watson, *Ssu-ma ch'ien*, p. 42.

51. Ibid., pp. 56–57.

52. Taylor, "The Centered Self."

53. Wu, "The Spiritual Autobiography of Te-ch'ing," pp. 68–69, 80.

54. Misch, *Geschichte der Autobiographie*, p. 1003.

55. Taylor, "The Centered Self," p. 281.

56. Peter H. Lee, *Celebration of Continuity: Themes in Classic East Asian Poetry* (Cambridge, Mass.: Harvard University Press, 1979), pp. 144–173. Friends are mentioned in traditional Chinese autobiographies, but nothing of basic importance attaches to them. All that Kao says about friendship is: "The river and the mountains were clear and inviting. Good friends urged me to drink more. . . . I suddenly felt unhappy. . . . I realized that being totally ignorant of the Way, my mind and body had nothing to draw on." Taylor, "The Centered Self," p. 278.

57. The concern of the sociology of consciousness is (1) to formulate an adequate description of the main variants of the shared symbolic forms demonstrably present in social behavior and subjective self-perceptions; (2) to locate these symbolic forms exactly in time and space, so that one could say when they begin and end, in what significant versions they present themselves, what transformations they undergo over time, and to whom, in what intensity, with what practical effects, and for how long they appeal in each of their transformations and variants; and (3) to identify the influences which operate, in various phases of these processes, to produce, change, undermine, and possibly revive such shared symbolic designs.

A civilizationally sensitized psychology would seek to open up and explicate the dynamic implications, the directionalities, mechanisms, and predicaments generated for human beings by each symbolic design of social behavior and subjective self-perception. Each of these designs—when fully developed—contains a largely implicit "psycho-logic." Cultural psychology may be conceived of as the systematic comparative study of such culturally differentiated, historically active "logics of the psyche."

58. Jean-Jacques Rousseau, *The Confessions* (Harmondsworth: Penguin Books, 1954), p. 17; John Stuart Mill, *Autobiography of John Stuart Mill* (New York: Columbia University Press, 1924), p. 1.

59. Giacomo Casanova, *History of My Life*, vols. 1 and 2 (New York: Harcourt, Brace and World, 1966), 1:28.

60. Johann Wolfgang von Goethe, *The Autobiography of Johann Wolfgang von Goethe* (Chicago: The University of Chicago Press, 1974), 1:8–9; 2:22.

61. Ibid., 1:2c, 3; 2:437.

62. Henry Adams, *The Education of Henry Adams: An Autobiography* (Boston: Houghton Mifflin Company, 1918), p. X.

63. Booker T. Washington, *Up from Slavery*, William E. B. DuBois, *The Souls of Black Folk*, James Weldon Johnson, *The Autobiography of an Ex-Colored Man* (New York: Avon Books, 1965).

64. Casanova, *History of My Life*, pp. 29, 31.

65. Mill, *Autobiography*, p. 1.

66. Casanova, *History of My Life*, p. 25.

67. Ibid., pp. 25, 38.

68. Rousseau, *The Confessions*, p. 262.

69. *The Nightwatches of Bonaventura* (Austin: University of Texas Press, 1971), p. 169.

70. Roger Rosenblatt, "Black Autobiography: Life as the Death Weapon," *The Yale Review* 65 (1976); 515–27, quote from pp. 522–24.

71. Charles Darwin, *The Autobiography of Charles Darwin 1809–1882* (New York: Harcourt, Brace and Company, 1958), pp. 21, 138–39. The experience of constriction was more general. George Rosen points out that, in the first half of the nineteenth century, "when the English lower classes were responding to messianic visions, intellectuals in many instances were exhibiting evidences of psychological disorder along very different lines. Feelings of isolation, loneliness, ennui, despair, and depression recur so frequently in the letters and writings of men like Charles Kingsley, Alfred Tennyson, John Stuart Mill, Thomas Carlyle, Arthur Hugh Clough, and others as to leave the impression of endemic psychopathology." "Emotion and Sensibility in Ages of Anxiety: A Comparative Historical Review," *American Journal of Psychiatry* 124 (1967): 782.

72. Edward Gibbon, *Memoirs of My Life* (New York: Funk and Wagnalls, 1969), p. 1.

73. Benjamin Franklin, *The Autobiography of Benjamin Franklin* (New Haven: Yale University Press, 1964), p. 43.

74. Gibbon, *Memoirs of My Life*.

75. Rousseau, *The Confessions*, p. 17.

76. Mill, *Autobiography*, pp. 1–2.

77. Rousseau, *The Confessions*, p. 456.

78. Ibid., pp. 386, 395.

79. John Stuart Mill, *On Liberty* (New York: W. W. Norton, 1975), p. 63.

80. *Harriet Martineau's Autobiography* (Boston: James R. Osgood and Company, 1877), 1:8; 2:113, 123–24.

81. Rousseau, *The Confessions*, p. 606.

82. Jean-Jacques Rousseau, *Reveries of the Solitary Walker* (Harmondsworth: Penguin Books, 1979), pp. 153–55.

83. Mill, *Autobiography*, p. 221.

84. Casanova, *History of My Life*, 12:238.

85. Gibbon, *Memoirs*, p. 189.

86. Glückel, *The Memoirs of Glückel of Hameln* (New York: Schocken Books, 1977), pp. 1–4.

87. Mary G. Mason, "The Other Voice: Autobiographies of Women Writers," in *Autobiography: Essays Theoretical and Critical*, ed. James Olney (Princeton, N.J.: Princeton University Press, 1980), pp. 207–235. Estelle C. Jelinek elaborates further: ". . . . women's autobiographies . . . emphasize to a much lesser extent the public aspects of their lives, the affairs of the world, or even their careers, and concentrate instead on their personal lives—domestic details, family difficulties, close friends, and especially people who influenced them . . . the idealization or aggrandizement found in male autobiographies is not typical of the female mode. . . . irregularity rather than orderliness informs the self-portraits by women. The narratives of their lives are often not chronological and progressive but disconnected, fragmentary, or organized into self-sustained units rather than connecting chapters." "Introduction: Women's Autobiography and the Male Tradition," in *Women's Autobiography: Essays in Criticism* ed. Estelle C. Jelinek (Bloomington: Indiana University Press, 1980), pp. 7–8, 15, 17. In line with the general tendency of the critical literature on autobiographies, Jelinek says "women's," when "Western women's" is meant. Not even eastern European women are included.

88. Georgia O'Keeffe, *Georgia O'Keeffe* (New York: The Viking Press, 1976).

89. George Sand, *My Life* (New York: Harper & Row, 1979), p. 240.

90. Julian of Norwich, *Revelations of Divine Love* (Baltimore, Md.: Penguin Books, 1966), pp. 63–64.

91. Maxim Gorky, *Autobiography of Maxim Gorky* (London: Eleh Books, 1953); Pitirim A. Sorokin, *A Long Journey* (New Haven, Conn.: College and University Press, 1963).

92. Glückel, *The Memoirs*, p. 4.

93. Ibid., p. 277.

94. Solomon Maimon, *An Autobiography* (New York: Schocken Books, 1967), p. 3.

95. Malcolm X, *The Autobiography of Malcolm X* (New York: Grove Press, 1966), p. 1.

96. Heinrich Heine, *Heinrich Heine's Memoirs. From his Works, Letters, and Conversations*, ed. Gustav Karpeles (New York: Arno Press, 1973), 1:4–5.

97. Ibid., 2:252–53.

98. Rosa Luxemburg, *The Letters of Rosa Luxemburg*, ed. Stephen Eric Bonner (Boulder, Colo.: Westview Press, 1978), pp. 178–79, 180, 203.

99. Sigmund Freud, *The Standard Edition of the Complete Psychological Works*, Vol. 20 (London: The Hogarth Press, 1959), p. 7; Gershom Scholem, *From Berlin to Jerusalem: Memoirs of My Youth* (New York: Schocken Books, 1980), p. 1.

100. Norman Mailer, *Advertisements for Myself* (New York: G. P. Putnam's Sons, 1959), pp. 15, 492–93.

101. Sigmund Diamond, *In Quest: Journal of an Unwanted Pilgrimage* (New York: Columbia University Press, 1980), p. 222.

102. Anne Roiphe, *Generations Without Memory: A Jewish Journey in Christian America* (New York: The Linden Press, 1981), pp. 172, 214.

103. Ibid., pp. 220–21.

104. Wolfgang Bauer, "Icherleben und Autobiographie im älteren China," *Heidelberger Jahrbücher* 8 (1964): 12–40; Wu, "Self-Eulogies," and "Self-Examination"; Taylor, "The Centered Self."

105. Miner, *Japanese Poetic Diaries;* Ackroyd, *Told Round a Brushwood Fire.*

106. Franz Rosenthal, "Die arabische Autobiographie," *Studia Arabica* (Roma: Pontificium Institutum Biblicum 1937): 1–40; Misch, *Geschichte der Autobiographie*, pp. 905–1076.

107. Sinha, *The Indian Autobiographies.*

108. Bauer, "Icherleben und Autobiographie," pp. 13–15, 17.

109. In a typically Chinese manner—combining, in the Confucian tradition, secular, ethical, authoritarian and lyrical emphases—Ch'ü Yüan represents a "Prometheus" who is (a) not an invented superhuman figure, but a real man, around whom both a literary and popular mythology have evolved; (b) originally not a rebel but a minister of the Ch'u state who, "out of loyalty to both king and country, and self-assurance of his 'purity' and the correctness of his ideas. . . . continually tried to remonstrate with the court and to express his uncompromising ideas"; (c) not guided by the moral considerations he himself evolves (as Prometheus did), but firmly supported by an existing tradition of moral expectations which prescribed this course of action as the obligation of the ideal man in his social position; and (d) not in need of others to describe his actions, but himself a poet of great power (and somewhat "Romantic" character). Lawrence A. Schneider, *A Madman of Ch'u: The Chinese View of Loyalty and Dissent* (Berkeley: University of California Press, 1980), p. 3.

110. Misch, *Geschichte der Autobiographie*, pp. 1008–1116.

111. Philip K. Hitti, trans., *Memoirs of an Arab-Syrian Gentleman; or an Arab Knight in the Crusades. Memoirs of Usāmah ibn-Munqidh* (Beirut: Khayats, 1964).

112. K. C. Yadav, "Introduction," *Autobiography of Dayanand Saraswati* (New Delhi: Manohar, 1978), p. 2.

113. Sinha, *The Indian Autobiographies*, p. 94.

114. Dayanand, *Autobiography*, pp. 22, 90.

115. Sinha, *The Indian Autobiographies,* p. 102.

116. Dayanand, *Autobiography,* p. 22.

117. The psychoanalytic approach would seem curiously inappropriate for those who are born into a world—unless psychoanalysis becomes necessary precisely in order to prove to them that they have been born into a family: a strategic resource in the battle between primordiality and modernism (or perhaps, in the specific historical context of its origin, between Judaism and secularity).

118. *Autobiography of Lutfullah, a Mohammedan Gentleman (Chiefly Resident in India;) and his Transactions with his Fellow-Creatures; Interspersed with Remarks on the Habits, Customs, and Character of the People with Whom He Had to Deal,* ed. Edward B. Eastwick, A New Edition (London: Smith, Elder, and Co., 1863), pp. III, 411.

119. Abdullah bin Abdul Kadir, *The Hikayat Abdullah* (Kuala Lampur: Oxford University Press, 1970), p. 29. On the history of Malayan autobiography, see A. H. Johns, "From Caricature and Vignette to Ambivalence and Angst: Changing Perceptions of Character in the Malay World," *Self and Biography: Essays on Individual and Society in Asia,* ed. Wang Gungwu (Sydney: Sydney University Press, 1975), pp. 29–54.

120. Arnold Krupat, "The Indian Autobiography: Origins, Type, and Function," *American Literature* 53 (March 1981): 22–42.

121. Avicenna's autobiography is translated in Arthur J. Arberry, *Avicenna on Theology* (London: John Murray, 1951), pp. 9–14. The quote is from p. 14.

122. Kadir, *The Hikayat Abdullah,* pp. 308–9.

123. Roiphe, *Generations without Memory,* pp. 218–19.

124. Kadir, *The Hikayat Abdullah,* pp. 310–16.

125. Amin Sweeney, *Reputations Live On: An Early Malay Autobiography* (Berkeley: University of California Press, 1980), pp. 51, 70.

126. Raden Adjeng Kartini, *Letters of a Javanese Princess* (New York: W. W. Norton, 1964), pp. 31, 246.

127. Yukichi Fukuzawa, *The Autobiography of Yukichi Fukuzawa* (New York: Columbia University Press, 1966), pp. 1, 336.

128. Ibid., pp. 182, 207.

129. Ivan Morris, *The Nobility of Failure: Tragic Heroes in the History of Japan* (New York: New American Library, 1976), p. 228.

130. "Jonas Basanavyczius," in *Lietuviszkieji rasztai ir rasztininkai. Raszliszka perżvalga parengta Lietuvos mylėtojo.* ed. Jonas Šliūpas (Tilžėje: Kaszta Baltimorės M. D. L. M. Draugystės, 1890), pp. 168–70. The second version of his autobiography, completed in 1922, and reprinted, with politically significant omissions, in Soviet Lithuania, begins in essentially the same way. Jonas Basanavičius, *Rinktiniai raštai* (Vilnius: Vaga, 1970), pp. 5–6. On the history of autobiographical writing in Lithuanian, which Basanavičius has initiated, see Vytautas Kavolis, "Pradžios ir pabaigos," *Metmenys,* no. 40 (1980): 5–32.

131. Chiang Yee, *A Chinese Childhood* (New York: W. W. Norton, 1963).

132. Czesław Miłosz, *Native Realm: A Search for Self-Definition* (Garden City, N.Y.: Doubleday & Company, 1968).

133. "Life-Record of an Immigrant," in William I. Thomas and Florian Znaniecki, *The Polish Peasant in Europe and America,* (New York: Alfred A. Knopf, 1927), 2:1915–2226; William Wolkowich-Valkavičius, "Lithuanian Immigrant Diary—A Rarity," *Lituanus* 27 (Spring 1981): 39–48. Extensive collections of peasant and worker autobiographies, mostly produced in public competitions, and going back to the first half of the nineteenth century, exist in Poland. They suggest a shift in the framework of self-comprehension from membership in the immediate familial-parochial setting to some degree of participation in national-organizational-movement activities in the early part of the twentieth century to a general culture-consumerist orientation in the generation born after 1930. This literature is reviewed in Józef Chalasiński, "The Life Records of the Young Generation of Polish Peasants as a

Manifestation of Contemporary Culture," in Daniel Bertaux, ed., *Biography and Society: The Life History Approach in the Social Sciences* (Beverly Hills, Calif.: Sage Publications, 1981), pp. 110–32.

134. Rožž Sabaliauskiené, *Prie Merkio mano kaimas. Atsiminimai* (Vilnius: Vaga, 1972), pp. 11–24 (quote from p. 14), 280.

135. James Olney, "The Value of Autobiography for Comparative Studies: African vs. Western Autobiography," *Comparative Civilizations Review*, no. 2. (Spring 1979): 52–64.

136. "Jonas Basanavyczius," *Lietuviszkieji*, pp. 194–95. The ending of the second version refers to a much later period—the Polish occupation of the capital of Lithuania, Vilnius, after World War I, "the persecutions of Lithuanians and of their language," and the intensification of Basanavičius' "nervous sickness as well as other processes of pathology in the organism. . . ." (Basanavičius, *Rinktiniai raštai*, pp. 51–52). Basanavičius writes in the manner of a "scientific autobiography" initiated by Cardano: extremely matter-of-factly and including all symptoms of all his sicknesses as well as a record of his visits, speeches, and conversations.

137. Alexander Herzen, *My Past and Thoughts* (New York: Vintage Books, 1974).

138. Fyodor Dystoyevsky, *Notes from the Underground* (New York: The New American Library, 1961), p. 96.

139. Simone de Beauvoir, *The Prime of Life* (New York: Harper & Row, 1962), pp. 24–25.

140. Henry James, *Autobiography* (New York: Criterion Books, 1956).

141. George Herbert Mead, *Mind, Self, and Society from the Standpoint of a Social Behaviorist* (Chicago: The University of Chicago Press, 1934); Erving Goffman, *The Presentation of Self in Everyday Life* (Garden City, N.Y.: Doubleday & Company, 1959).

142. Nicholas Berdyaev, *Dream and Reality* (New York: Collier Books, 1962), p. XI.

143. André Malraux, *Anti-Memoirs* (New York: Bantam Books, 1970), p. 1.

144. Carl Gustav Jung, *Memories, Dreams, Reflections* (New York: Pantheon Books, 1963), p. 3.

145. Rafael Alberti, *The Last Grove* (Berkeley: University of California Press, 1976), pp. 17–18.

146. Leon Trotsky, *My Life: An Attempt at Autobiography* (New York: Pathfinder Press, 1970), pp. 582–83.

147. Miłosz, *Native Realm*, p. 300.

148. Jung, *Memories*, p. 359.

149. Agehananda Bharati, *The Ochre Robe: An Autobiography* (Garden City, N. Y.: Doubleday & Company, 1970), pp. 275–76.

150. Malraux, *Anti-Memoirs*, pp. 511–12.

151. The protective return to the earliest sources underlies, at least in Europe, the great intellectual vitality of twentieth-century studies of Indo-European mythology. Such studies seem to have the most popular resonance in Eastern Europe.

152. In England, individuals who are born into the lower classes, such as Thomas Tryon, begin writing their autobiographies in the seventeenth century. The individuality of even a working-class person (and of an "ordinary" woman) first becomes of general interest to the Puritans. Margaret Spufford, "First Steps in Literacy: The Reading and Writing Experiences of the Humblest Seventeenth-Century Spiritual Autobiographers," *Social History*, 4 (October, 1979): 407–35. In continental Europe, working-class autobiographies started appearing, in individual cases, in the eighteenth century, became most numerous in the nineteenth and, except for the Soviet bloc of nations, have subsided after World War II. Workers' autobiographies frequently start with descriptions of poverty—sometimes, especially in the earlier period, coupled with pride in the honesty and hard work of the family line. No one in the history of autobiography has put a modest pride in the poor-but-honest tradition and the "tender conscience" of his family line closer to the beginning of his life story as the first German-speaking working-class autobiographer, the Pietist-influenced Swiss, Ulrich Bräker, 1735–1798. *Der arme Mann in Tockenburg* (Stuttgart: Reclam, 1977), pp. 11–13. (Pride in the

tender conscience of one's ancestors seems to be altogether missing in discussions of their family lines by non-Western autobiographers. In the sense of his life as a movement *from the honest family to the giving of thanks to God* Bräker is closest to Glückel; perhaps this form represents a "simple but devout-people's" self-comprehension that continued to exist in Europe, common to several religious traditions.) Most of the available working-class autobiographies in Europe have been produced under the impetus of the working-class movements of the nineteenth and early twentieth centuries and with the intention of promoting their goals. Thus they center on the economic conditions and their effects on individual and family lives, economic-political struggles, and frequently the tremendous efforts of the writer at acquiring a literary self-education. But of subjective self-revelation there is less than in bourgeois autobiographies, and no working-class autobiography in Western Europe attains to the literary status of Maxim Gorky's (or of Juozas Baltušis'). For these reasons, working-class autobiographies in Western Europe do not contribute as much to the history of self-comprehensions as they do to social history. Wolfgang Emmerich, ed., *Proletarische Lebensläufe: Autobiographische Dokumente zur Entstehung der Zweiten Kultur in Deutschland*, 2 vols. (Reinbek bei Hamburg: Rowohlt, 1974–1975); David Vincent, *Bread, Knowledge and Freedom: A Study of Nineteenth-Century Working Class Autobiography* (London: Europa Publications Limited, 1981).

153. William James, *The Varieties of Religious Experience: A Study in Human Nature* (London: Longmans, Green, and Co., 1916), p. 110.

154. An autobiography is "greater," to the extent that, in addition to recording the actions or revealing the experiences of an individual in an artistically effective manner, it also defines, and establishes in the history of consciousness, unforgettably, key elements of a widely shared self-comprehension (whether this self-comprehension is, at the time of writing, "emerging" or "disappearing" in society). But "second-rate" autobiographies, which merely illustrate key elements of widely shared self-comprehensions, are also essential sources of information in writing histories of selfhood.

Where the written record is inadequate, the flow of development of human consciousness will not coincide with the history (as written) of consciousness. This is always the case, but in Western history, especially since the Protestant Reformation (and particularly in England and France), less so than elsewhere, because of the abundance of autobiographical writing. The second half of the twentieth century has tended to replace the problem of insufficient information by that of non-congealment of scattergrams of phenomena into clearly outstanding paradigmatic patterns. But we always have too short a time perspective to discern with tolerable precision the layout of contemporary phenomena. The mind of the student of the contemporary consciousness "hangs in suspence," as Benedetto Croce concluded his *Autobiography* in 1915, "like a reflection upon stormy waters." (*An Autobiography* [Oxford: At the Clarendon Press, 1927], p. 116).

155. John Ruskin, *Praeterita* (Oxford: Oxford University Press, 1978); Oscar Wilde, *The Complete Works* (Garden City, N.Y.: Doubleday, Page and Company, 1923), vol. 11.

156. Michel Leiris, *Manhood: A Journey from Childhood into the Fierce Order of Virility* (New York: Grossman Publications, 1963); Malraux, *Anti-Memoirs.*

157. Norman Mailer, *The Armies of the Night: History as a Novel, The Novel as History* (New York: The New American Library, 1968), p. 5.

158. Piri Thomas, *Down These Mean Streets* (New York: Alfred A. Knopf, 1967), pp. 3–5, 329–31.

159. Alexis de Tocqueville, *Democracy in America* (New York: Vintage Books, 1957), 2:44: Nelson, "Self-Images.

160. Georgia O'Keeffe, *Georgia O'Keeffe*, unnumbered first page of text.

161. Simone de Beauvoir, *Memoirs of a Dutiful Daughter* (New York: Harper, 1974), p. 5.

162. *The Confessions of Lady Nijō* (Garden City, N.Y.: Anchor Press/Doubleday, 1973), p. 1.

163. Simone de Beauvoir, *Force of Circumstance* (New York: Harper & Row, 1977), 2:656–58.

164. O'Keeffe, *Georgia O'Keeffe,* unnumbered last page of text.

165. Welthy Honsinger Fisher, *To Light a Candle* (New York: McGraw-Hill Book Company, 1962), pp. 3, 279.

166. Kate Millett, *Flying* (New York: Alfred A. Knopf, 1974), pp. 3, 546.

167. Mohamed Choukri, *For Bread Alone* (London: Peter Owen, 1973), pp. 8, 150.

168. Oginga Odinga, *Not Yet Uhuru* (New York: Hill and Wang, 1967), pp. 1, 314–15.

169. Hsieh Ping-ying, *Autobiography of a Chinese Girl* (London: George Allen and Unwin, 1948), pp. 25, 216.

170. Te-kong Tong and Li Tsung-jen, *The Memoirs of Li Tsung-jen* (Boulder, Colo.: The Westview Press, 1977), pp. 3, 566.

171. John C. H. Wu, *Beyond East and West* (New York: Sheed and Ward, 1951); Chen-hua, "Random Talks." The quote is from *Chinese Sociology and Anthropology,* 14 (Spring 1982), p. 90.

Among Chinese autobiographies that are available in English, this pattern is more characteristic of those written by men than of those by women. Among twentieth-century texts, autobiographies by women appear to constitute a larger part of the total in the Chinese than in any other non-Western tradition. Chinese women's autobiographies (some of them written with the assistance of Western associates) generally move *from vivid event to vivid event* in personal experience (sometimes with considerable attention to individual psychology), whereas Chinese men's autobiographies tend to be more restrained, impersonal, and broadly descriptive and to move *from general situation to general situation,* where the situation is characteristic of China as a whole as envisioned by the author. This is especially true when the male autobiographer is a high official or advanced scholar, as most of them are. For aid in locating some twenty-five twentieth-century Chinese autobiographies, I am indebted to Guy S. Alitto.

172. Aisin-Gioro Pu Yi, *From Emperor to Citizen,* 2 vols. (Peking: Foreign Languages Press, 1979).

173. Sheng-Cheng, *A Son of China* (New York: W. W. Norton, 1930).

Sheng-Cheng's autobiography is partly the autobiography of his mother, presented in her own voice. In Europe, the counterpart to Sheng-Cheng is the nineteenth-century Lithuanian writer, Žemaitė, who devotes one-third of her autobiography to a description of her husband's life before meeting her, presented as his own tale. Žemaitė, "Autobiografija," *Raštai,* vol. 4 (Vilnius: Valstybinė Grožinės Literatūros Leidykla, 1959), pp. 291–422. Such "joint autobiographies," in which another person tells the story of his or her life at length within the autobiography of the writer, are entirely unknown among the major autobiographers of the West, whose individualism would not allow such a sharing of attention. Women autobiographers in the West have frequently included extensive descriptions of their husbands or, more recently, lovers, but not as if they were accounts spoken by these men themselves, as Sheng-Cheng and Žemaitė do.

174. Jawaharlal Nehru, *Toward Freedom* (New York: The John Day Company, 1941), p. 16.

175. Ibid., pp. 352–53.

176. Ibid., p. 353; Mohandas K. Gandhi, *An Autobiography: The Story of My Experiments with Truth* (Boston: Beacon Press, 1957), p. 505.

177. Nirad C. Chaudhuri, *The Autobiography of an Unknown Indian* (Berkeley: University of California Press, 1968), pp. VIII, 504.

178. Ibid., pp. 504–5.

179. Hazari, *An Indian Outcaste: The Autobiography of an Untouchable* (London: The Bannisdale Press, 1951), pp. 9, 151.

180. Sita Rathnamal, *Beyond the Jungle: A Tale of South India* (Edinburgh: William Blackwood and Sons Ltd., 1968), pp. 5–6, 251, 253.

181. Viveca Lindfors, *Viveka . . . Viveca* (New York: Everest House, 1981), pp. 9, 305.

182. Sukarno, *An Autobiography*. As told to Cindy Adams (Indianapolis: Bobbs-Merrill Company, 1965), pp. 1, 312.

183. Rato Khyongla Nawang Losang, *My Life and Lives: The Story of a Tibetan Incarnation* (New York: E. P. Dutton, 1977), pp. 230–31.

184. Carlos Bulosan, *America Is in the Heart: A Personal History* (New York: Harcourt, Brace and Company, 1946), p. 326.

185. Mark Vonnegut, *The Eden Express* (New York: Praeger Publishers, 1975), pp. 3–4, 207.

186. *The Letters of Abelard and Heloise*, p. 57.

II

The Languages of Selfhood:
Europe and Asia

2

Varieties of the Chinese Self

Pei-yi Wu

No single Chinese term matches the English *self* in versatility and flexibility. As a separate, freestanding noun, *chi* is equivalent to "self" in English, but *chi* is seldom used as a prefix, nor does it always connote reflexivity in the rather rare instances when it does appear as a suffix in a compound. *Tzu* resembles "self-" in English or *auto-* in Greek when it functions as prefix: e.g., *tzu-ai* "self-love," *tzu-hsin* "self-renewing," and *tzu-chuan* "autobiography."

Most Chinese pronouns of the first-person singular can be generalized to denote the "self," much in the same way as *moi* in French, which does not even have a term comparable to the limited *chi* in Chinese. Among such Chinese pronouns *wo* is most often pressed into this broader service, whereas *wu* is used much less frequently in this manner. Another distinction of the pronoun *wo* is its viability. It has survived in the standard modern vernacular, whereas its synonyms have not. Perhaps even in ancient times *wo* had already displayed too much vigor, for Confucius assigned an additional meaning to it and denounced it as a moral defect to be avoided. As he juxtaposed *wo* with *i* "wilfulness," *pi* "arbitrariness," and *ku* "obstinacy," its new meaning must have stood somewhere between "egotism" and "self-assertiveness."[1]

What philosophical implications, if any, are to be drawn from the linguistic facts of Chinese with regard to the representation or denotation of the self? Before we proceed any further, a recent discussion of a similar topic might be instructive. Comparing the differences between the English and the French approaches to the philosophical questions about the self, Stephen Toulmin believes the lack of a French term equivalent to the English "self" to be the main issue. To the French the problem of the self has to be formulated as the problem of the *moi* or the *soi*. "Having raised the issue in terms of personal pronouns which possess a variety of cases, rather than in terms of a case-neutral 'self,'" French philosophers

> are led to postulate alternative entities (different "selves") corresponding to the different cases of the pronoun: e.g. the nominative, *je,*

and the dative *moi*. So, one very early step in French discussions of the self is to question the relations between the *je* and the *moi*—i.e., between one supposed "self," which serves as the essential agent *(je)*, and another supposed "self," which serves as the essential patient *(moi)*.[2]

If the multiplicity of cases of the pronoun has led the French to be excessively analytical, the absence of case in Chinese has had the exact opposite effect on Chinese thinking with regard to the same problem of the self. As an illustration let us look at a much-quoted passage from the Confucian *Analects* as translated by James Legge.

> Yen Yüan asked about perfect virtue. The Master said, "to subdue one's self and return to propriety is perfect virtue. If a man can for one day subdue himself and return to propriety all under heaven will ascribe perfect virtue to him. Is the practice of perfect virtue from a man himself, or is it from others?"[3]

In the Chinese text the word *chi* (self) occurs three times, but it is translated variously as "one's self," "himself," and "a man himself." To some Chinese commentators there seems to be an apparent contradiction: the *chi* in the first two occurrences can not be the same *chi* in the last occurrence. A French philosopher, accustomed to the *je-moi* distinction, would not have minded this apparent contradiction, but no Chinese commentator has ever seen the *chi* in the first two occurrences as representing the "patient" aspect of the self and the last *chi* as representing the "agent" aspect. Most Sung commentators interpret the *chi* in the first two occurrences as standing for selfishness or the selfish desire of the self, apparently following Yang Hsiung (53 B.C.–A.D. 18), one of the earliest exponents of Confucian classics. But later exegetes have had difficulty in accepting this interpretation. Chiao Hung (1541–1620) after questioning the apparent contradictory roles of the same self arrives at an ingenious solution. To him the self is in itself forever free, but the one who holds on to his self always loses it; therefore, to subdue the self is to restore freedom to the self, the freedom to practice perfect virtue.[4]

The learned Buddhist monk Chih-hsü (1599–1655) in his commentary on the *Analects* passage in question states categorically that the *chi* can have only one meaning in its three occurrences. His solution is to read the word *k'e* not as to "subdue" but as "to be able to."[5] Thus with *chi* now assuming the role of an agent throughout, the first sentence, as Chih-hsü glosses it, is equivalent to "To be able by oneself to return to propriety is perfect virtue." His contemporary Mao Ch'i-Ling (1623–1716) also rejects the Sung interpretation of the first two occurrences of *chi*.[6] The controversy raged into the nineteenth century. Juan Yüan (1764–1849) maintains, like Chih-hsü, that *ji* has to be understood the same way in all its three occurrences.[7] He in turn was bitterly attacked by Fang Tung-shu (1772–1851).[8] Both polemicists deployed etymological evidence and cited historical usage, going back several centuries beyond Confucius. Nevertheless they only fought to a stalemate.

An established notion of case might have removed some of the contentiousness from the protracted debate, but no system of grammar could have solved all the problems that would arise in any discourse on the self. The difficulty lies in the very dual nature of the self: subject and object, agent and patient, observer and observed, the assertive and the receptive, the selfish and the selfless, and the like. Perhaps it is no accident that the passage from the *Analects* should have provoked so much polemics, for it hints at one of the fundamental paradoxes of the self, a problem with which moral philosophy and religion perennially have had to grapple. On the one hand the ego has to be restrained, denied, checked; on the other hand a strong will is required to accomplish these ends, as well as to resist temptations, and to redeem past wrongs that the self has committed. Self-effacement has to go hand in hand with firm resolution. In religious terms the self has to break out from its finite confinement in order to be reunited with the absolute or the transcendental: in doing so the self is both eradicated and exalted. This apparent contradiction, already hinted at in the *Analects,* was to haunt the Chinese discourse on the self for the next two thousand years.

The Expansive View of the Self

If the self acquired a moral opprobrium in the hands of Confucius when he placed it in the company of three other undesirable qualities, it fared somewhat better with Mencius who says: "All things are already complete in me *(wo).* There is no greater delight than to be sincere in self-examination."[9] The first sentence, in spite of its brevity and ambiguity, proves to be one of the most seminal statements in the subsequent development of the Chinese concept of the self. It is the origin of what may be called the expansive view of the self, which had its fullest expression during the Sung. In the intervening centuries several other thinkers contributed to the growth of this view. Chuang Tzu, in his attempt to establish relativism among all things, announces that "heaven and earth were born at the same time I was, and the ten thousand things are one with me."[10] When describing a holy man, Chuang Tzu has him utter: "I share light with sun and moon, and I am as constant as heaven and earth."[11] Such hyperbolic statements were frequently echoed in later times. Seng Chao (384–414), who expounds Buddhist doctrines with Taoist ideas, seems to be reiterating Chuang Tzu when he declares that "heaven and earth are of the same root as I am, and the ten thousand things form one body with me."[12]

The expansive view of the self received further impetus with the rise
of Ch'an Buddhism. Ch'an monks, disdainful of convention, doctrine, and
scriptural authority, which they considered as obstacles to truth, relied
entirely on what they called "seeing into one's self-nature." The excessive
reliance on each individual self and the manic exultation felt by the monks
after reaching illumination often led to nihilistic arrogance and mystical
solipsism. Ch'ang-sha Ching-ch'en, a ninth-century master, said in a ser-
mon that "the worlds in all directions are my eyes; the worlds in all directions are my whole body; the worlds in all directions are the brightness of
the self; the worlds in all directions are in the brightness of myself; in the
world in all directions there is not a person who is not myself."[13] A younger
member of his sect by the name of Chih-t'ung had the audacity to call
himself the "Great Ch'an Buddha."[14] One night he walked around the hall
shouting: "I am greatly illuminated!" When he was dying he uttered:

> Stretching my hand I clutch the Southern Dipper,
> Turning around I lean on the Morning Star.
> My head emerges beyond the Heavens;
> Do I see another man like me?[15]

His mystical aggrandizement of the self to cosmic proportions was echoed
by poets such as Su Shih (1037–1101), who wrote:

> When the self is expanded and raised,
> It hangs high as stars and Dippers.
> When the self is scattered and lowered.
> Would it not be mountains and rivers?[16]

Su's Neo-Confucian contemporaries had a more sober view of the self.
To them the self was to be expanded so as to broaden one's empathy with
all human and nonhuman beings. The ideal Confucian man, the man of *jen*
(humaneness, perfect virtue) widens the scope of his concerns and sym-
pathies until it envelops all the universe. One of the earliest expounders of
this view is Chang Tsai (1020–1077), whose book *Cheng Meng* has a chapter
entitled *Tai-hsin* (enlarging the mind).

When one enlarges his mind, he can incorporate all the things in the
world. As long as there is one thing that has not been incorporated,
there is still something external to his mind. The mind of the ordinary
people is limited by the narrowness of their sensory knowledge. A
sage, having fulfilled his nature, will not enfetter his mind by sensory
knowledge; in his view of the world, there is nothing that is not a part
of himself.[17]

Toward the end of his book Chang rephrases this concept in a more direct
way:

Heaven is my father and earth is my mother, and even such a small creature as I finds an intimate place in their midst.

Therefore that which extends throughout the universe I regard as my body and that which directs the universe I consider as my nature.

All people are my brothers and sisters, and all things are my companions.[18]

The same idea was echoed by Ch'eng Hao (1032–1085): "The man of *jen* considers heaven, earth, and all things as of one body: nothing is not a part of himself. Where would he not reach if he considers everything as himself?"[19]

Although Neo-Confucians always credited Mencius as the fountainhead of their assertion of a boundless, undifferentiated continuum of the self, running through all the human and nonhuman world, it is possible that they may have had other sources of inspiration. Ch'eng Hao's pronouncement looks almost like a rephrasing of Seng Chao's statement quoted earlier. One can also find in their view possible resonances from the Taoist insistence on the equality of all creation, the Mohist doctrine of universal love, or the Buddhist teaching of compassion for all sentient beings. In fact, some of the Sung Neo-Confucians felt uncomfortable with Chang Tsai's universalism, suspecting a non-Confucian origin for his seeming deemphasis of family obligations.

A more insidious temptation for the Neo-Confucian was that of unrestrained self-aggrandizement. Chang Tsai warns against such a temptation: "When I look at things from the point of view of the self, then I appear to be greater; when I incorporate things and the self into the Way, the Way appears to be greater. Therefore when a gentleman is great, he is great in the Way. He who considers himself great cannot avoid being deluded."[20] This warning was not heeded by Yang Chien (1141–1226), who wrote a most extraordinary essay on the self, equating it with, among other things, the *Book of Changes (I ching)*. To give an idea of the almost obsessive quality of Yang's long and effusive characterization of the self that borders on idolatry, I shall translate five sections of the long essay.

The *Book of Changes* is nothing but the self. It is not correct to take the *Book of Changes* to be a book and not the self. It is not correct to take the *Book of Changes* as representing the transformations of heaven and earth, and not the transformations of the self. Heaven and earth are my heaven and earth. The transformations are my transformations. They cannot be otherwise. He who is selfish separates the self from heaven and earth and the transformations. He who is selfish belittles himself.[21]

That which constitutes "I" is not only the sanguine forces and the physical form. My nature is clear, bright, and not material; it is transparent, boundless, and unmeasureable. Heaven is a sign of my nature; earth is a form of my nature.[22]

If I do not take heaven, earth, myriad of things, myriad of transformations and myriad of principles as the self, but only hold on to the ears, eyes, nose, and the limbs as the self, then I will have cut up my whole body and only held on to a square inch of the skin: I will have been imprisoned by my sanguine forces and become selfish. It is not true that my body is limited to a height of five or six feet. He who observes the heaven from the bottom of a well does not know how great the heaven is. He who observes the self with his sanguine forces does not know how extensive the self is.[23]

In my daily activities the ghosts and the spirits cannot understand me; the sages cannot fathom me. There are things about me even I myself do not know, how much less do the others. I am completely pure and impeccable as if bleached by the autumn sun; I am completely clean and immaculate as if washed by the water of the Han and the Yangtze Rivers. I am undifferentiable, boundless, limitless, without beginning, without end.[24]

The world is illuminated by the sun and moon, but does not know that the light comes from me; the world is moistened by the rain and dew but does not know that the water comes from me; the world fears the power of thunder and lightning but does not know that the fire comes from me. Day and night proceed from within me, yet the world does not know. It is not excessive to say that I cover and encircle heaven and earth or that I issue forth and nourish all living things. . . .[25]

The same hyperbolic language and sweeping assertions were used by Yang Chien to describe the mind (hsin) in another essay.

The mind of man is Spirit; the mind of man is the Way . . . The mind of man is not a part of the sanguine forces or the corporeal form. It is expansive without limits, ever-changing without regularities. Suddenly it sees, suddenly it hears, suddenly it speaks, and suddenly it moves. All of a sudden it arrives at a point a thousand miles away; all of a sudden it soars above the nine heavens. It is swift without hastening; it reaches without travelling. Is it not spiritual? Is it not coextensive with heaven and earth?[26]

Elsewhere Yang used similar language to characterize the mind. "The mind has no substance. It is clear and bright without limits. Originally it is coextensive with heaven and earth. Its scope distinguishes no inside or outside, nor does it have any boundaries in its nourishing the ten thousand things."[27] But he never explicitly identified the mind with the self. To him, as to all the Neo-Confucian philosophers, the mind-body problem, which is so important to modern philosophy, did not arise.

The expansive view of the self always included both the body and the mind, although it is not always easy to separate mystical and figurative elements from philosophical positions. In the passage quoted previously Chang Tsai says that "when one enlarges his mind, he can incorporate all things in the world." The "incorporate" is an inadequate rendering of the Chinese word *t'i*, whose basic meaning is "body." Used here as a verb, *t'i* can be interpreted either literally as "to include in one's body or to make something a part of one's body"; or more figuratively as "to treat someone or something as if it were part of oneself." Whichever way we choose to interpret the word *t'i*, it can be inferred that to Chang Tsai the self is a combination of mind and body, and that the two entities are closely linked. But on a more metaphysical level the mind is held by all Neo-Confucians to be eternal and universal, and as such its link with any particular body is provisional. The relation between the mind, the body, and the self, never explicitly formulated in Chinese philosophy, is best expressed in a poem by the Neo-Confucian philosopher Shao Yung (1011–1077):

The body was born after the heaven and earth,
The mind exists before the heaven and the earth.
As heaven and earth originate from myself,
How is the rest worth talking about?[28]

If the expansive view of the self never developed into a coherent theory, it nevertheless played an important role in shaping the expression of the individual self. In Neo-Confucian autobiography the discovery of this view and its subsequent confirmation is an important theme in the spiritual progress of the individual. This subgenre may have even owed its existence to the need to record the intense personal experience of the autobiographer as he in a sudden flash of insight came to the awareness of his oneness with the myriad things. The accompanying joy and sense of wonder compelled a new style of first-person narrative, a departure from the detached and objective prose of the historiographical model that Confucian autobiographers always followed until the mid-sixteenth century.

The Components of the Self

The self, complains John O. Lyons, "is a member of a group of terms which would be nice to keep distinct, but which in practice inevitably become muddled. This family includes *individual, person, ego,* the 'I,' *mind, will, soul, being,* and a litter of hyphenated combinations."[29] Such an embarrassment of related terms and allied concepts does not exist in China. Aside from the "I" and the *mind (hsin),* none of the words in Lyons' list has a counterpart in Chinese before the last years of the nineteenth century when the introduction of Western ideas forced a massive coinage of neologisms on the Chinese.

The idea of the soul played a very important part in the evolution of the Western self, for much of the content of the self in its modern usage was inherited from the soul in the early nineteenth century. A unitary and substantial soul, firmly and uniquely identified with its human host, does not seem to have been a part of indigenous Chinese religious belief. The earliest detailed statement on what in the West would be denoted as the soul was made in 535 B.C. by the statesman Tzu-ch'an:

> In man's life the first transformations are called the earthly aspect of the soul (p'o). After p'o has been produced, that which is strong and positive is called the heavenly aspect of the soul (hun). If he had an abundance in the use of material things and subtle essentials, his hun and p'o will become strong. From this are developed essence and understanding until there are spirit and intelligence. When an ordinary man or woman dies a violent death, the hun and p'o are still able to keep hanging about men and do evil and malicious things.[30]

What is interesting about this statement is that everything in it survived more or less intact in Chinese popular belief all the way to the nineteenth century, perhaps even to this day. Neither hun nor p'o has ever acquired the indestructibility of the Western soul, for the survival of both after the death of their host depends on so many contingencies. In any case, sooner or later, both of them will evaporate or join the primordial forces of nature. Nor can they be said to possess any individuality; being a pair neither can claim a unique identification with its host. In later centuries the number of hun and p'o in each person became greater: the Taoists believe that each human being has three hun and seven p'o. Some of these ethereal creatures might wander away from their host even when he is still alive, causing him illness or greater peril. The shamanistic practice of cajoling the ghostly truants to return to their proper place of domicile, a prominent theme in early Chinese poetry, persisted into this century.

Less shadowy than hun or p'o, but equally nebulous, is shen, which has been variously translated as "spirit," "consciousness," or "spiritual force." The same word can also mean "divinity," "mysterious," "subtle and ingenious," and the like. Opposite and complementary to shen is kuei, which is usually translated as "ghost." Most Neo-Confucian philosophers, in an attempt to link the two incorporeal pairs, identify shen with hun and kuei with p'o. From the beginning of Chinese philosophy shen has frequently been contrasted with hsing—"body," "form," "appearance," or "substance." In the shen-hsing polarity, shen represents the spiritual force, the vital power, the governing agent that reigns over the corporeal form. Sometimes the function of shen overlaps that of the mind (hsin). If shen is less furtive than hun, it is more playful than hsin. But the greatest advantage that shen has over hun and hsin is its association with the Chinese theory of painting; it was through this association that *shen* gradually acquired some of the attributes of the modern self.

Most painters looked down upon what they considered as mere copying of external shapes and forms. What they strove for was the expression through lines and color of the *spirit (shen)* of the object they were ostensibly depicting. In portraiture this preference was elevated to the status of a dogma, so much so that a respected portraitist was usually referred to or addressed by his honorific *ch'uan-shen*, literally someone who "transmits the spirit." Since *shen* could be visually, if somewhat symbolically, represented, it gained particularity as a concept. As the subject of a portraiture was presumably different from all other subjects, the *shen* of a person could only be uniquely identified with its human host. This idea is best stated in the two lines of a poem by P'u Tao-yuan (1260–1336), which he dedicated to a portrait painter.

> Men are endowed with myriad different spirits *(shen)* and appearances *(hsing)*.
> Master Liu achieves such diversity each time he wields his brush.[31]

Another aspect of the self, an aspect as much related to portrait painting as *shen,* is represented by the word *ying*. Like *shen* it covers a large semantic area and can denote several related ideas. Originally meaning "shadow," *ying* also denotes "reflection," "image," and somewhat later, "portrait." When photography was first introduced into China, *ying* was the word used to mean "photograph." The reflection/shadow of a person, although it resembles him closely and follows him intimately, is not, to modern mind, an essential or integral part of the person. To the primitive, however, in the words of Theodor H. Gaster, "the self, or identity, of a person is not limited to his physical being but embraces also everything associated with it and everything that can evoke his presence in another person's mind."[32] Among such things listed by Gaster are the shadow and the portrait—the two items that have much to do with the development of the Chinese sense of the self.

It is possible that at one time in the distant past the Chinese believed that a person consisted of the spirit/soul, the body, and the shadow/reflection. This tripartite composition was never explicitly formulated, but we can infer it from later writings. The earliest extant hint of this is provided by *Yen-tzu ch'un-ch'iu,* a work attributed to a sixth-century B.C. statesman. "A gentleman must not feel ashamed to his shadow when he stands alone; he must not feel ashamed to his soul *(hun)* when he sleeps alone."[33] The tripartite composition of the human person was more explicitly expressed by the poet T'ao Ch'ien (365–427) when he wrote a set of three poems, each representing the voice of one of the triad. The first poem is ostensibly the complaint of Form addresssed to the Shadow/Reflection *(ying)*, the second one purports to be the reply of Shadow/Reflection, whereas the third one represents the mediating words of Spirit *(shen)*, meant to soothe his two companions.[34] This decomposition of the person was most likely a literary device rather than an indication of T'ao's belief, but he may very well have echoed an ancient myth. The greatest import of T'ao's literary device is the personification of the components of a man: previously in literature *hun* had been usually mute and *shen* inarticulate, whereas the other components totally inanimate. T'ao's innovation was much emulated in later times; in fact the growing sense of the self as evidenced in the sixteenth-and seventeenth-century China owes much to the literary practice of inventing dialogues between the self and its image or composing pieces addressed to one's spirit.[35]

Strong emotional reactions to one's own image, whether a reflection, a shadow, or a painted likeness, were widespread in primitive societies, as documented by Frazer and other comparative mythologists. Georges Gusdorf, writing on European autobiography, has elaborated on this point:

> The subject who seizes on himself for object inverts the natural direction of attention; it appears that in acting thus he violates certain secret taboos of human nature. Sociology, depth psychology, psychoanalysis have revealed the complex and agonizing sense that the encounter of a man with his image carries. The image is another "myself," a double of my being but more fragile and vulnerable, invested with a sacred character that makes it at once fascinating and frightening. Narcissus, contemplating his face in the fountain's depth, is so fascinated with the apparition that he would die bending toward himself. According to most folklore and myth, the apparition of the double is a death sign.[36]

The myth of Narcissus does not seem to have a clearly identifiable variant in China, but there are numerous Chinese lores testifying to the universal shock of recognition triggered by a man's sudden encounter with his reflection in water. The shock sometimes had profound psychological and spiritual impact. Lu Yün (262–303), a prominent member of the literati, was a frequent victim of attacks of uncontrollable laughter, the first of which was brought on when he, having boarded a ship wearing mourning clothes, saw his image in the river. The ensuing laughing attack was so violent that he fell into the water and nearly drowned. With Chinese Buddhists the sudden confrontation with the reflected self seems to effect in the beholder more salutary, if equally drastic, changes. The Buddhist master Fu Ta-shih (479–569) reputedly achieved a sudden illumination upon seeing his own reflection in water. The same thing happened with the Ch'an monk Tungshan Liang-chieh (807–869). For a long time he pondered over a Ch'an puzzle: whether a real-life portrait could be made for his teacher Yün-yen after the master's death. One day while the monk was fording a river he saw his own reflection in the water and thereupon suddenly arrived at a total comprehension of the relation between the self and its visual representation. He expressed the liberating insight in verse:

> The worst thing is to seek him elsewhere
> —he would be far far away from me.
> Now that I am travelling alone,
> I meet him everywhere.
> Now he is simply me,
> But I am now not him.
> Only when this is understood
> Can the Absolute be comprehended![37]

Many other Chinese Buddhists were also fascinated with the complex of ideas that I call the problem of visual representation of the self. Portrait painting was a frequent theme in Ch'an discourse. The contemplation of the illusoriness of the image, whether on the surface of water or on a fragile piece of paper, should lead to the realization of the illusoriness of the self, which, though in a sense less unreal than its images, is also transitory and perishable. Such a sequence of reasoning, however, did not always lead the monks to a firm refusal when their disciples or lay devotees requested to have the masters' portraits painted. Nor did the Buddhist interdict against idolizing human beings prevent such portraits from becoming objects of adoration. After the ninth century the Ch'an masters not only acquiesced in the raging vogue of portraiture but went so far as to take up the practice of composing verses and inscribing them on their portraits, to the even greater joy of their admirers. The verses thus composed usually followed the format of *tsan* (eulogy), a minor genre of literature whose association with portrait painting began in the second century B.C. The *tsan* in its early days was short and perfunctory, but in the hands of Ch'an masters the self-eulogy *(tzu-tsan)* became a flexible and effective vehicle of self-expression.

A man's sight of his likeness in a newly painted portrait of his may bring about a disquietude and fascination that is probably similar to that which ensues from seeing his own reflection in water or in a mirror. It may well be this complex and powerful reaction that jolts the subject of a portrait out of his quotidian complacency and compels him to examine himself anew and, through writing a *tzu-tsan*, to attempt a new self-definition, the summing-up of the man in its entirety. This is probably the reason that *tzu-tsan* gradually spread beyond the Buddhist circles and became a very popular literary genre in the sixteenth and seventeenth centuries.

Self-Eulogies: An Autobiographical Mode in Traditional Chinese Literature[38]

A type of autobiographical information that is frequently present in a *tzu-tsan* is the description of the author as a person. Many strains went into the style of description, strains such as the usual self-effacement, the Ch'an masters' fondness for paradoxes, and a tendency to irony inherent in any discourse in which the narrator is also the subject. Tsung-kao (1089–1163), also known as Ta-hui P'u-chüeh, had an unusual career for a Ch'an monk. Involved in partisan politics, he was defrocked and exiled for fifteen years, but was eventually restored to the favor of the emperor. Perhaps it was inevitable that most of the forty *tzu-tsan* he wrote were colored by ambivalence and defiance. The following is a typical one:

> Should you be called a good man?
> You hate evil too much.
> Should you be called an evil man?
> You love sages and delight in doing good.
> Between the two roads of good and evil
> You have made your choice without regret.
> Alas, what a self-complacent man!
> You talk on without restraint
> Not rushing to attain Buddhahood or become a patriarch.
> This public case[39]
> Is to be turned over to Judge Chao![40]

The Ming Dynasty saw a proliferation of the *tzu-tsan,* and many non-Buddhists also wrote self-eulogies to be inscribed on their portraits. But the non-Buddhist participation had begun much earlier, although before Ming there were only a few specimens. The earliest one was written by P'ei Tu (765–838), the great T'ang general and minister:

> Your talent is not great,
> Your looks are not unusual.
> How can you be a general?
> How can you be a chief minister?
> Your inner self
> Can never be depicted in red and blue![41]

P'ei's ambivalent attitude toward both himself and the painting is similar to that of many of the Buddhist *tzu-tsan* writers. This suggests that he, the only T'ang non-Buddhist practitioner of the genre, may have been inspired by the Buddhists. The disbelief that the art of painting can faithfully represent the true self, or even the self at all, is a recurring theme in the *tzu-tsan* associated with portraiture. We have seen it expressed both in the previous example and in several Buddhist specimens. But to the Confucians, the phrase "red and blue," a metonymy for the art of painting, had a special meaning. Since the phrase stood for a particular type of portraiture, it had long been associated with the highest honors to which a Confucian could aspire. This linking goes back to the biography of Su Wu in the *Han shu.* Having withstood a long and harsh imprisonment without submission to his tormentors, the Huns, Su was entertained by Li Ling just after his release and before his triumphant return to China. Li as a Han defector was almost overwhelmed by the contrast between the two of them, but he congratulated Su for his sudden fame, saying, "Even those who were recorded in silk and bamboo or painted in red and blue from the time of antiquity cannot surpass you." In 51 B.C. Su Wu's own portrait was ordered by the emperor to be placed in the Unicorn Palace along with those of ten other meritorious generals and ministers. To a Confucian sitting for his portrait, the association of fame and honor with "red and blue" could hardly escape him. P'ei Tu alluded to this association, perhaps obliquely and even ironically, when he juxtaposed "general" and "minister" with "red and blue." But to a humbler self-eulogist the occasion could lead to an unfavorable comparison between his present station in life and the great aims on which he had been nourished since his childhood. Frequently a tinge of regret, or a defiant show of hope, is combined with the deprecation of the art of the "red and blue." Two Sung specimens illustrate this curious combination. Ch'en Liang (1140–1194) was a parlor general but a prolific writer. To that extent his *tzu-tsan* is autobiographical:

> His clothes are very ancient.
> Ancient, too, his looks.
> Shouting to the heavens,
> He dances brandishing a sword.
> Extremely foolish by nature,
> He often clashes with people.
> He sighs that he hasn't yet worn the garment
>   of vermillion and purple.[42]
> He ridicules the efforts to portray him in red
>   and blue.
> From a distance the portrait seems to be
>   Ch'en Liang's,
> A closer look reveals it to be that of T'ung-fu.[43]
> Let's not talk about the likeness of the portrait,
> But decide: Of the present generation
> Who is the dragon among men?
> Who is the tiger among writers?[44]

Ch'en Tung (1087–1128), the student movement leader, expressed similar sentiments:

> Life is but something borrowed;
> Who knows its reality?
> What is painted in red and blue
> Is not my spirit.
> Heaven and Earth have moved me
> To be Spring with all things.[45]

> I shall eventually find my way
> To the Unicorn Palace, high up![46]

The last Sung self-eulogist, Wen T'ien-hsiang (1236–1282), was the first one to write a *tzu-tsan* without any connections with a portrait. Written just before he was led to the execution ground, it is at once a historian's appraisal and a summary of the Confucian loyalist's credo:

> Confucius said, "Preserve your virtue"[47]
> Mencius said, "Choose the righteous"[48]
> Only when the righteous has been exhaustively served
> Is virtue attained.[49]
> Studying the books of the Sages
> What Have I learned?
> Now and hereafter
> Perhaps I have nothing to be ashamed of.[50]

Wen, the Sung chief minister who led the final resistance against the Mongols, was sustained during his three years of incarceration in Peking by historical precedents of heroism and the exhortations of Confucian masters. His determination to die for the lost cause was further strengthened by his confidence in his own place in history. Wen was also the first one to write an autobiography in the *nien-p'u* style. It must have seemed fitting for him, as a historian and biographer of himself, to write a *tsan* to an exemplary life.

Ming *tzu-tsan* writers were so diverse and numerous that they are here placed into groups on the basis of their backgrounds. The first may be considered as Neo-Confucians with more or less orthodox views. Their compositions are straightforward, prosaic, didactic, and free from paradox. Lo Ch'in-shun (1466–1547) a stalwart in the Ch'eng-Chu School and an opponent of Wang Yang-ming, seems to best represent this group:

> I have already served in the government for a decade,
> But have only followed my peers.
> Now that I am forty
> For the first time I have listened.
> What is it that I have heard?
> That the sages can be emulated.
> It is not that I did not hear this in the past,
> It is just that I did not wake up.
> Now that I have,
> I look into the mind of the sages.
> Rivers flow and mountains stand.
> The sun shines and the moon illuminates.
> Although with men there are ancients and moderns,
> With mind there is no difference.
> How do I keep within me the mind of the sages?

The only way is through reverence.
Reverence does not have an object.
The important thing lies in constant attention.
After keeping it long one becomes accustomed,
Yet in external behavior one should always be proper.
Tho' frequently in want, Yen Hui was always at ease,
Tseng Ts'an examined himself three times a day.
One should firmly set one's aims;
One should apply diligently.
Whether one's future is long or short,
There is no need to worry.
You have not come by this life easily:
Don't live it in vain![51]

Even though this *tzu-tsan* was inscribed on Lo's portrait, not a word was said either about the painting or about his own image. Nor is there anything resembling a eulogy or an appraisal. Keng Ting-hsiang (1524–1596) was a little more attentive to the portrait, but otherwise he also was plain:

White hair and loosened teeth:
I am old!
For what do I keep on going,
Waiting and hoping?
I study not Buddhist doctrine;
Nor do I seek Taoist secrets.
I preserve the Way and pass it on to the next generation.
This is all I do.
Therefore "there is nothing that I do that is not
Shown to you, my disciples."[52]

Even though Keng was grouped with the T'ai-chou School by Huang Tsung-hsi in the *Ming-ju hsüeh-an,* his relations with the more radical elements of the school were ambivalent at best. In this *tzu-tsan* Keng clearly identified himself with the Ch'eng-Chu orthodoxy.

The lives of these three Neo-Confucians span more than two centuries, yet there is an amazing continuity in their steadfast adherence to the "Way," their realistic and almost fatalistic appraisal of their times and their own place, and their unswerving faith in the Confucian classics.

The next group is designated, for lack of a better name, the divided Confucians, whose confidence in the rightness of things was eroded by the onslaught of Buddhism, personal defeats, or great national calamities. They could no longer find complete assurance from the Confucian doctrines, nor was their emulation of the ancient sages sufficient to allay their profound doubts. Their *tzu-tsan* are reminiscent of the Ch'an Buddhists' in their ambivalent tone, their ironical attitude toward the self, and their puzzlement over the dichotomy between appearance and reality. Occasion-

ally there is even a glimpse of some darkness at the core of their being that
is never shown in their other and more conventional writings.

The most ambiguous and allusive self-eulogizer of this group is Wang
Chi (1498–1583). A disciple of Wang Yang-ming, Wang Chi is closer to
Ch'an Buddhism and Taoism than almost all other Ming Neo-Confucians.
His *tzu-tsan* contains echoes from a disparate collection of sources, and it
throbs with an intensity not found in the three Confucian self-eulogies
previously quoted.

> His aims seem to be impractical yet he is self-confident;
> His steps seem to be unsteady yet he is self-possessed.
> His talents are worn with ease but seem limited;
> His knowledge is bubbling but seems concealed.
> In his daily conduct he seems both pure and corrupted;
> The Way in his grasp seems sometimes present and sometimes lost.[53]
> His vision seems to illuminate an eternity but does not go beyond a
>   foot;
> His capacity seems to comprehend all things but he differs not from
>   the commonplace.
> His illusory body resides in a pitcher which seems as large as the
>   universe.[54]
> A mere masked rider in a ceremonial procession, where the sleek
>   horses seem most dazzling.[55]

Hsü Wei (1521–1593) distinguished himself in several fields: poetry,
calligraphy, military strategy, and painting. Following the usual practice,
he commissioned an artisan to paint his portrait rather than doing it himself.

> I was fat at birth,
> But thin and emaciated in my teens.
> After thirty I began to put on weight again,
> To the point of obesity as shown in this painting.
> Now I am fifty.
> Yet how do I know that today's obesity
> Will not turn into thinness someday
> As to accord with a life in retirement?
> How can others hold on to this painting
> And expect me to remain forever unchanged?
> Alas! A dragon? A Pig?
> A crane? A wild duck?
> Is it a butterfly or Chuang Chou?[56]
> Who knows what it really is?[57]

Teng Huo-ch'ü (1498?–1577?), an enigmatic figure in the T'ai-chou
School, led a most unconventional life. Shuttling back and forth between
Confuciandom and the Buddhist monastic order, Teng antagonized most
of the official gentry members that he met during his perpetual wander-
ings over the length and breadth of China. He finally died unmourned in a

deserted temple. Only Li Chih appreciated his eccentricity and self-destructive arrogance, which are fully expressed in the following *tzu-tsan:*

> In solid substance he is like the Sung Confucians;
> In romantic temperament he is like the heroes of Chin.
> In freedom of spirit he is like T'ang poetry.
> In taste he goes beyond Fu-hsi.[58]
> He regards Heaven, Earth, and all things as straw dogs.[59]
> Appearance and body he considers as mud and weeds.
> All emotions and desires obey his orders;
> Frowns and laughs are for him unusual expressions.
> When he acts he shakes heaven and earth;
> When he retreats he covers all his tracks and footprints.
> He depends neither on men nor on Heaven.
> He is above all ranks and virtues![60]

When Huang Tsung-hsi (1610–1695), the scholar and Ming loyalist, was eighty years old, he had his portrait painted. For the occasion he chose to wear a cornered turban and a ceremonial robe. On his portrait he inscribed the following *tzu-tsan:*

> At first he was banned as a partisan;
> Then he was accused of being a roving knight;
> Finally he was placed in the Confucian academe.
> As a person he has changed three times.
> Was it because of the time?
> Or because he always had desertion in mind?[61]

Both the costume and the wording of the *tzu-tsan* were probably deliberately ambiguous, for Huang, the survivor of a valiant but futile resistance movement, was living under a hostile and alien rule. On the other hand, he may have mellowed sufficiently in his old age to fully appreciate the vagaries of fate, and the phrase "three changes *(san pien),*" recalling the same tortuous path that Wang Yang-ming had also traveled, may hint at a more sympathetic view, at eighty, toward the less correct ways of some of his fellow Neo-Confucians he had criticized in the *Ming-ju hsüeh-an.*

One more specimen written by a Buddhist monk concludes our enumeration of *tzu-tsan.* Chen-k'e (1543–1603), one of the three great Buddhist masters of late Ming, was throughout his life a passionate activist and heroic figure revered by Buddhists and Confucians alike. His deep involvement with several causes finally led to his death in prison. His self-eulogy, perhaps befitting a roaring Buddhist lion, was long and effusive.

> If you were I, you would have no sense;
> If I were you, I would be full of fantasies.
> When we are together, we are not one;
> We are even less, when we are separated.
> But nobody can tell us apart

Even though he be endowed with
Nāgārjuna's perspicacity and Śāriputra's wisdom.

By nature you are expansive and ebullient;
Direct and forthright, you cannot be trammeled.
Gain or loss are nothing to you.
You have the heart of a hero,
But not the ambition for fame or achievement.
Therefore you can hardly be fenced within the dusty world;
You should be let loose among rocks and fountains.

Furthermore, you are arrogant—
To you the Buddha and Patriarchs are nincompoops.
But a dusky slave or a white cow can be your friends.
Sometimes you quote doctrine to bear witness to Ch'an;
Sometimes you use Ch'an to confirm doctrine.
Sometimes thorns and debris are treasures to you;
Sometimes corals and agates are but dung and weeds.
Wagging your tongue, you praise and condemn without rule,
And turn right and wrong upside down.
Those who do you favors you treat no different from enemies;
Those who have no affection for you you like to be with.
You are happy and angry without reason, like an infant.
As I see it, you are totally ingenuous.
You start rambling and raving at the drop of a hat.
Others may hate you or love you,
You just go on freely like a crank.
You take such delight in wearing a red robe—
I am afraid if you are seen through by a clear-eyed lad,
You wouldn't be worth a dime!

Ha! Ha! Ha!
Who has recommended this man?
With the scale in his hand he can shift the balance at will,
Causing people to live or die as he wishes.[62]

Reading this exuberant self-depiction one cannot but feel that Chen-
k'e was vying with the portrait painter: the Ch'an master sweeps and
splashes across the vast silk texture with bold brush strokes and outrageous
colors. Indeed the vogue of the *tzu-tsan* may have resulted partly from the
writer's dissatisfaction with the painter, for the former demands an impossible delineation of the spirit of the man, a confirmation of his self-image,
whereas the latter, usually a humble and anonymous craftsman,[63] can do no
better than a more or less accurate execution within the contemporary
framework of stylization. To inscribe a *tsan* on a portrait can also be seen as
a part of the growing trend beginning in late Sung: the attempt of the
literary art to dominate the pictorial by means of all types of inscriptions
which almost fill up all the empty space in the painting.[64] But the *tzu-tsan*'s
accidental association with portraiture has other consequences. Because of
this association, the *tzu-tsan* author is essentially different from autobiog-

raphers in all other modes: he alone is confronted with the whole, concrete, palpable image of the self in the painting, whereas the others, in the absence of a direct and prompting visual immediacy, only recall past events or examine partial aspects of themselves.

From Nonself to the True Self

The existence of the self, or the reality of a substantial self, is a position inconsistent with Buddhist doctrine. To cling to the notion of the self would invariably obstruct understanding and hinder liberation. But the negation of the self, according to Buddhist teaching, is a notion to which one should not cling either, lest one is again led astray from the path to illumination. Hence the self is to be negated only at the right stage of the spiral ascension to wisdom: at a higher level the negation of the self and the negation of the nonself are united to form a higher truth. Although this kind of intricate and subtle reasoning is found in many Buddhist texts, its paradoxical and dialectical nature is best demonstrated in Ch'an discourse. As the following dialogue between the monk Wei-k'uan (755–817) and his disciple shows, any conceptual formulation has to be rejected if the Way is to be reached.

> A monk asks him: "Where is the Way?"
> The master says: "Right in front of your eyes."
> "Why is it that I don't see it?"
> The master replies: "It is because you have an 'I' that you do not see the Way."
> "I have an 'I', so I don't see the Way. Do you see it?"
> The master replies: "If there is a 'you,' then there is an 'I.' So the Way can not be seen."
> "If there is neither an 'I' nor a 'you,' can the Way be seen?"
> The master replies: "If there is neither a 'you' nor an 'I,' then who is it that seeks to see the Way?"[65]

The self is only a little more substantial in the neo-Taoist philosophy as formulated in *Chuang Tzu chu-shu,* an early fifth-century commentary on *Chuang Tzu.* Since everything in the universe changes ceaselessly, "the self of former times is no longer the self of the present moment. Both the self and the present move on: they are not something that can be kept or preserved. People of the world, not understanding this fact, stubbornly insist that what is encountered at any given present moment can be captured and held on to. Are they not ignorant?"[66] The impermanence of the self was echoed in a contemporary Buddhist treatise, the *Chao lun* by Seng-chao (384–414).

Thus we see that the minds of the sages are different from the views of the common people. Why? They say that a man possesses the same body in youth and in old age and that the same substance persists over a hundred years. They only know that the years pass on but do not realize that the body follows. A young ascetic seeking Nirvana left his family and when his hair had turned white, returned home. When his neighbors saw him and asked, "Is the man of the past still living?" he replied, "I look like the man of the past but I am not he." The neighbors were all startled and rejected his words.[67]

The discontinuity of individual identity, although a Buddhist and Taoist view, was never explicitly challenged by the Confucians. It prevails in literature, especially in the genre of *tzu-tsan* that was previously discussed. The most elegant literary expression of this view is in a poem by Wang An-shih (1021–1086) written when he came upon a portrait of him painted several years earlier by the well-known artist Li Kung-ling (1049–1106).

> Both I myself and my portrait are illusory beings:
> In the transformations of this world both will turn to dust.
> I only know that this thing is not that thing,
> But do not ask if the present person is the same as the former
>   person.[68]

The melancholy sentiment expressed in Wang's poem contrasts sharply with the strong will and great daring that he displayed in his younger days when his zeal for political and social change made him the foremost reformer in Chinese history. His skeptical attitude toward the self, however, was not so unusual for a Confucian. Earlier we have seen Confucius' admonitions against egotism. The submerging of the individual self in the service of the community and the state was always a basic tenet in the Confucian teaching. If few Confucians would accept the metaphysical position of the self's unreality or nonexistence, they would certainly exhort the ethical notion of selflessness. These two essentially different concepts were, as a result of the terseness of classical Chinese and the canon of rhetorical economy, represented by the same compound *wu-wo*. This curious linguistic accident would, as we shall see, result in the blurring of sectarian differences and the emergence of a syncretic attitude toward the self.

The term *wu-wo* is not present in any of the Confucian canonical texts. Neither does it appear in *Lao Tzu* or *Chuang Tzu*, but in the latter Taoist classic there is a similar expression, *wu chi:* "The great man has no self *(ta-jen wu chi)*."[69] *Chuang Tzu chu-shu,* the early fifth-century neo-Taoist work quoted previously, may have been the first non-Buddhist text in which *wu-wo* was used in the sense of "selflessness": "The holy man is the one who is selfless."[70] Sung Neo-Confucians, eclectic in their choice of words and expressions, heartily adopted *wu-wo*. Earlier in the discussion of the expansive view of the self we have seen Chang Tsai's idea about enlarging the self so as to encompass all creation in its empathy. Elsewhere in his book *Cheng meng* Chang says that "only when one is selfless *(wu wo)* can he enlarge himself."[71] Ch'eng Hao, perhaps alluding to *Chuang Tzu chu-shu*, stated the following about Yen Yüan, Confucius' favorite disciple. "If Master Yen had some imperfection, his would still be different from the imperfections of others. His lies only in that he still had a self *(yu chi)*. As for the one who is selfless *(wu wo)*, he is a holy man."[72]

Whereas the Sung Neo-Confucian philosophers were making statements on selflessness and the subduing of the individual self, the poets sung about another form of self-negation, the *true self (jen-wo* or *jen-wu)*. As a Buddhist concept, *jen-wo* stood for the real or nirvana self, as opposed to the illusory, and hence false, self. When all the impermanent constituents of the individual self are destroyed, the true self emerges. Su Shih expresses most eloquently the contrast between the ephemeral individual life and the indestructible true self:

> Things are born with forms and forms multiply:
> In a second rootless dreams grow into a mirage.
> A man dreaming takes nothing to be unreal,
> But everything will be different the instant the bubble is burst and
>   the reflected image lost.
> The morning dew is not yet dry, but the lightning has already
>   vanished.
> When all that is annihilatible is annihilated—there is my true self![73]

That the true self emerges when all extraneous layers of existence are stripped away is echoed by another poet:

> The leaves are gone, the water is low, exposing a thousand barren
>   crags;
> Clearly I too see my true self.[74]

To the Ming philosophers, whose nomenclature is even more eclectic than that of their Sung predecessors, the term *true self* was irresistible, notwithstanding its Buddhist origins and its strong negative implications. Wang Yang-ming (1492–1529) on one occasion equated the true self with innate knowledge *(liang-chih)*, the very foundation of his philosophical system:

> Basically the original substance of the mind is none other than the
> Principle of Nature, and is never out of accord with propriety. This is
> your true self. This true self is the master of the body. If there is no
> true self, there will be no body. Truly, with the true self, one lives;
> without it one dies. If you really want to do something for your bodily
> self, you must make use of this true self, always preserve its original
> substance, and be cautious over things not yet seen and apprehensive
> over things not yet heard of, for fear that true self be injured, even
> slightly.[75]

Some of these functions of the true self seem to be shared by the European soul, but the two are essentially different. The true self, unlike the Western soul, is devoid of individuality. None of the proponents of the true self makes any provision for the preservation of personal identity in the indestructible core of the individual, the true self. In fact, all the particularities of the individual are to be annihilated, as indicated by the two poets quoted. Furthermore, in the Buddhist theory of the true self there is the distinction between the little self *(hsiao-wo)* and the great self *(ta-wo);* the former is equated with the individual self whereas the latter is equated with the true self. The *hsiao-wo* and *ta-wo* distinction was adopted by the Confucians with the usual modification: ethical and social connotations were introduced at the expense of metaphysical meaning. The little self was to be subdued in the interest of the great self, which now was no longer identified with the Buddha or the nirvana but with humanity. The most representative of the syncretic discourse on the self is the *K'e-chi ming (An Inscription on the Subduing of the Self)* by Chao Chen-chi (1508–1576). He begins by repeating what by now was standard characterization of the self: "Heaven, earth, and all creation originally form one body with me." Echoing Cheng Hao's insight, Chao went on to praise *jen* (perfect virtue or humaneness). Ancient worthies "could complete themselves because they were selfless." Turning to himself, Chao exclaimed: "Alas, I have a great self which views all creation and observes heaven and earth. When the great self has not been achieved, the little self is rampant and growing; when the little self has been subdued, the great self is swift and flourishing." Going back to Confucius, but with a Buddhist vocabulary, Chao proclaimed: "The subdued self is selfless; the great self is the true self." He ended the piece optimistically, alluding to a Confucian admonition we have quoted at the beginning of this article: "The practice of perfect virtue is from the man himself."[76]

Notes

1. *Analects,* 9:4
2. Stephen Toulmin, "Self-Knowledge and Knowledge of the 'Self'," in *The Self,* ed. Theodore Mischel (Totowa, N. J.: Rowman and Littlefield, 1977), p. 297.
3. *Analects,* 12:1. *The Chinese Classics,* trans. James Legge (Oxford: Oxford University Press, 1893), 1:250.
4. Chiao Hung, *Pi-ch'eng hsü-chi,* (Ts'ung-shu chi-ch'eng ed.), p. 152.
5. Chih-hsü, *Ssu-shu Ou-i chieh* (Nanking: Chin-ling k'e-ching-ch'u, 1934), p. 129.
6. Cited in Fang Tung-shu, *Han-hsüeh shang-tui* (Hangchow: Che-chiang shu-chü, 1900), 2.48a.
7. Ibid., 2.48a–51b.
8. Ibid.
9. *Mencius,* 8, A:4. See *The Chinese Classics,* 2:450–51.

10. Chuang Chou, *Chuang Tzu: Basic Writings,* trans. Burton Watson (New York: Columbia University Press, 1964), p. 38.

11. Chuang Chou, *Chuang Tzu,* ed. Ssu-pu pei-yao, 4.19a–19b.

12. Seng Chao, *Chao lun,* in *Taishō Dai-zōkyō,* 45:159b.

13. Cited in *Ching-te ch'uan-teng lu,* comp. Tao-yüan (Taipei: Chen-shan-mei ch'u-pan-she, 1968), 10.171–72.

14. Ibid., 10.188.

15. Ibid.

16. Su Shih, *Su Tung-po chi* (Taipei: Shang-wu yin-shu-kuan, 1965), 10:36.

17. Chang Tsai, *Chang tzu ch'üan-shu,* (Ssu-pu pei-yao ed.), 2.21a.

18. Cited in *Sources of Chinese Tradition,* ed. Wm. Theodore deBary et al. (New York: Columbia University Press, 1960), p. 524.

19. *Erh Ch'eng i-shu,* (Ssu-pu pei-yao ed.), 2A:2a.

20. Chang Tsai, *Chang tzu ch'üan-shu,* 2.22b.

21. Yang Chien, *Tz'u-hu i-shu,* (Ssu-ming ts'ung-shu ed., 1934), 7.1a.

22. Ibid., 7.2a.

23. Ibid., 7.4a.

24. Ibid., 7.12b.

25. Ibid., 7.12b–13a.

26. Included in Lu Chiu-yüan, *Hsiang-shan ch'üan-chi,* (Ssu-pu pei-yao ed.), 36.26a.

27. Yang Chien, *Tz'u-hu i-shu,* 2.11a.

28. Shao Yung, *Yin-ch'uan chi-jang chi,* (Ssu-pu ts'ung-k'an ed.), 19.125b.

29. John O. Lyòns, *The Invention of the Self: The Hinge of Consciousness in the Eighteenth Century* (Carbondale and Edwardsville: Southern Illinois University Press, 1978), pp. 18–19.

30. Cited in *A Source Book in Chinese Philosophy,* trans. Wing-tsit Chan (Princeton University Press, 1963), p. 12.

31. P'u Tao-yüan, *Hsien chü ts'ung kao* (Taipei: National Central Library, 1970), 7.16b.

32. James George Frazer, *The New Golden Bough,* ed. Theodor H. Gaster (Garden City, N.Y.: Doubleday & Co., 1961), p. 76.

33. *Yen Tzu ch'un-ch'iu,* (Ssu-pu pei-yao ed.), 7.13b.

34. For a translation of these poems see *The Poetry of T'ao Ch'ien,* trans. James Robert Hightower (New York: Oxford University Press, 1970), pp. 42–44.

35. See my article "Self-Examination and Confession of Sins in Traditional China," *Harvard Journal of Asiatic Studies,* 39:1 (June 1979): 5–38.

36. Georges Gusdorf, "Conditions and Limits of Autobiography," trans. James Olney, in *Autobiography: Essays Theoretical and Critical,* ed. James Olney (Princeton: Princeton University Press, 1980), p. 32.

37. *Ching-te ch'uan-teng lu,* 15.101.

38. This section is based on exerpts from a paper presented before the University Seminar on Traditional China, Columbia University, 20 November 1973.

39. This *tzu-tsan* was inscribed on the portrait to be given to a judge. I have to translate the term *kung-an* rather than leave it in romanized form lest the pun be lost.

40. Tsung-kao, *Ta-hui P'u-chüeh ch'an-shih yü-lu,* in *Taishō Dai-zōkyō,* 47:860c–61a.

41. *Li-tai tzu-hsü-chuan wen-ch'ao,* comp. Kuo Teng-feng (Taipei: Shang-wu yin-shu-kuan, 1965), 2:534.

42. The garment of such colors was worn only by high officials.

43. Ch'en Liang's alternate name.

44. Kuo, 2:538.

45. An allusion to the *Chuang Tzu,* 5. Confucius is here alleged to have advised Duke Ai regarding the "alternations of the world, the workings of fate." "If you can harmonize and delight in them, master them and never be at a loss for joy, if you can do this day and night without break and make it be spring with everything, mingling with all and creating the

moment within your own mind—this is what I call being whole in power." (Watson translation)

46. Quoted in *Ch'ien-k'un cheng-ch'i chi* (1848 ed.), 61 : 3b.

47. Cf. *Analects*, 15 : 8: "The Master said: 'The determined scholar and the man of virtue will not seek to live at the expense of injuring their virtue. They will even sacrifice their lives to preserve their virtue complete.'" (Legge translation)

48. Cf. *Mencius*, 6, pt. 1 : 10: "So, I like life, and I also like righteousness. If I cannot keep the two together, I will let life go, and choose righteousness."

49. These two lines underscore Wen's determination to die in accordance with the teaching of the Confucian masters, after having done his utmost in the futile struggle against the Mongols.

50. Included in Kuo, 2 : 538.

51. Included in *Ming-jen tzu-chuan wen-ch'ao*, ed. Tu Lienche (Taipei: I-wen yin-shu-kuan, 1977), p. 384.

52. Included in Tu, p. 202. The quotation is from *Analects*, 7 : 23.

53. Cf. *Tao te ching*, 41.

54. This alludes to the story in *Yün chi ch'i chien* about a Taoist priest who sleeps in a pitcher which can hold a sun and a moon.

55. Quoted in *Wang Lung-hsi yü-lu* (Taipei: Kuang-wen shu-chü, 1967), "Wang Lung-hsi hsien-sheng chuan," 3b.

56. Cf. *Chuang Tzu*, 2: "Once Chuang Chou dreamt he was a butterfly, a butterfly flitting and fluttering around, happy with himself and doing as he pleased. He didn't know he was Chuang Chou. Suddenly he woke up and there he was, solid and unmistakable Chuang Chou. But he didn't know if he was Chuang Chou who had dreamt he was a butterfly, or a butterfly dreaming he was Chuang Chou. Between Chuang Chou and a butterfly there must be some distinction! This is called the transformation of things." (Watson translation)

57. Kuo, 2 : 549.

58. The first of the Three Legendary Emperors.

59. Cf. *Tao te ching*, 5:

> "Heaven and earth are not humane,
> They regard all things as straw dogs.
> The sage is not humane,
> He regards all people as straw dogs."
> (Wing-tsit Chan translation)

60. Teng Huo-ch'ü, *Nan-hsün lu* (1599), 43b. A rebel and vagabond when alive, Teng remains an outcast even to present-day anti-Confucian historians. For a brief sketch of his significance see my review of *Li Zhi: philosophe maudit* (1527–1602) by Jean-Francois Billeter, *Harvard Journal of Asiatic Studies*, 41 : 1 (June 1981), 308–12.

61. Quoted in *Ming-mo min-tzu i-jen chuan*, ed. Fu Pao-shih (Hong Kong: Li-wen ch'u-pan-she, 1971), p. 117.

62. Chen-k'e, *Tzu-po tsun-che ch'üan-chi* in *Dai-Nihon zoku-zōkyō*, Part 2, case 31, 5 : 474b–75a.

63. Prominent painters in traditional China seldom did portraits from life.

64. This is perhaps why the Mexican Revolution gave us Diego Rivera and Siqueiros while the Chinese Revolution gave us Quotations of Chairman Mao.

65. Cited in *Ching-te ch'uan-teng lu*, 7.127.

66. *Chuang Tzu chu-shu*, (Ku-i ts'ung-shu ed.), 3.12.

67. Quoted in Wing-tsit Chan, *A Source Book in Chinese Philosophy*, p. 348.

68. Wang An-shih, *Lin-ch'uan hsien-sheng wen-chi* (Peking: Chung-hua shu-chü, 1958), p. 326. It might be interesting to contrast Wang's doubts with the certitudes of John Locke, who proclaims that "as far as this consciousness can be extended backwards to any past action or thought, so far reaches the identity of that person; it is the same self now it was then; and it

is by the same self with this present one that now reflects on it, that that action was done." *Essay Concerning Human Understanding*, Everyman's Library (London: Dent, 1967), 1:281.

69. *Chuang Tzu*, 6.8b.

70. *Chuang Tzu chu-shu*, 1.43.

71. Chang Tsai, *Chang Tzu ch'üan-shu*, 2.14b.

72. *Erh Ch'eng yü-lu*, (Ts'ung-shu chi-ch'eng ed.), p. 90.

73. Su Shih, *Su Tung-po chi*, 7:6.

74. Cited in *Sung shih chi-shih*, comp. Li Ao (Taipei: Shang-wu yin-shu-kuan, 1968), 81.7a. The poem is attributed to Weng Sen.

75. Wang Yang-ming, *Instructions for Practical Living and Other Neo-Confucian Writings*, trans. Wing-tsit Chan (New York: Columbia University Press, 1963), p. 79.

76. Quoted in Huang Tsung-hsi, *Ming-ju hsüeh-an* (Taipei: Shih-chieh shu-chü, 1965), p. 334.

3

On the Self-Person Differentiation:
Universal Categories of Civilization and
Their Diverse Contents

Vytautas Kavolis

I

Much of the difference among civilizations derives from variations in the contents of "universal categories of the human mind" (or at least the literate mind) and in the linkages of meaning among these categories in particular linguistic universes at particular points in time.[1] A social psychology of the self or a theory of personality that does not reflect on the pressures exerted by the language, or languages, in which it has been conceived, on what and how of the human psyche it can comprehend, is bound to infiltrate hidden particularities into its conception of the universal.

An adequate comprehension of any category of thought is a prerequisite for using concepts that refer to it. Such a comprehension cannot be obtained without an examination of the range of meanings that have been attributed to the category and of their development over time within a particular linguistic tradition. The basic cognitive content (or the major alternative contents) of the category can be distilled by abstraction from the complete series of particular meanings that have been accepted sufficiently widely to have entered the list of the dictionary meanings of the term(s).

The area of meaning covered by a category may be circumscribed more precisely by asking which meaningful connections with other concepts the terms representing that category accept and which they reject. In English, "self-love" is an easily made connection of two concepts, whereas "person-love" is not. "Personal responsibility" is idiomatically acceptable, whereas "selfish responsibility" (or some equivalent thereof) is not. The English symbolic design of the "self" seems to point to something presumed to be capable of the emotion of love (turned inward), but not of the obligation of responsibility (turned outward).[2] The "person" is, in this respect, the inverse of the "self," but both can and ought to be "respected" (self-respect, respect for the person).

What is seen as being worthy of respect in the human being that is comprehended by the categories "self" and "person"? By looking more closely at the accumulated contents of the English categories "self" and "person,"[3] we observe that the diversity of meanings attached to the "person" contains four essential elements, the first two of which could be considered the historical foundations and the latter two the moral implications of the concept. In the approximate historical sequence of their emergence, these elements are:

1. *An artificial construction that retains its stability in the midst of surrounding change*—a mask, "a character sustained or assumed in a drama" that remains constant during a performance; the grammatical form indicating the author, the recipient, and the observer of an action; the "artificial person" of a corporation which retains its legal character however much everything changes around it. The Latin *persona* is perhaps derived from the Etruscan term, of Greek origin, for "masked figure," "orig. the embodiment of a god of the nether world whose office it was to receive the soul of the dead and to accompany it to Hades."[4] A mask is thus, in origin, an artificial— temporary, but for the time being, valid—godlikeness. In sociological usage, "The person is an individual who has status."[5] It is that within the human being which can be given a name by which he (or she) is publicly known. As symbolic constructions of the meaning of the human individual, the self relates to the person as the nameless relates to the named.[6]

2. What, as the object of human activity, is the artificial construction of a "mask" is, as the subject of human perception, *the external form of a metaphysical entity which makes its meaning understandable.* The Three Persons of the Trinity are comprehensible forms of the Godhead who, as the quality beyond the forms, escapes comprehension, but can only present itself, even to itself, through these forms.[7] In "crimes against the person," the "person" has physical tangibility, as "the living body of a human being" which has acquired the right not to be encroached upon by other persons. It is in this sense that a "viable" fetus, which is capable of surviving outside of the mother's body, is recognized as a legal person.

3. This "artificial" construction, which is, at the same time, the external form of something that is "really" there, has *the capacity to choose one's own purposes and to act reasonably in pursuit of them,* the most peculiarly Western element in the conception of personhood. This capacity, typically viewed as developed fully through education, thus "artificially," is what distinguishes a person "from a thing, or from lower animals" (or slaves, children, and the insane). A person is what is capable of "personal responsibility."[8] If an agent can legitimately refuse responsibility for its actions, either because (a) it acts under irresistible external direction, or (b) it lacks the capacity to understand the consequences of its own actions, it has been

substantively "depersonalized" into a "subject," a "patient," or a "victim" (as what used to be "persons" tend to become in the behavioral science-therapeutic tradition).[9]

4. The quality of *publicly recognized respect-worthiness, worthwhileness, valuableness* adheres inalienably, at least within the realm of human affairs, to this agent. A "person," and usually only a person, has legal rights. The person cannot be merely a tool, but is treated as an "end-in-himself." Only God (and sometimes his emanation, justice)[10] is permitted to be "no respecter of persons," presumably because he sees through this objectified shell of stability, reasonable agency, and publicly recognized respect-worthiness and observes directly the greater value beyond it—the "soul." But the "soul" is not directly accessible to mere mortals.[11] They, at least since the latter part of the Middle Ages, are in duty (or by contract) bound to be "respecters of persons."

The four elements of the category "person" are not necessarily all present when a reference is made to a "person." An act of communication presupposes the contents of a tradition of speaking but does not exhaustively represent it. Furthermore, terms may be given precise individual elaborations that are not a part of the generally shared linguistic tradition. Nevertheless, what is communicated by individual messages formed within a particular tradition of speaking is influenced even by the contents of this tradition that are not explicitly recognized or intended in the communicative act; to disregard the unintended contents is tantamount to a translation of the message into a foreign language.

II

Generally speaking, the "person," in the historical tradition of English usage, though grounded in a biological or metaphysical given that exists independently of anyone's consciousness of it, is also, and necessarily, an artificial construct (a theatrical "mask," a legal "fiction").[12] But, in contrast to dominant Indian traditions, in which what is human construction is not valid enough, it is a highly valuable artifice. It must be respected, it appears, for either (or both) of two different reasons: (1) by virtue of its own substantive—though perhaps artificially developed—character as the "rational agency" of what is there, and (2) because it is the cultural "form" in which the natural "substance" of what is worthwhile is preserved and through which it becomes accessible to others.

Whatever this "substance" is, it seems, in English usage, to include the "self", which, however, tends to be separated from the "rational agency" vested in the "person".[13] The basic elements of the English conception of the "self" are (1) *sameness of a substance* (as in "self good things"); (2) *unique essence* ("in contradistinction to what is adventitious") *or habitual condition of a conscious, though not necessarily rational, agent* ("true self" as contrasted to temporarily "not being one's own self"), this essence being "often identified with the soul or mind as opposed to the body"; and (3) *independence, capacity of acting alone* ("on one's own," but also a "self-acting mechanism"). In contrast to the independence of a person, which implies a reasonable understanding of one's own purposes, the independence of the self implies merely an ability to act by "one's own will or desire"[14]—a capacity that is also possessed by children, the insane, and animals, and, with will translated into a self-initiated response to changes in the environment, by automatic machinery.

Since approximately the seventeenth century, two additional meanings of the "self" have emerged into prominence in conventional English usage: (4) *one of several characters of which an individual is conscious within his personality,* either consecutively or simultaneously (e.g., the "natural self," "the sinful self," and the "spiritual self," 1703), all of them "true," but not consistent with each other;[15] and (5) *the agency within the personality pursuing selfish interests,* the specific antipode of a universal or at least socially shared morality. The very word "selfish" was said, in 1693, to be of the Presbyterians' "own new mint." "Synonyms current in the 17th cent. are *self-ended* and *self-ful.*" Much of the flavor of the seventeenth-century perception of the self is concentrated in: "Untimely Abortions of a Self-full, Distempered Spirit" (1693).[16] The "self" is now perceived as internally divided and the potential author of antisocial dynamism, whereas the "person" is usually, in modern usage, of one piece, indivisible, and a "rational being" (1659).

Whereas "selfish interests" are a quality of the self, only persons can have "personal belongings." Apparently the self—that part of human consciousness which is inherently there, a piece of "nature"—has the capacity to *seek* enjoyment from the acquisition or experience of objects. But only the person—that which is added to human nature, an artificial contrivance of "culture"—has the capacity to become bindingly *attached* to them.[17] This relatively stable attachment of the person to objects seems to transcend its merely legal right to possess objects. There can be "interpersonal relations," but no "interself relations." (Only an infusion of the "soul" into the "self" makes *Seelenfreundschaft* possible.) The self expands and contracts: it can fuse, either contemplatively or ecstatically, with the universe, but it can become separated, not only from other selves but also from other intrapsychic elements of the individual in which it is located, by its "selfishness."[18] It can even, perversely, alienate itself, by its own actions, from its own essence ("self-estrangement").

The person, in contrast, has unique and durable boundaries. In part precisely for this reason, in part perhaps by virtue of its ability to make "rational" choices and consequently to accept responsibility for them, the person also has a capacity—which the self apparently lacks—for making reliable attachments to other persons who are circumscribed by their own unique boundaries. To sustain such attachments, the person must be capable of generally (that is, both to self and to others) intelligible communication. The self can content itself with a completely internal "self-expression" or "self-contemplation" that is closed to others.

III

Any basic category of thought has a certain fundamental structure suggested, or made possible, by the language in which the concept representing it is being used. But the development of the latent possibilities of that structure—as well as, more slowly, of the language as a whole—is a historical process, influenced both by changes in the organization of society and by the partly independent intellectual dynamics of a variety of cultural movements (and by borrowing from initially alien traditions). History constantly throws new meanings at any major symbolic category to test what it will accept without breaking down (and casts off some of the old meanings in an effort to determine what a category can lose without ceasing to be itself). The method of concept linkages, by which it is determined with what other concepts a term is connected in a particular sociohistorical environment, provides one indicator of changes over time in the symbolic contents of such categories.

In English, the period from the second half of the sixteenth century to the eighteenth century has been particularly productive of *self*-compounds. There were, by my counting, thirty-two new self-compounds in the sixteenth century, eighty-one in the seventeenth century, and thirty-two in the eighteenth century. The peak of productivity of self-compounds in the seventeenth century suggests an increased preoccupation with the problem of the self and its relations with its semantic environment. Many of these new self-compounds have had a life span of "about 50 years (e.g., 1645–1690)"[19] and were, like "self-ill," subsequently rejected by the living language.

The typical self-compounds that appeared for the first time in written texts in the sixteenth century project the qualities, or potencies, of *self-sufficiency* ("self-born," "self-bred," "self-contained," "self-motion," "self-sufficient"), of *self-assertion* ("self-assurance," "self-conceit," "self-minded," "self-partial," "self-trust"), and of *self-enjoyment* ("self-delight," "self-glorious," "self-love," "self-pleaser," "self-pride"). The "self" that the self-compounds of the sixteenth century point to is an intrapsychic structure that produces its own unique pattern, performs it on a stage, and enjoys itself in the performance: *an amoral hedonistic self.*

In the seventeenth century, self-sufficiency and self-assertion become numerically still stronger, but they are, for the first time, strongly challenged by two new themes: *self-judgment,* resulting in self-condemnation ("self-accusation," "self-condemnation," "self-contempt," "self-judgment," "self-repugnance") and, even more strongly, *self-destruction,* not only physical (as in the few sixteenth-century terms of this type) but mainly psychological ("self-abasement," "self-annihilation," "self-deception," "self-despair," "self-ill," "self-slaughter," "self-torment"). The concept linkages of the self-compounds of the seventeenth century suggest a violent clash between the older ("Elizabethan") self-assertiveness and the new ("Puritan") self-criticism, both being approximately equal in numbers of variants. The self-repugnance arises in part through translations of the "self-repudiating" terms in the tradition of German mysticism, such as the works of Jakob Boehme. Whatever its origin, the seventeenth-century innovation in England is the *aggressively introspective self,* a self that has acquired the capacity of being its own judge and uses this capacity with ruthless intensity, regardless of the suffering it produces for itself in the process.

The symbolic counterpart of this process seems to be the incorporation of the category of the "soul," which had previously been structurally separated from, and superior to, the "self," into the structure of the latter, as one of its component parts. For Meister Eckhart, the "self" was a creaturely particle of nature that invaded the proper domain of the eternal "soul," alienating it from its destination. ". . . any soul that sees God must . . . have lost her own self."[20] Around 1700, in English usage, the "soul," as "spiritual self," becomes a part—though still the supremely valuable part—of the "self." It is the part capable of judging the rest.

In the eighteenth century, the themes of both self-judgment and self-destruction, on the one hand, and self-enjoyment, on the other, become less frequent among the newly emerging self-compounds. Self-sufficiency and self-assertion remain strong throughout the whole three-century period. But the assertive self of the eighteenth century has acquired trustworthy *self-control,* the one field of meaning in which new self-compounds now appear in increased numbers ("self-control," "self-government," "self-possession," "self-renunciation," "self-restraint"). What the new self-compounds of the eighteenth century point to is the emergence of a *balanced assertively controlled self,* the type that extends from the earl of Shaftesbury to John Stuart Mill and beyond (and includes many of the American Revolutionary leaders). It is this eighteenth-century self, capable of reliable self-direction, that becomes the object of "self-respect": the term "self-respect," which in the seventeenth century meant "a private, selfish end" (1613), and "self-love," "self-conceit" (1657), is now legitimated as "proper regard for the dignity of one's person" (1795–1814).[21] The self is entitled to self-respect only when it becomes certain of its capacity for self-control.

Religious thought apparently either initiates the move toward reliable self-control or registers it somewhat earlier than do changes in the general forms of language. The "norm of individual self-reliance in moral judg-

ments," "sustained by the belief that a person's inner resources are generally adequate to guide him in a morally sensible way through life," without
external guidance by authorities or the community, develops in English
sixteenth- and seventeenth-century sectarian Protestantism.[22] In psychiatric
thought, the idea of "moral management (that is, the care of the insane
without physical restraint and by appeal to conscience and will of the patient)" appears only toward the end of the eighteenth century. By the
middle of the nineteenth century, psychiatric literature treats "the power
of volition and self-control" as "the defining characteristic of sanity."[23] Even
the mentally disturbed are seen, in the first half of the nineteenth century,
as retaining this moral *Man's Power over Himself to Prevent or Control Insanity*
(the title of John Barlow's book, published in 1843), which they should
employ against areas of disorder in their own selves.[24]

Does the development of the "self" in English represent a general
structural sequence in which an intense self-searching, by the aggressively
introspective self, has to precede the emergence of adequate self-control?
Must self-control be forged in a battle between self-assertiveness and self-
condemnation, when both are equally strong? Is the amoral hedonistic
(and "theatrical") self incapable of being immediately transformed into the
responsible self, without undergoing the pains of self-repudiation?

Without having believed, in 1649, with great intensity, that "Antichrist
acteth selfe-hood and the lust of the flesh," can one, with full conviction,
declare, in 1858, "Their glorious self-hood and immortal liberty"? The
assertion of selfhood is immediately followed, in 1879, by "This extreme
development of . . . selfhood or self-feeling among the insane." It is the
balanced assertively controlled self of the eighteenth century, stronger in
England than in France or anywhere else at that time, achieved through
absorption of the "soul" into the "self" and through the attainment of
reliable control by the "person" over the "self", that is celebrated in the first
quote and revealed breaking down in the second.[25]

In the course of this breakdown, in the second half of the nineteenth
century, the theory of the moral responsibility of the patient is replaced by
his immutable hereditary character as the explanation of psychiatric illness.
When the "soul" evaporates from the "self" and the "person's" mastery is
undermined, only the body is left (or left over).

VI

Contemporary psychiatry preserves, not so much a positive conception
of the "person," as it does a residual notion of the effects of its absence.
From an analysis of the disappearance of the "person" in the psychiatric
state known as "depersonalization," the implied character of the missing
"person" may be reconstructed.

The language of psychiatry is a specialized language and might thus reveal not the general categories of the linguistic universe shared, to a greater or lesser extent, by all speakers of English (as presumably the seventeenth-century changes in self-compounds did), but a specialization that is peculiar only to itself. But against this interpretation one must contend that, even as a discursive specialty, psychiatry must be in touch with the general modes of organization of the linguistic universe of its patients—that is, largely of middle-class laymen—if it is to be of help to them. (If it proves not to be helpful enough, then we have to reconsider the issue: psychiatry may be categorizing experience in a manner too different from that of its patients.)

For our purposes, it is enough to discover how psychiatric language classifies, whatever the boundaries of this twentieth-century system of classification. Psychoanalytic usages of the term *depersonalization*—cited from Edith Jacobson, *Depression: Comparative Studies of Normal, Neurotic, and Psychotic Condition*—point to the following aspects of the relationship between "person" and "self" that is presumed in the Anglo-Germanic linguistic universe within which psychoanalysts think:

a. ". . . depersonalization . . . is an experience pertaining to the representation of the physical and mental self." The person is a symbolic ("cultural") *representation* of the contents of the initially nonsymbolic ("natural") self.

b. ". . . the person will complain that his body, or rather certain parts of the body, do not feel like his own, as belonging to him. He may describe them as being estranged from himself or as being dead"; "pathological processes causing severe emotional inhibition or blocking or affective emptiness may find expressions in states of emotional detachment to the point of depersonalization." The person, a symbolic representation, *attaches* the body and its organs, on the one hand, and the feelings of the individual, on the other, to a named identity. Only through such culturally mediated mutual attachments do both body and feelings become an individual's own, which they are not "by nature."

c. "Wherever the depersonalization extends to the mental self, there is a feeling of unreality of the self and of being 'outside of the self.'" Even the self needs to be appropriated by the person to be wholly "one's own." The person *confirms* the "at-homeness" of the self to the individual in whose experiences it has manifested itself.

d. "The depersonalized patient will think, react, act; but his experience is that of a detached spectator who is observing another person's performance. Not only his actions but his own thought processes appear to him unfamiliar and strange." What is given by nature alone to the individual is inherently alien to his consciousness—a "mechanism" that acquires his "spirit," and becomes his own, only when he succeeds in giving a symbolic interpretation to it that "it" accepts. The person *transforms* the "alien" into the "intimate" within the individual's experience of its own self.

e. "In psychotics, true experiences of depersonalization . . . develop as a kind of midway phenomenon in processes which eventually lead to generalized states of inner death, of self-extinction with loss of identity." "Instead of a punishing superego accusing the worthless self [as in depression], we find in depersonalization a detached, intact part of the ego observing the other—emotionally or physically dead—unacceptable part." The person protects life in the self by supplying to it a durable *conviction* that its contents are "proper" to the identity to which they belong.

f. "I believe that even in psychotics it [depersonalization] must be regarded as a defense of the ego which tries to recover and to maintain its intactness by opposing, detaching, and disowning the regressed, diseased parts."[26] The person is the *protective form* of the healthy self.

The person (or, in the transposition previously suggested, "culture") arises as a symbolic interpretation of the contents of the self (or of the "nature" of the human being). By this symbolic interpretation particular contents of the self are reliably attached to the identifiable totality of existence of an individual, given tangible form in it. By this very interpretation, by the "culture" which makes the "natural" contents of one's self intimately familiar to the individual, one also weighs these contents and, if one finds them adequate, decides to protect them, in one's life, from the fate of all natural things.

The person, that which in traditional legal usage makes it possible to choose one's own purposes and to act reasonably in their pursuit, is now viewed, in the psychiatric theory of "depersonalization," as that by which the individual interprets experiences coming to his attention and, when the interpretation is comprehensible, comes to sense those experiences as his own. The "person" is now apparently the agency both of instrumental rationality and of expressive coherence.

The suggested homology of self-person and nature-culture suggests that in English usage there is a tendency to perceive *culture as the artificial preservative of a piece of nature, which, left to itself, spoils.* (To speculate further: culture must protect nature from without, since "spirit," which preserved it from within, has been removed from nature.) To be sure, as we now know, preservatives may be poisonous. But it is not inherently necessary to poison nature to protect it from spoiling. Culture may be "unnatural," but it is, nevertheless, the condition, in the human being, of nature's ability to endure itself.

V

It is instructive to compare the English "self" with a pre-Christian peasant image of the self, gleaned from the corpus of the meanings of "self" in Lithuanian, possibly the most archaic of the living Indo-European languages.[27] The self appears here always in a sexually differentiated form and means, in one of its senses, "husband" and "wife" *(pats* and *pati)*. In this meaning, the "selves" specifically refer to adults in the working and managing age group, who are distinguished not only from the unmarried and the hired dependents but also from married but retired oldsters *(pats su pačia, duktė trečia, senis, senė ir piemenė*; rhymed description of the peasant household: "male self with female self, daughter the third, oldster, oldstress, and hired shepherdess").

The "self" in the sense of either husband or wife carries the connotation of a matter-of-fact, sober mastery in one's own household. The Lithuanian word for "self," *pats, pati,* derives from the same root as the Sanskrit *pat,* "to be master, reign, rule, govern, control, own, possess, dispose of."[28] The mastery connotation of the Lithuanian "self" is supported by two other meanings of the term, which refer to (a) independent capacity of acting alone, and (b) the capacity to possess property. These qualities may attach to any human being, to spiritual entities, and even to animals, but not to what in English would be "self-moving" mechanisms. Taken together, these meanings of the "self" constitute a kind of "householder self," which differs from the English, more Christianized (and more "civilized") self by the absence of introspective, "self-conscious" (as well as mechanized, "automatic") elements.

The "householder self" is coterminous with the body. It is outward-directed, has a commonsense, custom-defined moral responsibility and agency of reason in it, and is not concerned with explorations of its own subjectivity (which appears not to be differentiated from its mode of activity). It therefore has little need for the superimposition of the "person" on it (except when law replaces custom and one must be a person, in a formal sense, to be protected by the law.) Whereas the literate English self is "substantial" to the extent that it has inherited the structure (or memory) of the soul, in Lithuanian, which may express an older, "peasant" stratum of the history of (Indo-) European selfhood, the self draws its "substantiality" from its masterful participation in the smallest operational unit of society. The civilized (or esoteric) type of "self" is more likely to need an ideological foundation, whereas the peasant (or exoteric) type of "self" needs a social foundation to keep it from dissolving—into an escalating "self-consciousness" without an object in the first case, into a detail of earth-boundness in the second.[29] The psychological need for ideologies as confirmers of selfhood should increase with any weakening of the social foundations of selfhood and, specifically, with the transition from "peasantry" to "civilization."

In addition to the "householder self," there is a second set of meanings in the Lithuanian term for "self." In these semantic constructions, "self" points not necessarily to a human being (or a spiritual entity) but rather to some accented moment of the continuous flow of processes of nature and society. The moments of importance, of goodness, of plenty, of power, of special smallness, of the worst smell, of particular adequacy or appropriateness can all be semantically underlined by attaching the term "self" to them. The man at fifty is in his best years—that is, in "self-years" *(pačiuose metuose)*. The fox has carried away the very youngest chicken—that is, the "self-youngest" *(pačią jauniausią)*. He gave neither too much nor too little—that is, "in self-measure" or "in self-time" *(į patį sykį)*. The shoe is exactly as it is needed—that is, it is "self-it" *(pats tas)*.

In such constructions, "self" is not an objectified entity, but an accented (satisfactory, impressive, the most extreme, or the saddest) moment in time or space or cycles of nature or in social relations. It connotes the presence of the natural fullness or emptiness of things, their efflorescences, their times of plenitude and their sadness and smelliness. This construction may be termed "the ecological self"—the self as a temporarily accented moment in the universe, perceived by human consciousness. One can only speculate whether the identity of the terms for the "ecological self," which does not attach to the enduring pattern of an individual human being, and for the "householder self," which is attached (but in a manner not stressing his uniqueness) to the individual human being, has not suggested to the users of this language that the social self, the sober manager of its domestic affairs, is, simultaneously, but a temporarily accented moment in the continuous flow of natural events, a socionatural phenomenon not justified in claiming any unique dignity.

In contrast to the primordial rootedness of the "self," the older Lithuanian term for the "person," *asaba,* documented as far back as the sixteenth century, is a Slavic loanword, meaning (1) "person," "personality," (2) "picture," (3) "face," "appearance," unless otherwise qualified, an impressive or beautiful appearance. In current usage, this term usually suggests a pretentious "personage."

The contemporary Lithuanian term for the "person," *asmuo,* is a neologism introduced in late nineteenth- and twentieth-century texts and, in addition to its legal and grammatical uses, means "free and reasonable individual," "separate individual," but an individual in a formal sense, the generic "human being," whose very identity (and name) is attached not to the "person," but to the "personality" ("tonight three persons were arrested, but their personalities have not yet been established," *šią naktį suėmė tris asmenis, bet jų asmenybė dar nepaaiškėjo).*[30] *Asmuo,* which is an initially not clearly differentiated version of *esmuo,* "essence," is a semantically flatter symbolism with no mythological depth and fewer meaning-associations than "person" has in English.

The meaning-contents of the Lithuanian "person" have historically evolved (first under the impact of an Eastern European and later under the influence of a Western European tradition) from "appearance" to "essence." But the transition has occurred only recently, and through the replacement of *asaba* by *asmuo,* the sense of continuity of this development and the older, more evocative levels of the meaning of the term "person" have been irretrievably lost, as they have not been in the West European languages.

VI

The structure of Lithuanian does not suggest any Eckhartian Latin-Germanic distinction between the "person" and its "essence." The "essence" embodied in the term *asmuo* seems to be the "generic humanity" defined not by any spiritual qualities (other than reason) or by any metaphysical connotations of mystery and significance, but by its mere physical presence, by its "being a human life there." It is the essence not of the godlike "spirit," but of the "nature" of man. It would be difficult to find any of the recognition in English of the valid element of "artifice," "mask," or "legal fiction"—in short, of "culture"—in the structures made available in Lithuanian for comprehending the person.

The "self," a temporarily accented detail of nature without any semblance of "soul" in it, is more completely embedded in nature in Lithuanian than it is in English. But the "person" in Lithuanian is also nothing other than the essence, a concentrate, of that detail of nature. If, as has been previously suggested, the relationship between "self" and "person" is homologous, at least in the European languages, to the relationship between "nature" and "culture," the hypothesis emerges that in the realm of experience defined by traditional Lithuanian, *culture is the essence of nature comprehended by man.* This reading is supported by the oldest recorded meaning of the Lithuanian word for nature, *gamta,* "virtue" (*Nesuskaitomas garbas ir gamtas savas pasauliui rodė* 1599, in contemporary Lithuanian: "He showed his innumerable honors and natures to the world.")[31] Nature coincides with the moral (and therefore cultural) sphere of the "virtuous." What "nature" can be contrasted with is not culture but the "artificial"—which, if nature is virtuous, must be virtueless and therefore not truly cultural. We are in a linguistic universe that is more similar to that of the speakers of Chinese than of English.

The English "self" and "person," "nature" and "culture" is not isomorphic with their Lithuanian equivalents. It seems likely therefore that psychological, legal, and philosophical texts in which these terms are used cannot be translated from one language into the other without changing their impact upon the reader. The question arises even whether the individual who has acquired English rather than Lithuanian as his or her language of common discourse (or, in the case of bilinguals, as their first language) will not *experience* himself or herself more disjunctively (with a sharper separation of "self" and "person," the Meadian "I" and "me") and therefore more "self-consciously," as well as less "naturally" (with artificial elements of the "person" occupying more important places in such "self"-perceptions). Preoccupation with the self is inconceivable in Lithuanian, except as a translation from a foreign language.

VII

The native East European symbolic designs of the "person" do not place much stress on the rational capacity of the human being to choose his, or her, own purposes. The "person" in Romance languages seems to be an entity more capable of emotionality than it is in English. There are even clearer differences among the forms suggested by the various European languages for the comprehension of "selfhood." What, we may ask, are the nationally specific trajectories of the development of, and the interactions between, the categories of "self" and "person"? And are both of these structural categories of the meaning of the empirical individual distin-guishable—perhaps under names not translatable as "self" and "person"—outside of Western traditions?

The semantic contents of non-Western categories also change over historical time, although a Western observer is more impressed by con-tinuity than by change. Future research may yet uncover unknown depths of cultural change in non-Western traditions as well. But, for the time being, we concentrate on the "structural" questions: (1) whether categories comparable to self and person exist in non-Western languages, (2) if these *general* categories are in evidence, how their *particular* contents differ from those of their Western equivalents, and (3) whether the hypothesized homology of categories self-person to categories nature-culture obtains in non-Western languages as well.

In China, the "self" is explicitly recognized as the "agency of selfishness" and is associated with the sphere of privacy. "The word 'ssu' (selfishness) . . . refers to a private self or something or person belonging to someone. This meaning is often contrasted with that of the term 'kung' (the public or belonging to the public that is identified with a society, or an organization, or a state)."[32] However, Chinese self-compounds, constructed mostly but not always with *tzu,* "self" (a term used only in self-compounds), suggest that the self partakes of such moral functions as "self-indictment," *tzu-sung,* "self-reproach," *tzu-tse,* or "self-realization" (in ethics), *tzu-ch'eng* or *tzu wo shih hsien.*[33] The self evoked by these terms is not a substantial entity, but the initiating capacity of various kinds of moral functions that operates from within the nature of these functions. This capacity is apparently homogeneous, not divisible into multiple selves, as the English "self" is. What is potentially divisible in Chinese is "I," *wu,* a term that, however, does not suggest the possibility of separating it from "me."[34] If psychological theories are influenced by the nature of the linguistic universe in which they are developed, a Confucian George Herbert Mead might have had to conceive of the "I" as an individual aesthetic sensibility, "inner spontaneity," or *ch'i-yün,* "spirit consonance," an emotional participation in the animating qualities of nature.[35] Mead would presumably have had to think of the "me" as *jen,* the voice of humanity in the individual, its obligations graded in accordance with one's objective position in the kinship and administrative structures.

The basic Chinese term for the "person," *jen,* refers to humanity and to the individual as part of humanity. The Chinese "person," *jen,* is neither the grammatical "person," *wei tz'u,* nor the person that has "freedom of the person" in constitutional law, *min shen tzu yu,* nor does it own "personal property," *tung ch'an, tung tzu,* the latter meaning "property of the self" (which can be selfish in a way in which the person, in its basic meaning as *jen,* is not). *Jen* appears, however, in connection with *ssu,* "private" (suggestive of selfishness) in the concept of "private citizen," *ssu jen* (which evokes more a "selfish person" than the Anglo-Saxon "private citizen"). [36] In contrast to English usage, the basic Chinese conception of the person has nothing to do with a highly respected legal idea of the "person" (and therefore with "personal rights").

"The word *'jen'* . . . is mentioned only occasionally in pre-Confucian texts, and in all these cases it denoted a particular virtue of kindness, more especially the kindness of a ruler to its subjects."[37] Thus the Chinese "person" originates not in a god's mask, a significant artifice, as it does in Europe, but in the spontaneously obligatory—naturally moral—kindness of a human ruler, an expression of the Chinese tendency toward secularity and naturalism of moral thought. In Confucian usage, the person stands for the social obligations of the individual, which it is his nature to fulfill. The person is "natural," with "culture" permitting him to express his "nature" more perfectly. The person is located within the moral order embracing both "nature" and "culture" as one continuous whole,[38] *culture being nature's own spontaneous morality, recognized by man* (though apparently not or not to the same degree by woman). But since the person is anchored in the recognition of the obligations emerging from nature, it represents "the structured," in contrast to the "energetic" of the self.

The Chinese counterpart of the English "self" is *either* "selfish" (when concerned with its own small particular interests and, in this case, an expression of an "unnatural" deflection toward disorder that alienates itself from both nature and culture) *or* the processual location of the sense from which all things arise, partaking of the qualities of both "nature," *tzu-jan* (literally "being thus of itself") and of "freedom," *tzu-yu* (literally "self-initiating").[39] But these qualities in conjunction are proper only to Tao. Thus the self, in the great depth of its being (in contrast to its superficial and eccentric "selfish" excrescences), belongs to the self-initiating, self-regulating Tao and is *beyond* both nature and culture, which are structures regulated by something beyond themselves, namely by Tao. Being so assimilated to Tao, the self at its deepest must be coextensive with the universe and, as a component of the individual, it cannot have any unique substance of its own. (In Chang Lü-hsiang's seventeenth-century treatise on self-compounds, however, the self creates individual distinctiveness by its free, self-initiating choices.)[40]

The categories of nature vs. culture do not identify the fundamental distinction between the Chinese self and person. Placed in a universe in which nature and culture are (at least from the Confucian point of view) continuous, self and person can rather be described as the "unstructured, determining" vs. the "structured, determined" *levels* of the nature-culture continuum in the human being.

But these levels are not as rigorously separated from one another as they would be in most Western traditions of thought—or as the language of "levels" implies. What we call "levels" relates to each other in China, perhaps, as what we call "religions" do: permeatively. This fundamental, pretheoretical configuration, anchored in the organization and "spirit" of the Chinese language, seems to accommodate both Taoist and Buddhist theories of the self and the Confucian theory of the person (to use a Western distinction); it also helps to explain the confluences among these theories and the directions of change possible for them.

VIII

Equivalents of the "person" and "self" appear to be clearly present, but with contents different from their European counterparts, in Japan. On the *person*: ". . . we are struck by the problem of the 'public personality' in Japanese history. . . . The man himself . . . became the office. . . . In Tokugawa times, . . . role playing was further supported by an ethic which held that a man was true to his own moral essence when he selflessly fulfilled the demands of his station or role." The *self* is expressed more directly in fiction: "Edwin McClellan has pointed out that even modern Japanese writers feel that plot is mechanical and that fleeting poetic moments are more real, and they are often critical of the sustained personalities in Western novels as forced and unreal. . . . The fusing of self with nature lets self see in nature moods corresponding to its own."[41] What have here been conceived as "person" and "self" seem to be equivalent to the traditional Japanese distinction between "*giri* and *ninjo*—roughly translatable as social obligation and human feeling. . . ."[42]

The Japanese equivalent of the "person" does not incorporate the capacity to choose one's own purposes and to act reasonably in pursuit of them, and the "self" is built less around sameness of substance and willfullness of initiative than is the "self" in English usage. Man's *social* morality, in the sense of strict obedience to the obligations of his formal position in society (and, indirectly, of the policy of his organization), is located in his public person. His *natural* "moral purity" is diffused throughout his inner self. The natural self is much more sharply separated from the public person than is the case in China and, consequently, its "moral purity" is largely impotent in public life.[43] The matter is complicated by the presence of "a variety of different and distinct terms that translate as 'self.'"[44] Whereas there is a "primitive self," *waga* or *ga,* comparable to the "id in Freudian terms," which must be "killed" *(waga o korom),*[45] the "self" is also something that seems close to what "spirit consonance" is in China—the highly regarded locus of one's "aesthetic flavor." This self, merged with an insubstantial "soul" (or "spirit"), is placed within the sphere of "nature" that is seen as continuous with the *expressive* side of "culture." The self does not participate in the *obligatory* side of "culture" to which the public personality, with its "moral essence," belongs. Thus both the self and the person belong to (different components of) "culture," whereas the self, but not the person, also belongs to "nature." The self is not perceived as a decisive moral agent.

The self, in Japanese usage, is not intrinsically subversive of the sphere of moral obligation, but is childlikely dependent on it and aware of its dependence (as the Chinese self is not). On the one hand, the Japanese "self" is obligated to bottle itself into the "person": "The Japanese *Bildungsroman* is not so much about the self's discovery of the self as the self's discipline of itself into a production model hierarchically classified and blueprinted in detail by society at large."[46] On the other hand, the Japanese "self" *(jibun,* also translatable as "identity") appears to be powerless to survive without support by its "public personality." "The expression *jibun ga aru,* 'to have a self,' or *jibun ga nai,* 'to have no self,' is probably peculiar to Japanese . . . the group for [the Japanese] is basically a vital spiritual prop, to be isolated from which would be, more than anything else, to lose his 'self' completely in a way that would be intolerable to him. . . ."[47]

But the "person" which, in Japan, seems more rigidly in control over "self" than in the West—outside of the English gentleman—is actually more intimately informed by it. "In Japan, the practice of self-control in role behavior differs somewhat from that in the West in that Japanese depend very heavily on mechanisms of suppression, whereas Western Europeans or Americans tend to practice repression. That is to say, Japanese very often are totally aware of their underlying emotional states when those emotions are not appropriate to expected role behavior, but they choose to suppress them."[48] The relationship between the contents of the individual that Western observers translate as "person" and "self" is, in Japan, one of *rigid intimacy.*

IX

The volatilization of the *self* in the advanced industrial societies (foreshadowed in Emerson)[49] might portend, in the symbolic organization of the individual, a quasi-Japanization of the West: a moody, "de-souled" self located within, but not communicating through, a public personality identified with the mode of operation of an office, a profession, a technology, or a scholarly discipline.[50] In contrast to the Japanese tradition however, the contemporary "impulsive" self tends to be not only "de-souled" but also "de-natured." It is neither directed by the enduring essence of a "soul" nor obligated (or even reliably inclined) to act within the enduring framework of "nature."[51]

In the absence of the categories of *both* "soul" and "nature" from its design the self is bound to appear tawdry, a sociological triviality: "an intersubjective atrocity, a mouth, a maw" perpetually greedy for new experiences, unable to find a center of gravity or its appropriate place in any of them.[52] When both nature and soul disappear from it, the self exists solely as an imitation of the contents it no longer contains and therefore cannot get in touch with anywhere else either.

This kind of self is, however, still a variant, fully present only in Goffman's cautionary tales. "Nature" is still active in the self through the body and its "discontents" (Freud). And even the "soul" occasionally speaks, if only as the capacity for resurrecting the precise shapes of memorable moments and ideas that have crumbled into dust. In this notion of the soul the post-modern West may also be moving closer to old Japan.

The distinctiveness of the Western conception of the person is still confirmed especially by the legal tradition. But even in the law the meaning of the person is shifting, in American usage, in the direction of the possessor of rights and away from the agent with a rational capacity who is therefore responsible for his actions (e.g., the unborn child is now a legal person, with enforceable rights for support payments by the father).[53]

The person is becoming a "human form which other human forms are obligated to respect," regardless of what capacities it possesses or what responsibilities it is capable or willing to assume. The "person" is thus virtually identical with the "human being," conceived, however, not as part of humanity in the Confucian manner, but as an isolated possessor of "human rights," for which there is no analogous concept of "human responsibilities."

If one looks at the usage of language in practical discourse, the person is becoming a more formal, less substantive category, a perspective for looking at the individual, not the individual's comprehension of intrinsic qualities of himself/herself. The person seems to be reverting to a (nonindividualized) mask. It is a mask increasingly not of a god, but of legal definition. The old gods struggle to be dissolved into new legislative claims.

Notes

1. Marcel Mauss, "A Category of the Human Mind: The Notion of Person, the Notion of 'Self,'" *Sociology and Psychology. Essays* (London: Routledge & Kegan Paul, 1979), pp. 57–94.

2. But in the courtly poetry of feudal Japan, "such expressions as 'person' *(hito)* often prepare us for a love allegory," suggesting that in this sociohistorical setting emotion is central to personhood. Robert H. Brower and Earl Miner, *Japanese Court Poetry* (Stanford, Calif.: Stanford University Press, 1961), p. 16. In ancient Chinese philosophy, *jen*, "humanity" or "human-heartedness," but also "person," is "equated . . . with love." Wing-tsit Chan, "The Evolution of the Confucian Concept Jên," *Philosophy East and West* 4 (January 1955): 299.

3. Sir James A. H. Murray, ed., *A New English Dictionary on Historical Principles* (Oxford: The Clarendon Press, 1888–1928), 7:724–28; 8, Part 2:409–427.

4. Ernest Klein, *A Comprehensive Etymological Dictionary of the English Language* (Amsterdam: Elsevier, 1967), 2:1163. The "person" arises as a shamanistic production, the dramatic *representation* of a spirit located wholly outside of the human being that "empowers" the human being to whom it is affixed to preside, as a "master of ceremonies," over the transitoriness of human existence. But the worldwide shamanistic figure becomes a reasonable person only in Western Europe.

5. Robert E. Park and Ernest W. Burgess, *Introduction to the Science of Sociology* (Chicago: University of Chicago Press, 1921), p. 55.

6. "To the degree that the person, or aspects of the person, are not named, to that degree the person remains a 'stranger,' even within the group." Stanley Diamond, *In Search of the Primitive: A Critique of Civilization* (New Brunswick, N.J.: Transaction Books, 1974), p. 156. The "self" of an individual is a "stranger" to the group of which, as a "person," he is a member. The "self" (at least in the language in which Diamond is writing) is accessible only through its own introspection and is unavailable to a public examination. The "person" must translate the "self" to make it presentable to society.

7. "—What is a Person in the Trinity?—A Person is that which preserves its own rational individuality apart from any other distinct Person. . . .—What is the essence of the three Persons in the Trinity?—That which, impartible, contains all things impartibly while of itself it neither generates nor produces things. . . . one Person begets the others. Essence begets not." Franz Pfeiffer, *Meister Eckhart*, trans. C. de B. Evans (London: John M. Watkins, 1956), pp. 392–93, 382. Compare this with Emerson's: "Souls never touch their objects."

8. The present tendency in legal usage is to separate what might be called "formal" from "substantial" personhood, the first always and the second only conditionally attaching to the living human being. The widely used American Law Institute test for determining criminal responsibility states that "a *person* is *not responsible* for criminal conduct if at the time of such conduct, as a result of mental disease or defect he lacks the substantial capacity, either to appreciate the criminality (wrongfulness) of his conduct or to conform his conduct to the requirements of the law." Cited from *The New York Times*, October 3, 1975, p. 12 (italics mine).

9. As one of the values of "the counseling ideology," Paul Halmos lists the belief that: "The notion of blameworthiness, of moral responsibility, of culpability, and the correlate sentiments of punitiveness, avengefulness, and the like are senseless, and, therefore morally wrong in a universe in which we cannot control the most decisive phase of our learning," which takes place "in intimate social relationships and mostly so in the initial years of life. . . ." *The Personal Service Society* (New York: Schocken Books, 1970), pp. 16, 18.

10. Louis Segal, ed., *New Complete Russian-English Dictionary* (New York: G. E. Stechert & Company, 1942), p. 325.

11. Though the mystic commands: "The eternal word never put on a person. So do thou strip thyself of everything personal and selfish and keep just thy bare humanity; . . ." Franz Pfeiffer, *Meister Eckhart*, p. 236.

12. In Spanish and in French the artificial elements of the *personne* tend to be consigned

to the *personnage* (where *personnage* meant first, in 1250, ecclesiastical dignitary, then celebrity, historical figure, or character in a play). In contrast, the *personne* is the embodiment of spontaneous human authenticity, roughly analogous to the English "true selfhood." In English, the distinction between "person" and "personage" tends to get blurred by the possibility of designating an actor in a role as a "dramatic person." It would seem that the English symbolic design of "person" permits a greater appreciation of the "artificial elements" in the meaning of the individual than is possible in the Romance languages (or in Russian). But this is a rather impressionistic hypothesis.

13. In continental West European usage, the "self" appears to be more frequently associated with rational discourse and the efforts toward self-knowledge (e.g., in Descartes and the whole Cartesian tradition), and the "person" is more emotionally defined than it is in English. The distinction between "self" and "person" seems less clearly drawn.

14. Apparently the oldest documented of the English self-compounds, *self-will*, in its earliest usage meant simply "one's own will or desire" (888), so that *self-willing* could mean "spontaneous" (1000) and "self-willingness" constitutes a translation of *spontaneitas* (1674). The morally derogatory sense of "willful or obstinate persistence in following one's own desires or opinions" became attached to *self-will* later (1489). Murray, *A New English Dictionary*, 8, Part 2:424.

15. The consecutive ordering of multiple selves makes it possible to retain the "selves" of the past as a part of one's psychic construction, not merely as memories but as dynamic agents ("his self of two hours ago was looking at him reproachfully"; "this was my twelve-year-old self acting"). The gradual recognition of these layers of selfhood as a coherent personality constitutes Marcel Proust's "search for lost time" (*A la recherche du temps perdu*, familiarly translated as *Remembrance of Things Past*).

In contrast to the potentially pluralistic self the person is "lawfully" homogeneous and "magically" ageless, like Dorian Gray's picture. One cannot put one's "best person" forward, as one can one's "best self." If the person were merely an artificial construction, one could construct any number of them. But, by the rigorous virtue of grammar, law, and ordinary language, one person is all one has got—even in cases where the "personality" is "split" or "marketable."

"Persons" are plural only (a) when the individual is divided into the "person" that acts and the "person" that judges its actions, as in Adam Smith (who anticipates here Mead's distinction between the "I" and the "me"), or (b) when "persons" are assimilated to "souls" or to myths working themselves through individual lives, as in archetypal psychology. "The many persons which play their parts through an individual have differing paths to follow, different moments of rise and decay, different Gods to obey. The doctrine . . . about two or more different kinds of soul (in China, Egypt, and Greece) also presents these souls as undergoing different destinies." James Hillman, *Re-Visioning Psychology* (New York: Harper & Row, 1975), p. 88. Neither of these usages of the "person" has become established in the common consciousness of English speakers.

16. Murray, *A New English Dictionary*, pp. 421, 419. The newness of "selfish" refers to events in 1641.

17. Strictly speaking, the "self" *begins* as "nature" (though one which may contain "soul" or "spirit" within itself). Certain—though not all—elements of "culture" arise from it or are implanted into it. The "person" *begins*, in the classical tradition, as (god-given) "culture." It may become "naturalized" by becoming attached to, and eventually implanted into, certain, but not all, elements of "nature" (such as a human, but not an animal, body).

18. If one grants what seems to have been a part of the human experience—the capacity of what he (or someone else) calls the "self" of an empirically concrete individual to identify with the moral core of the universe (the universal Self of Hindu philosophy) and to contract to one among several psychic impulses within the empirically concrete individual, it seems awfully naive still to argue that the self is only "the unique combination of the roles we play in

relation to others." Victor Ferkiss, *The Future of Technological Civilization* (New York: George Braziller, 1974), p. 151.

19. Murray, *A New English Dictionary*, 8, Part 2:411.

20. Franz Pfeiffer, *Meister Eckhart*, p. 173.

21. Murray, *A New English Dictionary*, p. 425.

22. Edmund Leites, "Conscience, Casuistry, and Moral Decision: Some Historical Perspectives," *Journal of Chinese Philosophy* 2 (1974):41–58; quotes from pp. 42–43. There is an analogous change, at the same time, in both religious and legal thought, toward the conception of voluntary consent of individuals in society as the basis of law and true order. David Little, *Religion, Order, and Law: A Study in Pre-Revolutionary England* (New York: Harper & Row, 1969).

23. Vieda Skultans, *Madness and Morals: Ideas on Insanity in the Nineteenth Century* (London: Routledge & Kegan Paul, 1975), pp. 2, 14, 25.

24. Barlow's title is virtually a translation of Kant's earlier essay "Von der Macht des Gemüths, durch den blossen Vorsatz seiner krankhaften Gefühle Meister zu sein." Ernst Cassirer, ed., *Immanuel Kants Werke* (Berlin: Bruno Cassirer, 1916), 7:411–31.

25. The control by the "person" over the "self" is presupposed in English mid-nineteenth-century psychiatric thought, such as the statement that one of the essential characteristics of insanity is "the *destruction or impairment of moral liberty*, or a notable diminution of that controlling power over self which belongs to every soundly-constituted person. . . ." Daniel Noble, *Elements of Psychological Medicine* (London: John Churchill, 1853), pp. 11–12, cited from Skultans, *Madness and Morals*, p. 170.

26. Edith Jacobson, *Depression: Comparative Studies of Normal, Neurotic, and Psychotic Condition* (New York: International Universities Press, Inc., 1971), pp. 137–39, 163–64.

27. Lietuvos TSR Mokslų Akademija. Lietuvių Kalbos ir Literatūros Institutas. *Lietuvių Kalbos Žodynas*, (Vilnius: "Minties" Leidykla, 1973), 9:633–38.

28. Sir Monier-Williams, *A Sanskrit-English Dictionary, Etymologically and Philologically arranged with Special Reference to Cognate Indo-European Languages*, new ed. (Oxford: At the Clarendon Press, 1899), p. 580.

29. On issues relating to the esoteric-exoteric differentiation, see Ralph L. Slotten, "Exoteric and Esoteric Forms of Apprehension," *Sociological Analysis* 38 (1977):185–208; and Vytautas Kavolis, "Structure and Energy: Toward a Civilization-Analytic Perspective," *Comparative Civilizations Review* 1 (Winter 1979):21–41.

30. Lietuvos, *Lietuvių Kalbos Žodynas*, 1:324–328.

31. Ibid., 3:93. The older meaning of Lithuanian *gamta* points in the direction of the Indian employment of the word *dharma* "for the 'essential nature of things' (*vastusvabhāvaḥ*) on the one hand, and for 'moral duties' on the other." Dayanand Bhargava, *Jaina Ethics* (Delhi: Motilal Banarsidass, 1968), p. 12.

32. Chung-ying Cheng, *Tai Chên's Inquiry into Goodness* (Honolulu: East-West Center Press, 1971), p. 158. "Private," in the sense of "not official or public," is *ssu, ssu tzu, ssu hsia*. It is, in modern Chinese, possible to speak of "private virtue," *ssu te*, in contrast to "public morality," *kung te*, thus suggesting that the sphere of privacy is no longer wholly "selfish." The term for "selfish" is most frequently, but not always, made with *ssu*, "private": *yu ssu hsin, tse ssu, ku chi, wei chi, yu wo, tzu ku tzu, tzu chih yu chi pu chih yu jen*. K. Hemeling, *English-Chinese Dictionary of the Standard Chinese Spoken Language* (Shanghai: Statistical Department of the Inspectorate General of Customs, 1916), pp. 1103, 1287–88.

33. Pei-yi Wu, "The Role of Confession in Chinese Religion and Moral Culture," paper presented at the Columbia University Seminar on Traditional China, December 14, 1976; Hemeling, *English-Chinese Dictionary*.

34. "Notions of multiple selves are not too common in China. When they do arise, the word for 'self' is usually one of the words which are normally first-person singular pronouns. For instance, 'wu' or 'wo,' which both mean 'I' or 'me,' can be used in contrasting compounds

such as 'ta-wo' and 'hsiao-wo' (the great self and the small self). I have seen the compound 'jen-wu' (true self), but I don't recall seeing the hypothetical compound 'chia-wu' (false self). . . . The notions of 'the self of today' and 'the self of tomorrow,' though expressible in Chinese, are imports brought in around 1900." Letter from Pei-yi Wu of March 20, 1978.

35. Joseph R. Levenson, *Confucian China and Its Modern Fate: A Trilogy* (Berkeley: University of California Press, 1972), 1:23, 35; James F. Cahill, "Confucian Elements in the Theory of Painting," in *The Confucian Persuasion* ed., Arthur F. Wright (Stanford, Calif.: Stanford University Press, 1960), pp. 115–40.

36. Other terms for the "person," in the sense of "human being," are *wei, jen ko, ko jen, jen k'on*, of which only *wei* does not contain some reference to *jen*. Hemeling, *English-Chinese Dictionary*, pp. 1103–28.

37. Chan, "Evolution of Confucian Concept," p. 295. See also Wei-ming Tu, "The Creative Tension Between Jên and Li," *Philosophy East and West* 18 (January–April 1968): 29–39. There is a Chinese equivalent to the concept of "depersonalization," formulated by Hsieh Liang-tso (1050–1130): "We call paralysis of the body and the unconsciousness of feeling the absence of *jên*." Quoted from Chan, "Evolution of Confucian Concept," p. 313.

38. "It *(jen)* is extended not only to include all human beings but the universe in its totality, man and the universe thus forming one body." Chan, "Evolution of Confucian Concept," p. 319.

39. Wolfgang Bauer, *China and the Search for Happiness: Recurring Themes in Four Thousand Years of Chinese Cultural History* (New York: The Seabury Press, 1976), pp. 140–42.

40. Pei-yi Wu, "Sources of the Chinese Self," prepared for the meeting "Individualism and Social Role," January 14–16, 1977, Columbia University; "The Guilty Confucian: Wei Hsi and his Dreams," in Edmund Leites, ed., *Life Histories as Civilizational Texts*, International Society for the Comparative Study of Civilizations Occasional Papers No. 1 (1977), pp. 40–48.

41. Albert M. Craig, "Introduction: Perspectives on Personality in Japanese History," in *Personality in Japanese History* ed., Albert M. Craig and Donald H. Shively (Berkeley: University of California Press, 1970), pp. 5–7, 18–19, 23.

42. Takeo Doi, *The Anatomy of Dependence* (Tokyo: Kodansha International Ltd., 1973), p. 33.

43. Takie Sugiyama Lebra, *Japanese Patterns of Behavior* (Honolulu: The University Press of Hawaii, 1976), pp. 161–63. "Morality is not summoned up from the depths of the individual; on the contrary, it has its roots outside of the individual. . . . The identification of morality with power meant that pure inner morality (as opposed to the external type) was always regarded as 'impotent' and therefore worthless." Masao Maruyama, *Thought and Behaviour in Modern Japanese Politics*, Expanded Ed., Edited by Ivan Morris (London: Oxford University Press, 1969).

44. Thomas P. Rohlen, "The Promise of Adulthood in Japanese Spiritualism," *Daedalus* 105 (Spring 1976): 142.

45. Thomas P. Rohlen, "'Spiritual Education' in a Japanese Bank," *American Anthropologist* 75 (October 1973): 1542–62.

46. Masao Miyoshi, *Accomplices of Silence: The Modern Japanese Novel* (Berkeley: University of California Press, 1974), p. XI.

47. Doi, *Anatomy of Dependence*, pp. 132, 135.

48. Hiroshi Wagatsuma, "Status and Role Behavior in Changing Japan: Psychocultural Continuities," in George A. De Vos, with contributions by Hiroshi Wagatsuma, William Caudill, and Keiichi Mizushima, *Socialization for Achievement: Essays on the Cultural Psychology of the Japanese* (Berkeley: University of California Press, 1973), pp. 34–35.

49. "One of Emerson's most surprising ideas is his conception of the self as an exemplary fluid consciousness . . . 'fluid consciousness' in that man is best pictured as a medium of flowing perceptions, not as a social or historical type. There is nothing like this conception in the European writers Emerson favored—Wordsworth, Carlyle, Goethe, Swedenborg, even Col-

eridge. . . ." James McIntosh, "Emerson's Unmoored Self," *The Yale Review* 65 (Winter 1976): 232.

50. Wylie Sypher, *Loss of the Self in Modern Literature and Art* (New York: Vintage, 1962); Robert Jay Lifton, *Boundaries: Psychological Man in Revolution* (New York: Vintage, 1970); Gerald Graff, "Babbitt at the Abyss: The Social Context of Postmodern American Fiction," *Tri-Quarterly* no. 33 (Spring 1975): 305–337.

51. Ralph H. Turner, "The Real Self: From Institution to Impulse," *American Journal of Sociology* 81 (March 1976): pp. 989–1016.

52. Donald Barthelme, *Sadness* (New York: Farrar, Straus and Giroux, 1972), p. 169.

53. "Rights of Fetus Upheld by Court," *The Washington Post,* December 10, 1975, p. 10.

III

Traditions and Countertraditions
in Indian Self-Comprehensions

4

The Idea of Self in the Countertraditions
of Bengali Hinduism

David Kopf

This attempt to understand the Hindu concept of self in the historical
context of the relationship between orthodox tradition and countertradition in Bengali medieval Hinduism is part of a larger project that addresses
itself to the need for a new history of medieval Hinduism which is free of
puritanical bias as well as historical, critical, multidisciplinary, comprehensive, and synthetic. Hindu scholarship has been predominantly classical-
Brahmanical or contemporary village-oriented.[1] The rich regional
traditions of the middle period, which gave birth to Hinduism as we know
it, have been largely ignored,[2] particularly the Hindu countertraditions
which emerged at given times in opposition to systems of orthodoxy. The
history of the Hindus is not as static, amorphous, or chaotic as others make
it out to be. To understand ideas such as self it is necessary to reconstruct
the histories of both the Brahmanic traditions of migrant Aryans as well as
the indigenously rooted, regionally oriented countertraditions. The confrontation and accommodation of interests between these two forces could
very well constitute the "true" history of Hindu civilization in South Asia.[3]

The beginnings of Hindu orthodoxy go back to the second millennium
B.C., when an Indo-European tribe of aggressive migrants known as
Aryans intruded themselves upon the indigenous Indus civilization and
imposed upon them a set of values, beliefs, and institutions. Curiously
though the archeological remains of the Indus civilization still exist,
whereas the material remains of the Aryan barbarians during the time of
encounter do not, it is the latter culture that is taken as the starting point of
Hindu history.[4]

There seems little doubt that the emphasis on closed hierarchies—
what is called the Great Tradition of Hindu orthodoxy—was worked out by

the Aryans centuries after their initial intrusion, seemingly without benefit
of synthesis with the indigenes' traditions. Apparently, the Aryans
operated a rather tight system based on obligations and privileges according to the class or caste into which one was born. It is difficult if not
impossible to say with precision what features or functions of the *varna* or
divisions of Aryan society were. We would err if we made *varna* the pivot of
the system. In the first place, *jati* and not *varna* seems to be more characteristic of the actual Hindu system of caste and *jati* probably did not exist then;
it came later and under different historical circumstances. Second, if we
remember that Sanskrit terms such as Brahman, Kshatriya, Vaishya, and
Sudra respectively, meant priest-intelligentsia, warrior-ruler, merchant,
and cultivator, then we could be describing the stratification system in any
of a number of sedentary civilizations.[5]

Like other orthodoxies, Aryan orthodoxy seems to have been a system
of requirements, duties, external religious practices, and ceremonies. The
crucial idea of *dharma* meant strict adherence to the legal and ethical code,
the correct performance of which protected the society against disharmony
and chaos.[6] Classical notions like *karma* (awareness of the consequences of
one's behavior), *kama* (pursuit of pleasure), *artha* (pursuit of economic and
political gain), or even *moksha* (pursuit of salvation by means of individual
self-realization) were later subsequently integrated into the Great Tradition. Not only is it historiographically confusing and ahistorical to lump all
these ideas together in one grand Hindu orthodoxy but the probability that
they were originally conceived in protest against the earlier pattern of
Aryan orthodoxy is obscured. These ethical notions all represent extensions of self, and self was surely not the core issue of Aryan theology.
Aryans valued an exacting performance of rites and rituals, a knowledge of
magic and esoteric formulas, and complete devotion to accepted legal,
ethical, and social norms and traditions.

The notion of self among Indians was a product of the earliest notable
countertraditions that challenged the sterility of Aryan orthodoxy. Historically, an intellectual revolt of momentous importance took place in the first
millennium B.C., a movement that paved the way for the assimilation of
karma, kama, artha, and *moksha* into orthodoxy. Not only are these ideas
alien to second millennium B.C. Aryan religion, they are also blatantly
existential, that is, they represent a veritable extraction of self from the
collectivity-consciousness of the ritual system.[6] *Karma* particularizes the self
as doer of good and evil; *kama* is self-fulfillment of the body; *artha* represents individual strategies of self-aggrandizement, those of Machiavellian
and of economic man; and *moksha* postulates transformation and transcendence of a self entity.

The Upanishads (circa 900–600 B.C.) as well as the appearance of
Buddha's and other ideologies of salvation in the sixth century B.C. were

conspicuous examples of the intellectual revolt. Jainism, a creed that, un-like that of Buddha, survives in India today also swelled the wave of protest against orthodoxy. These ideas and the subsequent movement that took place *outside* of Aryavarta, in the least Aryanized regions of the eastern Gangetic plains of Bihar and Bengal, have usually been interpreted as protest against Brahman casteism, as reformation of Brahman religion, and as expressions of economic grievance against the excesses of a violent era.[7] All these and other interpretations, which are not mutually exclusive, are undoubtedly true, yet scholars have not sufficiently heeded a remark-able aspect of all those major contemporary forms of protest: the shift of focus from the external collectivity to the internal soul—from a belief in the efficacy of external manipulations of magic to coerce the supernatural, to a belief in the power of self that could only be achieved by a rigorous mental, ethical, and ascetic program.[8]

The Upanishads constitute the earliest known Indian challenge to the values and ideas of the Brahman establishment. The dialogues express a pronounced skepticism of the efficacy of everything Brahmanic—from mechanistic rites to the Vedic concept of cosmos.[9] The Upanishadic au-thors not only taught the unity behind apparent diversity (monism) but they equated self *(atma)* (not to be confused with ego, or *ahamkara*) with the absolute principle *(Brahma)*. The *Mundaka Upanishad,* for example, tells us that

> Finite and transient are the fruits of sacrificial rites . . . Living in the abyss of ignorance, yet wise in their conceit, the deluded go round and round, like the blind led by the blind. Living in the abyss of ignorance the deluded think themselves blest. Attached to works, they know not Brahma . . . Considering religion to be observance of rituals and per-formance of acts . . . the deluded remain ignorant of the highest good. . . . But wise, self-controlled, and tranquil souls, who are con-tented in spirit, and who practice austerity and meditation in solitude and silence, are freed from all impurity, and attain liberation. . . .[10]

The clue to what is really being sought in the Upanishads may be ascertained from the scant attention the authors devote to defining the attributes of the absolute principle and the enormous attention they give to the means necessary to understand the true Self. The Upanishads are about Self and not about God or gods. When one is liberated from ego (*ahamkara*—not to be confused with the Freudian metaphor), which is confined in bondage to externalities *(maya)*, then one achieves true Self, a state identical with nonillusory reality. The Upanishads challenge the Vedic preoccupation with things external by turning the acts of salvation inward to self-consciousness. According to the *Katha Upanishad,*

The ego made the senses turn outward. Accordingly, man looks toward what is without, and sees not what is within. Rare is he who, longing for immortality, shuts his eyes to what is without and beholds the Self.[11]

The formulation of an ethical program to emancipate the Self is really the contribution of Buddha and Mahavira. It is no accident that Buddha was rediscovered by twentieth-century existentialists as one of their own.[12] Buddha placed *experience* and the will to transcend an ego-centered life at the core of his ideology. Buddha's message is the affirmation of individual integrity and an enlightened consciousness in a world in which God is dead. Every individual must work strenuously through continuous self-examination to overcome the blind urges and ignorant strivings of a shallow, meaningless life. Priestly intercession or adherence to intricate metaphysical systems are to no avail because salvation lies in the cultivation of consciousness within each individual personality.[13] Though Buddha's ultimate purpose was *nirvana,* or the release from the cycle of birth and rebirth, still his eightfold path from right understanding to right concentration constitutes one of the most practical programs ever conceived for developing a super consciousness by means of a superhuman will.[14] Yoga, which was constructed precisely along these lines, was perhaps the most important legacy of Buddhism to Hinduism.[15] To Eliade, who has written a superb book on the philosophy of yoga,

> liberation cannot occur if one is not first "detached" from the world, if one has not begun by withdrawing from the cosmic circuit. For without doing so, one could never succeed in finding or mastering oneself. Yoga implies a preliminary detachment from matter, emancipation with respect to the world. The emphasis is laid on man's *effort* (to yoke), on his self-discipline. . . .[16]

In the next thousand years, a period sometimes called India's classical age, the earlier Brahmanic orthodoxy had incorporated much of the countertraditional ideology to form a new establishment religion (the Upanishads had become Vedanta or "end" of the Vedas, for example).[17] In addition, the earlier rebellious salvation ideologies had become orthodoxies of their own. Buddha was himself an atheist, certainly a humanist, and not inconceivably, in the context of his own times, an existentialist. Surely, he saw no value in divine intervention or intellectual mystifications as sources of individual salvation. Centuries later, Buddha himself was deified and there were innumerable Buddhas, all icons.[18] Buddhism became an elaborate intellectual pursuit, while Buddhist monasticism developed into a wealthy and materialistic social institution.[19] When Hinduism revived in South India as a new ideology of protest (seventh century A.D.), the Buddhist leadership could be said to have been hardly indistinguishable from other privileged urban elites who were the dominant class not only in India but in every one of the Eurasian classical civilizations.[20]

It was an age of great empires, great cities, and international trade. It also produced great art, great literature, and exceedingly refined philosophies that brought the thought of each civilization to its ultimate perfection as an articulate statement of each culture's intellectual contribution. Not only did its benefactors bemoan the decline and fall of the classical world, but for generations of subsequent neoclassicists the demise was so colossal in import that human civilization never quite recovered from the disaster. According to the Indologist Van Buitenen, the classical age of India

> was the most acquisitive and the most successful in the history of India. . . . In northern India . . . the (classical) age extended from the first until the seventh century A.D., reaching its zenith in the fourth and fifth centuries under the Gupta dynasty. It witnessed the meteoric rise of great trade cities, where Alexandrian brokers bargained with Chinese silk merchants and where Romans kept factors. It was also the age when Indian merchants set sail eastwards to seek gold and in passing sparked a splendid culture to which Angkor Wat and Borobodur are the perennial monuments. A dozen great cities, many of them on the Ganges and its tributaries, gave shape to the golden age. . . . What remains of these once splendid cities is a sleepy provincial town, Ujjain, and a village called Tamluk which is now far from the river and the bay that once carried its merchantmen. It seems as though the urban culture quietly went to sleep for a thousand years. After the Hindus had broken up the Indian empire and the lucrative Western trade had declined with the fall of the Roman empire, the yawns of village India finally drowned out the cries of the city barkers. . . .[21]

This is obviously an idealized picture of an age that may have once been all that Van Buitenen says it was; yet in its later stages it was also decadent and oppressive. It is not unlikely that this era promoted the conservation of tradition to rescue its civilization from a deepening crisis. Why did Christianity spread so rapidly in the Roman Empire? Why did Islam meet so little resistance among Zoroastrians in the Iran of the Sassanids? Why did Hinduism sweep South India so completely at the expense of such classical survivals as Buddhism and Jainism? How else can we explain the mass conversion of Chinese to Mahayana Buddhism after the disintegration of the Han Empire? Contrary to their later establishmentarianism, these universal religions as they appeared during the first millennium A.D. were radical countertraditions in opposition to the dominant ideologies of the classical world.[22]

When Brahmanic Hinduism finally came to Bengal in 1125 A.D. with the Sena Dynasty, its anti-Buddhism was no longer radical but constituted a new orthodoxy that was rigid, dogmatic, and elitist. Bengal is interesting to study historically because it has always been one of the most fertile areas in all India for the birth of countertraditions.[23] In the first place, it was never fully Aryanized during the Vedic period.[24] Second, along with Bihar, Bengal proved highly receptive to pristine Buddhism and Jainism.[25] Third, Buddhism survived here longer than anywhere else in India under the Pala Dynasty (725–1100) though in a Tantric form.[26] Fourth, although the Sena-imposed social hierarchy endured into the nineteenth century among Kulin Brahmans, the dynasty perished early in 1225, a victim of Muslim conquest. Fifth, in few other regions of India did so many people convert to Islam, with the result that today the majority of Bengalis are Muslim and reside in the highly Islamicized republic of Bangladesh. The likely reason for this is that the heterodox Bengalis resisted Sena Hindu orthodoxy by responding positively to Islam as introduced by the countertraditional Muslim mystics known as Sufis.[27]

But some Bengali Hindus also remained within the fold to form countertraditions against Hindu orthodoxy. Before turning to a discussion of their situation however, we should describe medieval Hindu orthodoxy, which in Bengal was based on Kulinism, an established Hindu aristocracy with rigorous qualifications for purity and behavior.[28] The core concept of the orthodox system was *achar,* the medieval equivalent of the Vedic idea of *dharma. Achar* may be loosely translated as rules of behavior to which all good Hindus must conform.[29] It is certainly pre-Upanishadic in the way that it ignores the search for self, for the examined moral life, and for a developed consciousness. Here was a return to the priestly demand for unquestioned obedience to priestly law and caste rigidity.

The source that best illustrates *achar* in Bengal was compiled by Raghunanda Bhattacharya in the sixteenth century.[30] This source still serves as a fundamental text for orthodox Hindus. In brief, Bhattacharya has made a comprehensive list of requirements covering every major activity in the human cycle.[31] Precise details are given even on which foods are to be eaten on which days.[32] It has been suggested that the undue emphasis on food taboos in medieval Hindu orthodoxy stems from a sharp reaction by Brahmanic purists to Tantric Buddhist eating habits. Because Tantrics believed that everything in creation was holy, they allegedly ate everything including a putrifying human corpse.[33] In this way, Brahman scholars justify the orthodoxy of Bhattacharya as the natural reaction to the extreme moral laxity attributed to Tantric Buddhist society.[34] The imposition of a rigorous code for marriage and the family is also justified along these lines. One literary historian of Bengal, Dinesh Chandra Sen, implies that Tantric Buddhists had no formal marriage.[35] He claims that in one Buddhist version of the *Ramayana,* Sita is represented as the sister of Rama, who at the same time marries her.[36] The only problem with this explanation of Hindu orthodoxy is that neither *dharma* nor *achar* really encouraged awareness of true morality (as opposed to convention) since they compel obedience to rules and do not allow struggle over alternative possibilities, freedom of thought, or the determination to arrive at rationally understood distinctions between good and evil.

The medieval countertraditions seem to have a common set of presuppositions that reappear again and again in the fresh beginnings of new religious cults.[37] When a cult becomes rigid through the routinization of charisma and crystallizes as a system, a new cult invariably emerges to challenge what has become the orthodoxy. Common features of the countertraditions were a softening of patriarchal authoritarian values; a concept of love distinguished from lust and representing a sanctified view of sexuality; an erotic vision of divinity or the use of sexual bliss as a metaphor of spiritual bliss; a deepening interest in feeling or emotion; and a sympathetic depiction of women as human beings.[38] Some cults were founded on the worship of woman as god.[39] Other cults stressed the belief in god as the man in the heart.[40] There were other features, such as the familiar distrust of externalities like prayer in holy places, the efficacy of rites and rituals, and the value of priestly intercession. And yet cults in the Middle Ages seemed also to favor esoteric symbols and magic.

These attributes of medieval countertraditions suggest that a new stress on sexuality and women modified the older notions of self-liberation. No higher unity was possible without the act of copulation.[41] The idea of *shakti* or the belief that the true source of energy was female rather than male seems to have become widespread.[42] Icons of male gods were increasingly concretized with their consorts or shaktis.[43] In Bengali Vaishnava literature woman became symbolic of soul engaged in the eternal *lila,* or sacred drama, which reenacted the erotic interaction of the soul as female with the male god, Krishna.[44] Sexuality, sensuality, love, and an elevated image of woman dominate every new countertradition throughout this period. The idea of love or *prem* is especially significant because of the mistaken notion that only the Europeans invented love or feelings that transcended carnal desire.[45] Translations are often misleading since the Bengali *prem* has been defined as sacred love, a concept that we with our heritage of puritanism confuse with a pure spiritual love completely separated from the physical. In medieval Bengal, *prem* or sanctified love was frankly physical and was always depicted in erotic terms. Contrary to the cynical views of Jewish, Christian, and Islamic puritans, the Hindus believed that natural sexual relations could be transformed into an act that was aesthetically, spiritually, and even ethically uplifting. *Sahajiya,* which was perhaps the most important style of worship and belief among the Vaishnavas in Bengal, was rooted in the idea of *sahaja,* which Edward Dimock translates as "easy or natural."[46] Sahajiya Vaishnavism, Dimock asserts, rested on the fundamental belief that "the natural qualities of the senses should be used, not denied or oppressed."[47]

If the Hindu idea of sanctified love is difficult to grasp, it seems even more difficult to achieve. The fourteenth-century erotic religious poet Chandidas, who was an avid exponent of Sahajiya, once wrote that "everyone speaks of Sahajiya but who knows what it really means? One who has crossed from the region of darkness in the land of carnal passion can alone experience the light of Sahajiya."[48] Nowhere does Chandidas abjure the act of copulation, which he feels one must indulge in freely as a spiritual person. But the object is not physical catharsis (kama), which leads to a renewed emptiness; rather the aim is a love (prem) that fills the self with the radiant experience of divine joy. There is a key line in one of Chandidas' poems that suggests that the path of self-transformation by means of a sexualized yoga was exceedingly demanding, difficult, even dangerous. According to Chandidas, "to be a true lover, one must be able to make a frog dance in the mouth of a snake."[49]

Basic to the new attitude that distinguished prem from kama, at least among initiates, was the view that woman must cease to become a mere sex object but instead must become a subject commanding respect and even worship. The historical background to this important social change is still unclear at this early stage of my research. But the evidence from literature is intriguing. Chandidas, for example, chose for his love a washerwoman whom he treated like a goddess—at least in his poetry. In the following selection from one of his poems, Chandidas expresses a concept of love and a sense of consciousness and self which the love inspires:

> O my love! I have taken refuge at your feet, knowing, they have a soothing effect on my burning heart. I adore your beaming virginal beauty, which inspires no lust. When I do not see you, my mind grows restless; and when I see you, my heart is calm. Oh, washerwoman, my lady, you are to me what parents are to helpless children. The three prayers that a Brahman offers daily to his god, I offer to you. You are to me as holy as Gayatri from which the Vedas originated. I know you to be the goddess, Saraswati, who inspires songs. I know you to be the goddess, Parvati, the goddess of the mountains. You are the garland of my neck, my heaven and earth, my whole universe! You are the star of my eyes. Without you a darkness descends. My eyes no longer sting at the sight of you. The day I do not see your moon-like face, I remain like a corpse. I cannot, even for a moment, forget your grace and beauty. Oh, tell me how I may win you! You are my sacred hymns and the essence of my prayers. My love for you, beautiful one, far transcends physical desire. Says Chandidas, the love of the washerwoman is pure gold tested by touch-stone.[50]

It might seem from this passage that Chandidas was expressing a love akin to the idealized love of an adolescent. But, in fact, as described in other passages, the poet has no intention of sublimating his sexuality. An attitude of affection and tenderness helped the loving couple transport themselves from the mundane to the realm of the gods. By following the Tantric way, the medieval countertraditions made a radical departure from classical ascetic notions about sex. As intimated earlier, Tantric permissiveness on sex was part of a larger program allowing indulgence in more forbidden acts including the consumption of animal flesh. Such behavior was justified by the argument that since people did these things anyway for the pure pleasure or power, why not appropriate this vast area of profane human indulgence to the service of a higher and divine purpose?[51]

Herbert Guenther maintains that Tantrism has been greatly misunderstood by Westerners who use only the sexual aspect of the religion to bolster their own narrow, ego-centered pursuit of the cosmic orgasm. Guenther writes, "pleasurable experience may provide a temporary escape but . . . it is not the solution to man's burning problem to find himself."[52] Tantrism, he goes on to say, must not be equated with the "sexual act as proof of one's masculinity which is the paranoid Western conception."[53] Guenther believes that Western man "tries to make the woman responsible for the action of satisfying his needs." Simultaneously, "he identifies himself with his sexuality and this identification becomes the basis for his idea of power, preferably of omnipotence."[54] The following quotation by Guenther about Tantrism in comparative perspective contains one of the most incisive summaries of precisely what these countertraditions in eastern India were all about:

> Tantrism is certainly not on the side of asceticism, but it would be wrong to conclude that therefore it must of necessity advocate libertinism and that its appeal to Western man, reared in an atmosphere hostile to women, pleasure, and life, is due to the fact that Tantrism approves of women and of sex and, by implication can serve as the moral justification for the sex addict's compulsion. It is true, Tantrism recognizes pleasure as valuable and positive, but more than mere pleasure-seeking is involved. It is equally true that in its Hinduistic form it combines power with pleasure which is essentially appreciation and is meant to lead to aesthetic enjoyment, and so has a positive content, unlike Christianity which advocates the impotence of man, denounces pleasure and condemns its source, woman. Buddhist Tantrism dispenses with the idea of power, which it sees as a remnant of subjectivistic philosophy, and even goes beyond mere pleasure to the enjoyment of being and of enlightenment unattainable without a woman.[55]

An additional point that can be made in light of Guenther's perceptive reference to power in Hindu Tantrism is that most Bengali Hindus today are known as *Shaktos*, which means that they worship woman as god because she alone possesses Shakti or the source of all energy and power. This is not to say that in modern times the women of Bengal have played the dominant sexual role in society and culture; the contrary seems to have been true.[56] On the eve of the modern era, both Vaishnavism and Shaktism in Bengal were systems of male-dominated orthodoxy against which socioreligious reform movements, such as the Brahmo Samaj, launched attacks in the name of humanitarian morality.[57] Nevertheless, it must have been different for women in the early days when Shaktism swept the culture in the form of a counter tradition.

It is historically meaningful that the most important religious festival in Bengal remains Durga Puja, which is dedicated to a manifestation of woman as god. It is also meaningful from literary evidence that in Bengal, at the same time Siva worship declined, Shakti worship developed.[58] In Bengal, the image of Siva is hardly that of the powerful lingam to whom Vishnu and Brahman once prostrated themselves in adoration.[59] In Bengal he is a rather passive god, inert, undemanding; Shakti, on the other hand, is creative, energetic, and always in the process of becoming. Sexually she is Kali, straddling Siva and sucking every drop of power-inflated joy from his rocklike lingam. The evidence suggests that Siva worshipers did put up a struggle against Shaktos but lost. As Dinesh Chandra Sen has written in his magnum opus on the history of Bengali language and literature:

> Bengali literature begins, so to speak, with this account of a fight between the Saivas and the worshippers of those local deities who claimed to be Shakti but whom worshippers of Siva called witches and regarded as quite unworthy of worship. At a later time the Saiva creed was blended with the Shakti cult, even its local forms, but this could not happen before a hard contested fight on either side.[60]

By way of conclusion, we may ask whether the medieval countertradition emphasis on sexuality diminished or heightened the earlier countertradition emphasis on existential self-realization. The worship of woman likely equalized the role of the sexes and thus curbed the ego-centered will of man to be dominant. Perhaps it was felt that only within the corridors of a receptive vagina could a man demolish the artificial wall of ego by means of selfless reciprocity. The Kundalini yoga concept of the coiled serpent constituted a frank rejection of the classical idea that transcendence could be achieved by sexual abstinence. The doorway to power and superconsciousness was in sexual ecstasy with a woman. As Guenther puts its, "woman became an education in loving, and an adventure in fulfillment, a search for higher integration."[61] The medieval Indian notion of self was in fact a sublime concept that in no way violated the objective of the classical countertraditions. Writes Guenther, in this final quotation:

> we begin with sex which quite literally is the beginning of ourselves, but sex is not a mere manipulation of organs, it generates an awareness

which may turn into undemanding love, and it is through such love that we see the world and ourselves in a different light, and develop an unclouded awareness of the value of being. What on the previous level was a cold abstraction became now a living symbol pointing to the source, Being-as-such, and through its experience we return to the world differently.[62]

Notes

1. The University of Wisconsin Indian Civilization course, which was funded by the United States government and organized with the help of over twenty scholars from North America and England, began its survey with village India today and devoted most of the remaining sections of lectures to classical, Brahmanic, or the Great Tradition of India. Conspicuously underemphasized were the fields of modern Indian history and regional South Asia as well as Islamic civilization. *Civilization of India Syllabus* ed. J. W. Elder *et al.* (Madison, Wis.: University of Wisconsin, 1965).

2. In recent decades, however, regional studies of South Asia have been emphasized. For a study of the American contribution to Bengal studies, as one regional case in point, see D. Kopf, "A Bibliographical Essay on Bengal Studies in the United States," *Aspects of Bengali History and Society,* ed. R. V. M. Baumer (Honolulu: University of Hawaii Press, 1975), pp. 200–242.

3. Bengali scholars have begun to accommodate these two historical forces in regional histories. For a pioneering work, see *The History of Bengal,* ed. R. C. Majumdar (Dacca: University of Dacca, 1943).

4. This process has been recently reversed by historians with a regional orientation who believe that the Aryan historiography has distorted the true history of the Indian people. For a good monograph from this point of view, which places indigenous matriarchy against Aryan patriarchy, see N. N. Bhattacharyya, *The Indian Mother Goddess* (New Delhi: Monohar, 1977).

5. For a fair analysis of caste and class in ancient India, see A. L. Basham, *The Wonder That Was India* (New York: Hawthorn Books, Inc., 1963), pp. 138–52.

6. For a good general understanding of *dharma* in its classical sense, see *Sources of Indian Tradition,* ed. T. De Bary (New York: Columbia University Press, 1958), 2:211–30.

7. For an interesting composite view of Buddha's protest, see A. de Riencourt, "The Twilight of Culture: Buddha," *The Soul of India* (New York: Harper & Brothers, 1960), pp. 56–76.

8. For a comparative approach to Buddha and other contemporary reformers, see E. Farmer, et al, "The Crisis and Ethical Protest in the Mid-First Millennium B.C.," *Comparative History of Civilizations in Asia* (Reading, Mass.: Addison-Wesley Publishing Company, 1977), vol. 1, pp. 82–124. See also K. Jaspers, *Socrates/Buddha/Confucius/Jesus* (New York: Harvest Books, 1957).

9. The Isa Upanishad, for example, is strongly ethical but not in the Vedic sense of *dharma* or caste duty; it is almost Buddhist in the way the authors stress doing good to others. Morality is derived from within the individual and not from without by means of sacred ritual and knowledge. See *Isa Upanishad,* trans. P. Lal (Calcutta: Writers Workshop, 1968), pp. 4–5.

10. *The Upanishads.* Trans. S. Prabhavananda, F. Manchester (New York: Mentor Religious Classic, 1957), p. 44.

11. Ibid., p. 20.

12. For an imaginative analysis of Buddhism in the light of modern existential philosophy, see W. Liebenthal, *Existentialism and Buddhism* (Santineketan, West Bengal: Visva-Bharati Press, n.d.).

13. For an excellent survey of Buddha's revolutionary ideas, allegedly his own, see *The*

Teachings of the Compassionate Buddha, ed. E. A. Burtt (New York: Mentor Religious Classic, 1959), p. 52.

14. In terms of the sociology of religion, it should not be forgotten that Buddhism appealed to the merchant classes, who according to one scholar "were the main support of the Buddhist revolution." See de Riencourt, "Twilight of Culture," p. 74.

15. Mircea Eliade offers an interesting quote from Emile Senart that is appropriate here: "it was on the terrain of Yoga that Buddhism arose; Whatever innovations he was able to introduce into it, the mold of yoga was that in which his thought was formed." M. Eliade, *Yoga: Immortality and Freedom* (New York: Bollingen Foundation, Inc., 1954), p. 162.

16. Ibid, p. 5.

17. Basham, *Wonder That Was India,* pp. 330–31.

18. For a lucid account of Buddhist thought after Buddha, see Burtt, *Teachings,* pp. 123–41.

19. See, for example, for Bengal, Majumdar, "Buddhism", *History of Bengal,* pp. 411–20.

20. There is an elaborate historiography on the decline of Buddhism in India with varied explanations. For an excellent source, see R. C. Mitra, *The Decline of Buddhism in India* (Calcutta: Visva-Bharati, 1954).

21. J. A. B. Van Buitenen, *Tales of Ancient India* (New York: Bantam Books, 1961), pp. 3–4.

22. For a processual analysis of universal religions from this perspective, see Farmer, *Comparative History of Civilizations in Asia,* pp. 225–81.

23. For an excellent study of these countertraditions, see S. Dasgupta, *Obscure Religious Cults* (Calcutta: Firma KLM Private Limited, 1976).

24. The area now known as Bengal is not mentioned in the Vedas. See Majumdar, *History of Bengal,* pp. 7–10.

25. Ibid, pp. 409–18.

26. For a well-documented historical discussion of the origins and development of Tantric Buddhism in Bengal from the vantage point of the history of ideas, see Dasgupta, *Obscure Religious Cults,* pp. 9–34.

27. For a critical analysis of the impact of Sufism on Bengal, as viewed in historical literature, see D. Kopf, "Bibliographical Notes on Early, Medieval and Modern Sufism with Special Reference to its Bengali-Indian Development," *Folklore* 3 (February 1962): 69–84.

287. N. Kunder, "Caste And Class in Pre-Muslim Bengal" (Ph.D. diss., University of London, 1963), pp. 167–85.

29. D. C. Sen, *History of Bengali Language and Literature* (Calcutta: University of Calcutta, 1954), p. 83.

30. Ibid.

31. Ibid., pp. 83–84.

32. Ibid., pp. 84, 87–88.

33. Ibid., p. 86.

34. Majumdar, *History of Bengal,* p. 612.

35. Sen, *History of Bengali Language,* p. 87.

36. Ibid., p. 86.

37. Dasgupta traces the process back to the Upanishads rather much as has been done in this article. For an interesting discussion of the process with reference to Sahajiya, see Dasgupta, *Obscure Religious Cults,* pp. 61–86.

38. For a superb treatment of how all these factors came together in the Vaishnava Sahajiya cult of Bengal, see E. Dimock, *The Place of the Hidden Moon* (Chicago: The University of Chicago Press, 1966).

39. In India, the ideological system founded on such worship is known as *Saktism.* For a brief but excellent discussion of its relation to Tantrism, one of the more important countertraditions, see Bhattacharyya, *Indian Mother Goddess,* pp. 222–32.

40. For a well-researched analysis of the Baul countertradition, which still stresses this belief, see Dasgupta, *Obscure Religious Cults,* pp. 157–87.

41. It should be stressed, however, that such sexoyogic practices were confined to the left-hand cults, which are here equated with countertraditions. The right-hand, or conservative, cults never actually defied sex and other taboos but sublimated them in various ways.

42. It was widespread in the sense that it was reflected in a vast corpus of epic literature in which the goddess is the central figure. There is no demographic evidence except in partly verifiable assumptions by historians that Saktism was numerically superior to Vaishnavism in late medieval Bengal. For an excellent monograph, which analyzes contemporary materials to prove Sakti dominance in Bengal, see T. Raychaudhuri, *Bengal Under Akbar and Jahangir* (Calcutta: A. Mukherjee and Co., Ltd., 1953), pp. 98–99.

43. N. N. Bhattacharyya, *History of the Sakta Religion* (New Delhi: M. Manoharlal Publishers Pvt. Ltd., 1974), pp. 67–68.

44. Dimock, *Place of the Hidden Moon,* pp. 15, 101, 138–40.

45. For a definition of *prem,* see ibid., pp. 14–16; for a comparative study of such love, East and West, see ibid., pp. 1–14.

46. Ibid., p. 35.

47. Ibid.

48. This is my translation of the Bengali passage attributed to Chandidas in Sen, *History of Bengali Language,* p. 44.

49. Ibid., p. 45.

50. Ibid., pp. 47–48.

51. Dimock, *Place of the Hidden Moon,* pp. 14–18, 101–9.

52. H. V. Guenther, *The Tantric View of Life* (London: Shambhala, 1976), p. 57.

53. Ibid., p. 64.

54. Ibid.

55. Ibid., pp. 65–66.

56. For a brief but thought-provoking discussion on this very point, see W. C. Beane, *Myth, Cult and Symbols in Sakta Hinduism* (Leiden: E. J. Brill, 1977), pp. 266–67.

57. For a description of Brahmo concerns about female emancipation, see D. Kopf, *The Brahmo Samaj and the Shaping of the Modern Indian Mind* (Princeton, N.J.: Princeton University Press, 1978), pp. 31–41.

58. Sen, *History of Bengali Language,* pp. 216–17.

59. I am referring here to the myth of "The Origin of the Lingam," which is retold in H. Zimmer, *Myths and Symbols in Indian Art and Civilization,* ed. J. Campbell (Princeton, N.J.: Princeton University Press, 1974), pp. 128–30.

60. Sen, *History of Bengali Language,* pp. 229–30.

61. Guenther, *Tantric View of Life,* p. 74.

62. Ibid., p. 76.

5

The Self in India and America: Toward a Psychoanalysis of Social and Cultural Contexts

Alan Roland

[This chapter is a result of a psychoanalytic research project in India, 1977–78 and the summer of 1980, while the author was on research Fellowships from the American Institute of Indian Studies. The National Psychological Association for Psychoanalysis in New York City was the sponsoring organization. In India, affiliating organizations were the Centre for the Study of Developing Societies in Delhi, the National Institute for Mental Health and Neuro Sciences in Bangalore, and the Indian Council for Mental Health in Bombay, which graciously arranged for most of my clinical work.

Shorter versions of this paper have been presented to the International Society for the Comparative Study of Civilizations, May, 1980, Syracuse; and the Midwinter Meeting of the American Psychoanalytic Association, December 1980 New York City.]

From my clinical psychoanalytic work in India, along with ongoing discussions with Indian psychoanalysts and other mental health professionals and social scientists, it is apparent that there is a radically different development, structuralization, and functioning of the self in India and in America.[1] In effect, there are different inner psychological developments for functioning effectively in hierarchical and egalitarian social relationships in these two cultures which are so civilizationally varied. The intrapsychic development and organization of the self are congruent with the sociocultural patterns of each society. Thus, the person will actually have a somewhat different experiential, emotional sense of self and relationships, as well as cognitively internalized varying world views in each culture.

This raises profound issues and implications concerning the necessity

170

for psychoanalysis to be far more integrated with highly varying social and cultural contexts than is customarily the case—with rare, notable exceptions such as Erikson.[2] One far-reaching implication involves the problem of theoretical analyses of the Indian psyche: just how suitable are the very categories of psychoanalysis, and the psychoanalytic vocabulary of basic concepts, which are so completely based on the data of Western personality and culture with its highly individualistic psychology? Another implication concerns the necessity for not only seriously questioning the oft-criticized psychoanalytic assumption of the primacy of psychic reality over cultural, social, and historical factors but also Erikson's far more sophisticated schema of universal, developmental, or epigenetic stages influenced by the cultural patterns of a given society. Such central aspects of Erikson's life cycle as autonomy, initiative, and identity crises and syntheses do not appear to be pertinent to the traditional Indian life cycle, but rather are profoundly rooted in Western, if not American, individualistic psychological development. Other important elements of universalistic theorizing in psychoanalysis are also open to serious question and revision. Still another implication involves the necessity for a psychoanalytic psychology of the self to take into account the structure and quality of kinship relationships—not only between America and India but also within the various ethnic groups in America coming from a diversity of European backgrounds as well as from Africa and other non-Western countries.

A psychoanalysis of social and cultural contexts is already gradually developing through psychoanalytic work in major non-Western cultures, such as India and Japan, where there are established psychoanalytic movements.[3] Actual clinical psychoanalytic work in India and Japan affords a giant methodological step over the usual psychoanalytic-anthropological research: it affords direct access into unconscious motivation and structures in major, complex cultures in contrast to nonclinical observations in far less developed societies. It also affords the use of the major psychoanalytic tools of disciplined subjectivity through trained empathy and introspection that enables the observer to understand inner psychological makeup and processes of others, rather than evaluations based on behavioral assessments. By drawing upon the observations and insights of indigenous psychoanalytic therapists, it is possible to extend vastly the sampling of patients and to reach some degree of consensual validation.

Based on my clinical psychoanalytic work in India,[4] a new theoretical paradigm is presented here that uses broad psychoanalytic categories for analysis, such as psychic structures, conscience, and narcissism—in the sense of psychological processes related to the development and maintenance of self-regard, self-object—or the meaning of the other to oneself, self, and object representations or internal objects (from a more Kleinian standpoint)—the inner psychic structuring of images of self and other, psychosexual and psychosocial stages of development, ego functioning and ego boundaries, the structuring of aggression, sexuality and affect, and unconscious motivation and conflicts. This paradigm recognizes that the various inner psychological structures involved in or through these categories in India are often quite differently constituted from those of most Americans, and function and develop differently. Further, it is necessary at times to reformulate some very basic psychoanalytic concepts to accommodate a psychological reality and mode of relationship in India that have no parallels in America. This paradigm seeks to avoid a normality-pathology model that all too often subtly or openly imperialistically imposes a Western psychoanalytic psychology, where all the norms for mental health are implicitly Western, and deviations in individuals in non-Western societies are implicitly regarded as pathological or inferior, which, of course, supports the old Western notion of superiority.[5] Instead, the emphasis here is on the congruency and adaptation of the psychological to sociocultural contexts. Inner psychological structures that are highly congruent and adaptive in one society and culture will often obviously not be so in another.

The concept of the self is used here in a few different ways. One is Hartmann's concept of self as an organizing principle of the psyche,[6] which is preferred to identity because Erikson's important formulations around identity syntheses and conflicts are not all that accurate a representation of the traditional Indian psyche—though it is highly relevant to Indians who are exposed to Westernization.[7] A second use of self is related to Kohut's emphasis on the self as developing through bipolar internalization processes.[8] Self is also considered in terms of an intrinsic authenticity that must be actualized—related to Winnicott's true and false self, and also to related concepts of the Menakers, Loewald, and Kohut.[9] Finally, self is viewed through Indian categories as *jiva* (finite) and *Atman* (Infinite) with highly differing experiential components of consciousness and being in each.[10]

In comparing the development of the psyche in Indian and American societies, we must talk of three different selves: *the familial self, the individualized self, and the Transcendent Self.* That is, the self forms meaningful and identifiable gestalts in these three different catagories, though any given person has a more or less unitary self—subject, of course, to a variety of possible splits in the overall organization of the self.[11] The traditional Indian person has varying integrations of a familial self with a transcendent self, with little if any development of a more individualized self. This contrasts dramatically with contemporary Americans in whom the individualized self is the dominant note, with only background chords of the familial self—varying in intensity with the ethnic and national background as well as quite frequently with the sex of the person—and traditionally with a more or less deaf ear turned to the transcendent self, with only occasional echoes coming from certain philosophical and artistic quarters. In both countries, especially in the urban areas, there are significant changes taking place. In India, it is the growing individualization within the dominant gestalts of the familial-transcendent selves, whereas in America, there is a serious developing involvement in the realization of the transcendent self within the dominant mode of the individualized self. This whole topic of social and intrapsychic change obviously requires an entirely separate study and conceptualization to cover the subject adequately.

Within the broad organizational gestalt of the Indian familial self are important recognizable subgestalts, all of which are oriented toward functioning within various kinds of hierarchical relationships that pervade Indian society; symbiotic modes of relating in affectional intimacy relationships, the structuring of narcissism, and the Hindu conscience with its mythic orientation that internalizes traditionally defined reciprocal responsibilities and obligations in a complexity of different contexts, which thus comprises one's *dharma*. By delving into these three specific subgestalts in some depth, correlating intrapsychic structures and their development with functioning in the Indian extended family, the Indian familial self can be contrasted with the American individualized self, and a psychoanalysis of sociocultural contexts can begun to be demonstrated. A further aspect will be to indicate some of the continuities and counterpoints of the gestalt of the transcendent self with the familial self. Unfortunately, there is not sufficient space here to go into a number of issues, including the differences in ego functioning and modes of cognition.

These two societies are significantly different for individual functioning. *The pervasive dominance of the extended family is a constant throughout the enormous heterogeneity of Indian society, and is the social and psychological locus throughout life (with the exception of the renouncer) of almost all Indians.* Whether the family is living in a nuclear or joint household, *extended family relationships predominate.* Moreover, the nuclear or unitary household may well change to a joint one with a change in the life cycle—such as one or more sons marrying and bringing a wife home, and eventually having a child— only to change at another point to a unitary household if the original parents die or the son(s) decide(s) to establish a separate household from his parents and/or brother.[12] Or even if a given family is living in a unitary household, decisions may still be made jointly by family elders, marriages arranged through the extended family female network, property held jointly, mutual obligations still maintained, and meetings take place with the extended family on important ritual occasions (*samskaras*) such as births, deaths, and marriages as well as certain festivals. What is even more important is that even when a family may be living in its cycle as a unitary household, the models for the relationships still strongly remain those of a joint household—sanctioned by centuries of tradition and given extensive meaning from a vitally alive mythology derived from the *Puranas* and from local folklore.

It is essential to note that in this paradigmatic joint family the whole is not only greater than the sum of its component parts *but far more important; the joint family paradigm significantly transforms its component parts.* All relationships and roles are governed by the overall needs of the joint family with individual needs almost always subordinate to the needs of the joint family. Conjugal love is therefore generally subordinate to hierarchical love in a traditional Indian family, or at the very least does not supplant hierarchical love, with husband and wife spending little time together and showing no overt display of affection to each other in the presence of his parents or others of the joint family. Nor are husband and wife to exhibit any favoritism or possessiveness toward their own children, but rather they are to allow the children to be shared and raised by other members of the family. Filial and fraternal attachments are very strong with hierarchical roles and responsibilities well defined. Nuclear family units are always subordinate to the extended family. The woman only attains status in Hindu society as a mother, and the mother-child relationship is generally far more intense than the husband-wife one, in which the husband remains strongly attached to his mother throughout life, having to carefully balance his involvements with both his mother and wife.

The model for joint family functioning, which also predominates in unitary households, is profoundly based on structural hierarchical role relationships (in contrast to hierarchy by quality), the structural hierarchy being fundamentally based on kinship status, which, in turn, is primarily based on deference and subordination for age and seniority on one hand, and for sex (the female toward the male) on the other. Wives derive their status from the position of their husbands in the family, as well as from becoming mothers. Kinship terms in India are much more precise for all variations of relationship than in the West, and are used differentially in various social contexts to take into account the complexity of multiple kinship relationships and the varied statuses accorded them.[13] Complicated exchanges of gifts, foods, and the like define and express these relationships and statuses, as do the timeless models from the rich Indian mythology. *Correct behavior is much more oriented toward what is expected in the specific contexts of a variety of roles and relationships, rather than any unchanging norm for all situations.* Obviously, contexts and correct behavior or *dharma* will shift depending on what part of the life cycle the person is in and what kinship status he or she occupies at a particular time, as well as the particular makeup of the persons involved.

The reputation and status of the family is of central concern to its members because this is a key factor in the arrangement of the marriages within its *jati* or community (caste). This is apparently as true of the low castes and even the scheduled castes (untouchables) as it is of the high castes.[14] Friendships and even ongoing professional relationships become subsumed within extended family relationships. Children and adolescents are therefore predominantly with parents and other family elders, there being no real separation of age groups. Individual achievement and success are oriented not so much toward individual mobility as toward family status and mobility, and ultimately the mobility of the *jati*. *Major life decisions are rarely left to the individual*, though among the urban educated there is more of a tendency to take into account the wishes of the child both in occupation and in marriage. In traditional India marriages are always arranged, whereas in modern middle- and upper-middle-class urban India the great majority of marriages are still arranged with most of the "love marriages" being based on parental consent. Formerly, sons automatically followed their father's occupation, which was *jati* based, and is still the case in many communities; whereas among the urban educated, the son is usually guided by the parents and other family elders into what type of education and career would be most suitable, taking the boy's (and increasingly the girl's) wishes and inclinations into account to varying extents.

A deeply etched millennia old-world view on the meaning of the life cycle is profoundly internalized into the preconscious of Hindus. This comprises the four goals of life—*dharma* (right conduct in specific struc-tural hierarchical relationships), *artha* (attainment of material goods and power), *kama* (fulfillment of desire), and *moksha* (spiritual realization)—and the four *ashramas* or stages of life (the student, the householder, the house-holder who begins retiring from life to pursue spiritual attainment, and the renouncer who is devoted entirely to spiritual pursuits). However much a Hindu Indian does or does not follow this schema, it is still somewhere in the back of his or her mind.

The Indian closely knit hierarchical kinship relationships contrast strongly to the nuclear and now even split family of contemporary Ameri-can urban society, where peer groups and various other extrafamilial social groups assume increasingly dominant proportions as a child grows into an adolescent and becomes part of social groups separated by age and genera-tion. Moreover, the ideal of hierarchical relationships contrasts strongly with that of egalitarian relationships. Whereas major life decisions are made by the family for the individual in India, autonomy is granted if not imposed on the adolescent and young adult in America to choose between a variety of social options including a mate, friends, social affiliations, edu-cation, vocation, and even a value system or ideology—for which there is presently nothing approaching any social consensus. Whereas the social options are obviously more or less limited depending on one's social class, the pervasive ideology of individualistic choice and initiative is present throughout most of the society. *It is not too much to generalize that Indian society stresses far more the extended family, community or jati (caste), hierarchy, a millennia old-world view and the continuity of traditions than American society, which is so oriented toward social change, social and physical mobility, a multiplicity of social options, considerable autonomy of the individual, and an ideology of egali-tarian-contractual relationships and individualism.*

In line with Francis Hsu's emphasis on intimacy relationships in non-Western societies,[15] the quality of affectional relationships is much stronger within the Indian extended family than in most northern European-American ones. This qualitatively different mode of relating with its congruent intrapsychic structures can be termed "symbiotic reciprocity" although this phrase contains antithetical elements in contemporary psychoanalytic theory, where symbiosis implies a clinging dependency in relationships and a tendency toward inner fusion of self and object representations, and reciprocity or mutuality connotes a far more mature level of inner development and relatedness. The problem is in finding a suitable phrase for Indian emotional intimacy relationships that are simply of a different quality and order than in the northern European-American culture belt. Takeo Doi approached this problem in depicting Japanese intimacy relationships by discarding psychoanalytic theorizing as implicitly being too Western to fit Japanese psychological reality, instead relying on a subtle psychological exegesis of indigenous Japanese concepts, particularly of *amae*[16]—intense dependency needs and strivings.

In the Indian context what is meant by symbiotic reciprocity is the strong mutual caring for, and depending on, a tremendously heightened asking and giving (for an American) in an emotional atmosphere of affection and warmth, where emotional connectedness is always central and any feelings disruptive to the relationship are contained or inhibited, or sometimes unconsciously displaced or turned against the self, especially ambivalent ones. Ego boundaries are more open to others and there is relatively little psychological space around oneself; that is, the person is much less self-contained than in America. Although there is great consideration, care, and giving to others, there are strong expectations of reciprocity. When these expectations are not fulfilled, there can be intense angry feelings generated by disappointment and hurt.

Thus, inclinations to give and to ask become greatly magnified, sometimes with a relative disregard of either one's own needs or those of the other. Often, the asking is not done directly, but through subtle communication or setting up of an interpersonal situation so that the other volunteers. In this way there is no threat either to one's own or the other's self-regard if the other refuses the request. I have found myself in different situations volunteering to help out one or another person without being asked for anything, then realizing later that the whole situation had been set up that way from the beginning. It is not that the "demands" were unreasonable, or that I wouldn't have agreed to help if I were asked directly. What strikes me is rather the subtlety of the communication.

Let me give a brief example. At one psychiatric facility I visited, the head of the department wanted me to hear a case one of the staff had treated in psychotherapy. The woman who presented displayed a most unusual sensitivity and ability to do psychoanalytically oriented psychotherapy, especially with very little training. I suggested to the head psychiatrist the possibility of her getting a couple of years training abroad in psychoanalytic therapy, which I would look into. He agreed that this was an excellent idea. From a later remark he made, it dawned on me that that was exactly what he had had in mind and was the reason he wanted me to hear this woman present in the first place. At a more extreme point in this continuum, I have heard an Indian colleague complain that he had just done something that he never would have done, had he been asked directly, but had been subtly and successfully maneuvered into it.

Favors may at times be freely asked of another, even a stranger, who may find it difficult to refuse the request if it plays on unconscious identifications with the selfless mother. A family member, or even those working in an organization, who find it difficult to assert their own wishes or needs to someone higher in the authority hierarchy, may pick on another who is more in favor to voice their wishes. The other, even while realizing that the full weight of displeasure will fall on herself or himself, will nevertheless do what is asked. To give an example, in a large social service department in a highly regarded institution, many of the women were apparently afraid of asserting their own strong dissatisfactions with certain practices and rules. In a subtle way, they settled on one of the strongest of them to fight with the authority figures to win their points. This particular woman could not say no and fought the battle successfully, even though knowing it would cost her her well-regarded position there—which it did.

Udayan Patel, a Bombay psychoanalyst, told me about a patient who had received a telephone call from the former employer of this man's servant, strongly requesting that he send the girl servant back to the former employer since the latter's wife was having a breakdown and missed this servant. The patient's strong initial reaction was that of compliance, regardless of any inconvenience to his own family or of any wishes or feelings of the girl. How could he be so selfish as to keep the girl? It was only with the reflection of analysis that he decided to ask his servant how she felt about it. He then learned that she had left the former employer because of his proximity to her frequently drunken father who had been rather brutal to her. She obviously did not want to return. The man then had to deal with his own unconscious identification with the selfless mother in finally refusing the other's demand.

Relationships are thus of overriding importance to the Indian, much more so than to an American. Kakar pointedly states, "The yearning for the confirming presence of the loved person . . . the distress aroused by her or his unavailability or unresponsiveness in time of need—is the dominant modality of social relationships in India, especially within the extended family."[17]

Thus, Hindu social organization accentuates the continued existence of the child in the adult and elaborates the care-taking function of society to protect and provide for the security of its individual members. . . . Indian society . . . attempts to alleviate *dukha* (anxiety and suffering) by addressing itself to deep needs for connection and relationship to other human beings in an enduring and trustworthy fashion and for ongoing mentorship, guidance and help in getting through life . . . .

Or again, "From the earliest years, the Indian child learns that the core of any social relationship . . . is the process of caring and mutual involvement . . . he should be sensitive to the relationship itself, the unfolding of emotional affinity"[17]—citing Pande's observation that in the West, intimacy grows more out of shared activities rather than simply being together.[18]

Inner psychological structures develop that enable the person to develop an unusually high degree of empathy and emotional sensitivity to others' dependency needs and self-regard, with heightened sensitivity to subtle, nonverbal communication. This contrasts with far less sensitivity in Americans; where empathic awareness is present, it is usually oriented toward others' needs for autonomy, self-expression, and individuation. An American psychoanalytic colleague aptly put it, "When someone is highly sensitive and intuitive in America, you tend to comment on it. While in Indian relationships, it is the necessary and normal mode of relating."[19] The Indian experiential sense of self is more organized around "we," "our," and "us,"[20] or an "I" that is always closely related to a "you,"[21] than the American highly individualistic sense of "I" and "me," with its inherent duality between "I" and "you." The other as self-object always remains in closer inner proximity to the self, with strong expectations of mirroring no matter which end of the hierarchy one is in. Frequently the other as self-object is invested with intense idealizations when the hierarchical relationship is based on quality and the veneration is reasonably earned.[22] Sometimes the person idealized coincides with the person who is superior in the structural hierarchy; at other times the idealized person may be junior or a female. This degree of mirroring and idealization in the other as self-object completely transcends what is present in American relationships, except perhaps in childhood. There is probably somewhat less differentiation of self and object representations (images of self and other) in Indians than in Americans, both structures being highly adaptive to their respective societies.

Another psychological structure involved in symbiotic reciprocity is a strong libidinal wishing, wanting self. In contrast, the accent in American relationships and development is on a strong degree of separation and autonomy, inwardly and in relationships, and in a highly developed individuation of ego skills and in the realization of a highly individualized identity. The intrinsic need for mirroring and idealizing relationships, especially in childhood, has recently been recognized in American psychoanalysis, but even in this work the dominant chord is still a high degree of individual autonomy and individualization.[23]

Implicit in this mode of relating is a relative lack of any regard for, and at times definite discouragement of, separation and autonomy, and too great social individuation—though this is changing somewhat in urban areas and is vital to the thesis of an evolving self in Indians. The phrase *social individuation* is stressed here because it is evident that there are two kinds of individuation in Indian culture, one relating to the social sphere and the other to the inner realization of the spiritual or transcendent self— what a major Indian psychiatrist, Professor Neki, terms "individuation apart from society."[24] The latter kind of individuation is stressed far more in traditional Indian culture than the former, where the various degrees and skills of ego functioning and development of the self seem closely related to the particular family culture one is brought up in and broadly to the *jati* norms of which the family is a part. Individuation in the social sphere for Indians is not nearly as closely associated with the separation process as it is for Americans.[25] The lack of regard for separation and autonomy is experienced by Westerners who live in India for some time, and even by Indians who return home after having been abroad for some time in the West, as being "swallowed up" in Indian relationships. The normal separateness, privacy, and autonomy of Western relationships and the psychological space around oneself dissolves into the more symbiotic world of giving and asking, of caring and depending on, of close, warm emotional connectedness, and of relationships transcending the separate or individualized self. Conversely, Indians going to the West find relationships far too distant and people uncaring, and they personally yearn for the emotional, sensuous intimacy of the Indian extended family.[26]

The quality of communication is often highly subtle and nonverbal— often relying on facial expressions and eye movements—and may be taken on different levels. Communication is frequently oriented around not hurting another's feelings and not threatening that person's status and self-esteem in observing the correct form of a situation, while still expressing what one feels or wants. Some Indians feel that these two levels of communication are *always* present to some degree, and may be particularly so with women since extended family morality and expectations are stricter for them. Other Indians are acutely attuned to these various cues, if not always able to resolve the ambiguities. A striking example of this multiple level of communication is given in Veena Das's paper "Masks and Faces. . . ."[27] A young husband responded to the complaints of his mother and sisters about his wife by dutifully scolding and beating his wife—thus fulfilling his primary responsibilities to his mother and sisters as determined by the role hierarchies of the joint family. That night, however, he made love to his wife in such an indiscreet manner that his mother and sisters could hear, thus nonverbally communicating his love and preference for his wife over his mother and sisters, who were apparently crestfallen the next day over his covertly communicated preference. Americans, on the other hand, tend to be much more openly vocal and direct in their communication and can become quite disturbed when they are in the midst of this characteristic multilevel communication and indirectness of normal Indian communication.

In India, the inner development of the self along the lines described comes from the highly emotionally gratifying, sensuous, and physical closeness of mothering person(s) with the child through the first three to four years of life, during which aspects of separation and autonomy are not particularly encouraged if not discouraged. Some Indian writers emphasize indulgence, but that is clearly from a more Western perspective. Weaning in India does not take place till the second or third year, and there is a great deal of sensuous, physical closeness in the ways of handling and carrying the child, who is rarely left alone. This is especially true of the sleeping arrangements. Even where there is enough room, and there often is not, the infant and toddler is in the mother's or parental bed until displaced by the next sibling, or until he or she is two to five years of age. The youngest child may sleep with his or her mother for a number of years, and especially if the child is a girl, she may continue to sleep with her mother into her teens and even until her marriage. When the child leaves the maternal bed, it is to sleep with another sibling, aunt, or uncle, and almost never alone. Separation and aloneness are to be avoided at all costs in Indian family relationships. To the extent the mothering person(s) can do so—and various responsibilities at times prevent her from doing so—she will handle her infant's or young child's frustrations, anxieties, and unhappiness by instant gratification. As Kakar rightly stresses, the degree of maternal gratification and close mother-child relationship in India are of a completely different magnitude from normal mothering in the northern European-American culture belt.[28]

It is evident that this type of symbiotic mothering with a definite discouragement of separation and autonomy is considered clearly psychopathological within an American context by major psychoanalytic writers such as Mahler and Jacobson.[29] They view such mothering as resulting in severe psychopathology in the child, and instead emphasize the whole process of separation and individuation, by which an American child gains the increasing skill and autonomy needed to function more and more independently within adolescent and adult social contexts. What these writers overlook is that for an American mother (from northern European ethnic groups) to function as an Indian mother does would tend to imply that the American mother would probably be a disturbed person to be so at odds with her own social patterns, whereas Indian mothering is highly congruent and adaptive within Indian patterns and evidently does not usually result in any severe psychopathology.

Thus, maternal patterning (Indian) in infancy through a highly symbiotic mode of child rearing with a strong discouragement of separation and a limited encouragement of certain kinds of individuation, as compared to an alternate patterning (American) where symbiotic modes are downplayed and separation and individuation are stressed, *result in different psychological structures and modes of relating which are noticeable as early as the age of two-and-a-half.* It is instructive to note the observations of Bim Bissel, director of a progressive nursery school and kindergarten in New Delhi consisting of 80 percent Indian children—from upper-caste, upper-class Westernized families—and 15 percent Western children (the remainder being Japanese). Bissel observed that the Indian children, even at the age of two-and-a-half, were far more sensitive to relationships within the group, to each other, and to the teacher, whereas Western children were more autonomous in approaching their tasks with greater initiative and independence.[30] The effects of this early child rearing are apparent, as is the manner in which they are basically adaptive to functioning in particular social and cultural milieus.

Or on a more informal level, consider the comments by sixteen-year-old-girl college students at Jai Hind College in Bombay upon seeing a Canadian film of two- and three-year-olds in a nursery school and at home. These students found the children in the film to be far more exploratory of their environment and involved with toys than Indian children of the same age, whereas the nursery school teacher and mother seemed far less involved and protective than the typical Indian mothering person—at least from the Indian middle- and upper middle-class families.[31] The implication is that the two- and three-year-old Indian child looks much more to the relationship, and the Western child looks more to what is in the environment; the latter was confirmed by the work of Margaret Mahler and her associates.[32]

The tendency to see non-Western cultures and psychological functioning through the lens of Western psychoanalytic norms is exemplified by Warner Muensterberger, a psychoanalyst who was trained in anthropology. Muensterberger delineates a number of developmental dimensions in an important, summary paper citing the results of the separation and individuation process in psychoanalytically oriented, anthropological fieldwork in a number of non-Western cultures, including India.[33] In his attempt to arrive at rigorous, psychoanalytic scientific formulations, Muensterberger surprisingly and blatantly exhibits coloniallike attitudes, clearly asserting superiority of Western culture over non-Western, which is equated with primitive, utilizing the model of Western personality as the measuring stick against which all other psychological development is assessed. Thus, Muensterberger asserts that the non-Western type of child rearing interferes with the formation of normal ego boundaries, with the development of intellectual development and abstract conceptualization, with the differentiation between representations of the self and other, with reality testing in causing less distinction between reality and fantasy, with the internalization of superego regulatory functions making the individual more depen-

dent on regulation from external figures, with ego autonomy from
instinctual drive involvement, with developing optimal frustration-
tolerance, and in general with the whole separation and individuation
processes resulting in a far less differentiated personality. He completes
this litany by a final assertion that this kind of child rearing is done by a
"not good-enough mothering"—in contrast to Winnicott's concept of
"good-enough mothering."[34]

Although Muensterberger makes some valuable observations in this
paper—such as the child being less involved with transitional objects because of the continued availability of mothering persons,[35] and the symbiotic, libidinal tie to the mother being transferred to the kinship group—
as well as some incorrect ones on intellectual development, achievement,
and the superego—serious deficiencies result from this imposition of Western cultural standards. *Even more to the point, Muensterberger does not recognize
that other kinds of intrapsychic structures can be formed which are highly adaptive to
the different sociocultural contexts of non-Western societies such as India.* To emphasize this point from another angle, an American for instance, with the
kind of inner psychological structures developed through American child
rearing, would usually have an extraordinarily difficult time functioning
well within an Indian extended family.

The second and third major gestalts of the Indian familial self involve
functioning within traditionally defined hierarchical relationships within
the kinship and other groups of Indian society, with the attendant responsibilities and obligation from both ends of the hierarchy. Hierarchical relationships in India are basically of two different kinds that may at times be
congruent, but at other times are in a constant dynamic interrelationship.
The first type can be termed "structural hierarchy," which, as referred to
previously, is governed by age and seniority on the one hand and sex on
the other (the female being subordinate to the male). Roles and responsibilities in this type of hierarchy within a diversity of social contexts are
usually traditionally well defined, and are given timeless meanings and
models from a vitally alive mythology from the *Puranas* as well as from
folklore. The second type of hierarchy is governed more by quality, in
which persons are highly respected and venerated for their personal qualities, in contrast to the deference displayed toward the person at the top of
the structural hierarchy. The person who is venerated may or may not be at
the top of the structural hierarchy; frequently it may be someone lower in
the structural hierarchy, e.g., a younger brother.

To function well within hierarchical relationships requires a different
psychological organization of narcissistic structures and a different kind of
conscience from that of an American, whose inner structures are oriented
toward functioning in more egalitarian relationships. The Indian individual usually identifies so profoundly with the status and reputation of the
extended family that we must speak of an inner narcissistic structure of

high *self-we regard* that can also extend itself to a number of hierarchical relationships. This contrasts sharply with the more individualistic self-regard of Americans. In fact, when an American tends to enhance self-regard primarily through association with another, psychoanalytically it is looked upon as immaturity, psychopathology, or making up psychologically for some childhood deficit.

One can sense within most Indians an inner core of heightened narcissism, with great sensitivity to maintaining self-we regard in others and oneself through continuous consideration of this dimension in relationships. Issues can become very secondary to the narcissistic factor in relationships, a strong contrast to most American relationships. This inner core of self and self-we regard has a number of implications; it often inures Indians to considerable later deprivation. Much of the pervasive multileveled communication has a strong narcissistic dimension in the sense of always overtly showing proper deference and respect while nonverbally sometimes conveying quite different feelings. The narcissistic investment in what might be termed "life space" is primarily with the body ego, the self, and the extended family, outside of which is something of a no-man's land.

To illustrate this point, Bassa observed in the slums of a suburb of Bombay that even in the most squalid and abject of conditions, personal grooming is relatively good and the inside of the small huts are invariably neat and clean.[36] Oddly enough, the same observation can be made about persons of the middle- and upper-middle classes and their living conditions. Personal grooming is fastidious; in the luxury buildings the flats are usually well taken care of—in some cases they are sumptuous—but the hallways and other public spaces are almost invariably in a poor to very poor condition—often reminiscent of a New York City slum tenement building. Almost the worst of these I frequented is interestingly enough a high rental building in an excellent location filled with a variety of medical practitioners. The public areas are thus a striking contrast to the family areas of the flats and personal grooming. *This indicates that the individual's narcissistic investment extends to the individual body-ego and self-image, and clearly also to the "we" of the extended family, but outside the family it is a no-man's land.*

A related aspect to life space is what I have called "interpersonal space," as contrasted to Eliade's sacred and profane or secular space. By this I mean that even so-called "objective" space in a Western sense is related to in terms of relationships by Indians. An example will illustrate this concept. My wife gave me directions to meet her at one of her Indian colleague's home in Bandra, a suburb of Bombay. In good American spatial terms, she first told me which road to take, then to make a sharp right turn to another road, and then to go to the fifth building from the corner. I had some difficulty finding the house only because it was the third, not the fifth house from the corner. Our Indian hosts declared that there would have been no difficulty whatsoever in finding their flat if only my wife had told me that it was in the building immediately adjacent to the burned-out house. It was only then that it fully dawned on me that almost every direction I had ever been given was basically in relationship to another building, or landmark, or such. Nothing was ever given in geometrical, objective space—with the exception of those Westernized New Delhi planners who have taken extra pains to lay out their housing colonies in the most systematic, geometric way imaginable—but rather in relationship to another place. *This is a carry-over of a profound Indian perception of the world as being based on interpersonal relationships; one relates oneself to so-called objective reality in terms of relationship, not some kind of impersonal abstraction or geometry as in America.* In India one is thus always located in *relationship* to others, in one or another context, not as an impersonal, individual monad—such as the third or fifth house from the corner.

The Indian's narcissistic cathexis of life space within the extended family contrasts with the American's, in which there is far less involvement with the extended family and more investment in public space. Still another contrast concerns the inner emotional core of high self-we regard that is totally consistent with the Hindu philosophical formulation of Atman-Brahman; that is, that the individual soul is one with the Godhead. This, of course, contrasts strongly with the Christian doctrine of original sin and self-denigration with characteristically far less positive early mirroring toward the young child.

From the standpoint of child rearing, this inner core derives primarily from intense, prolonged maternal mirroring and involvement. Additional important factors are the strong idealizations to the point of veneration that are culturally supported in the child's relationship with family elders at all stages of the child's development, including adolescence. Parental figures are seen as embodiments of the gods and goddesses, and as being contiguous with the latter. Moreover, this process of idealization and identification, greatly enhancing self and self-we regard, proceeds throughout life in hierarchical relationships governed by quality where the other is highly respected. Further, there are no separate age groups in India, the child and adolescent being constantly with family elders, thus further intensifying the identification process and internalization of the norms, customs, and traditions of family and *jati*.[37] The child rearing contrasts considerably with most American ethnic groups, in which there is far less maternal mirroring and more limited periods of culturally supported idealization, with idealizations in general being less intense in egalitarian relationships. Moreover, separate age groups, particularly at the time of adolescence, tend to greatly diminish the identification process with their parents.

A third major organizing gestalt of the familial self is the Hindu conscience, which is oriented around the concept of *dharma*. *Dharma*, or right action, takes into account mutual responsibilities and obligations according to one's kinship status and stage in the life cycle as well as the norms of one's *jati,* specific contexts and situations of multiple kinship and caste hierarchical relationships, and to some extent the persons' psychological makeup in the hierarchical relationship, termed here the Hindu conscience, a "socially contextual ego-ideal rooted in a mythic consciousness." There is the inner psychological structure of extreme sensitivity to proper behavior and how one will be regarded within a number of specific, hierarchical social contexts, often traditionally defined—serving the narcissistic function of maintaining the ego-ideal and the inner sense of high self-we regard that is unconsciously invested in the ego-ideal. The Hindu conscience is far more oriented toward the ego-ideal than a superego—that is, of living up to certain internalized ideals, but *ideals rooted in specific contextual, hierarchical relationships,* with expectations and sensitivity to the constant approbation of others no matter which end of the hierarchical relationship one may be in.

The Western and American conscience in terms of superego in contrast is metaphorically more of a gyroscope, enabling the individual to sail the seas of innumerable social situations by keeping his balance around more abstract, universalistic principles of behavior. As Riesman's work has indicated, the ego-ideal of the American may be strongly geared to the specific social group in which the person is functioning.[38] This type of superego and ego-ideal guides the more autonomous, mobile individual, who may have to adapt or function within a number of groups, but does *not* have to deal with traditionally defined, complex, multiple kinship relationships—not to mention complex, well-defined, hierarchical relationships in other groups as well. The American ego-ideal further incorporates strong values of individualism, autonomy, and self-reliance, with less narcissistic involvement than the Indian. Although the American conscience is somewhat contextual with regard to the social group one is in, it is still much more universalistic than the Indian conscience. A further dramatic contrast between Indian and American consciences is the strong mythic consciousness and orientation in the Hindu ego-ideal. Through a vitally alive, richly complex mythology that elaborates a large number of mythic models and relationships, the Indian child who has learned them from a variety of mothering figures from early childhood venerates elders as living manifestations of the gods and goddesses, and gradually identifies with one or more of these models on the basis of temperament, inclination, and cognitive style. Families from one or another *jati* will emphasize different mythic models to their children, depending on the norms of the *jati;* e.g. heroic military myths will be emphasized to a child of Rajput (princely) background.[39] These mythic models also give norms for correct behavior and attitudes, as well as negative images, in a variety of kinship relationships and situations. Timeless models and meanings are available for almost any situation or relationship. Thus, mythic models and relationships are deeply internalized within the preconscious of the Indian self, and are vitally integrated with self and object-representations throughout life. These models not only orient persons to their own responsibilities or *dharma* but also implicitly to the reciprocal responsibilities of others in the complex, hierarchical kinship relationships.[40] In Hindu cognition, the mythic image is experienced as contiguous or metonymic with the other person or icon or idol and not as a symbol or representation of it.[41]

This understanding of the Hindu conscience has strong implications for what has been termed "compartmentalization" by the anthropologist Milton Singer.[42] In studying various aspects of social change, Singer noted contemporary, urban Indians functioning in different group settings in ways that would be considered highly contradictory to a Western conscience. For example, men would work in a Westernized setting in which they would dress in Western clothes, eat with members of any caste, and, in general, follow a number of practices that would be completely different from those they followed at home. What might seem to a Westerner as inconsistent, unprincipled, or at best compartmentalized is actually totally consistent to an Indian since the Indian conscience is a socially contextual one oriented through a high sensitivity to the norms of a particular group. The main abstract principle is to act properly within the given context. These men are thus acting in a wholly consistent way through the inner ideals of their consciences. In line with this, there is a strong tendency within Indians to contextualize any new situation; i.e., to define carefully what is expected, proper behavior appropriate to that situation. As Singer duly noted, a foreign, innovative institution is ultimately accepted into Indian culture when it becomes traditional.

Almost all of the psychoanalytic-anthropological work on the conscience in India and other non-Western countries sees this type of conscience as lacking the internalized structures of the Western superego, and as being basically dependent on externalized controls and guides such as the elders of the family.[43] Implicitly, this is considered to be inferior. From my own psychoanalytic work with Indian patients, I view the Indian conscience as being profoundly internalized into psychic structures that are of a somewhat different nature from those of most Westerners, and which function in a different way.

In terms of child rearing, in the earlier most symbiotic stage of the first few years, gratification is used to distract the child from any wrongdoing or unwanted behavior. Psychoanalytic observations of infant-mother interactions also indicate that the child is enormously sensitive to the mothering person's moods, and may desist from doing something if the child senses that the mother may be upset or angry, even though the mother may not overtly communicate this.[44] This probably becomes the bedrock for the later enormous sensitivity to nonverbal communication, to approbation and criticism from others, and for the splitting of the goddess into benevolent and fierce forms.[45] The child through these first three to four years is regarded as an innocent sent by the gods, and is not viewed as being particularly responsible for his or her own actions.

Around the ages of four to six through most of adolescence there is usually a strong crackdown for proper behavior and attitudes within the various kinship relationships, which seemingly occurs more suddenly for boys and more gradually for girls.[46] Shaming is frequently and successfully used, probably because of the child's enormous investment in maintaining a high self-we regard. The ego-ideal is constantly appealed to, such as, you are children of the same family, how can you fight? Boys tend to be more gratified than girls, who are raised at an earlier age into competency. After the crackdown the child feels that all eyes are on him or her, and proper respect and behavior must be instituted to gain the elders' approbation. Expectations are profoundly integrated with the mythic models and stories that have been internalized from early childhood.

The development of the Indian conscience around aggression and sexuality is wholly consonant with functioning within hierarchical, extended family relationships, and is much more related to ego-ideal than superego functioning. Within close, extended family relationships all kinds of anger and hostility have to be contained and controlled by the individual members in order "not to spoil the atmosphere within which one lives," or to interrupt the strong emotional connectedness.[47] As a result, anger is often unconsciously split off and displaced to extrafamilial relationships, or may frequently be conveyed by all kinds of nonverbal cues, such as suddenly stopping talking, leaving the room, walking around with an unhappy look, or not eating the next meal while conveying the impression that you are feeling perfectly fine. Anger may sometimes be unconsciously displaced to those lower in the hierarchy, or unconsciously turned against the self in the form of depression or not infrequent somatizations.

Sexuality and sensuality is generally more developed in Indian personality than in Western as a result of the prolonged sensuous contacts of early childhood. In contrast to aggression, sensuality is kept within the family, especially with girls. The girl deeply internalizes familial attitudes that she be scrupulously well-behaved in public, avoiding contact with boys so that she may maintain family honor and reputation upon which the arranged marriages are so dependent. Although there is often segregation of the sexes within a traditional Indian household, there are also close contacts between cousins, and with uncles and aunts, and not so infrequent infatuations, with the parents often looking the other way. What is kept within the family will not hurt its reputation.

I have posited the gestalt of the transcendent or spiritual self to take into account the central emphasis in Hindu culture on inner spiritual realization. The transcendent self is both continuous with and counterpoints the familial self. It is clear that the first three aspects of the four Hindu goals of life are more oriented around the familial self—*dharma* (reciprocal responsibilities), *artha* (wealth and power), and *kama* (desire)—whereas *moksha* (spiritual realization and freedom) relates exclusively to the transcendent self. However, it is usually considered necessary to fulfill these first three goals in order to eventually realize the last. Similarly, the first two *ashramas* (stages) in the life cycle are related more to the familial self—student and householder—whereas the last two, as the person fulfills family responsibilities, increasingly relate to spiritual realization. The continuity of the transcendent self with the familial self is mainly through mythic consciousness. That is, the myth deals with both the involved kinship relationships and a spiritual consciousness, the two becoming inseparable as parental figures and elders are experienced as living manifestations of the gods and goddesses. A further aspect of continuity involves the various exchanges and transactions that many anthropologists have emphasized as leading to subtle, inner transformations, the goal being to advance from grosser to more subtle qualities.[48] Then, there is the psychological internalization of a world view of a soul in pilgrimage through many reincarnations, its progression being largely dependent on its *karma* and *samsaras* from past lives and efforts made in the current life.

The counterpoint of the transcendent self with the familial self is present through far greater emphasis on separation, privacy, and individuation within the spiritual sphere than in family relationships. Spiritual practices are based to a considerable extent on individual cognitive style, temperament, emotional makeup, inclinations, motivation and aspirations, talent and capacity, and level of attainment. This degree of individuation is not present in other parts of the culture that are related to the familial self. There is a further aspect of counterpoint in the traditional emphasis on detachment, in which the mind begins to focus on spiritual realization and begins to loosen its emotional involvement in the intense, symbiotic, familial relationships. It is not that the person abandons the responsibilities of the relationship but rather the intense emotional expectations that are a normal part of living in India.[49] This is a far different orientation from the emphasis on separation and individuation in contemporary psychoanalysis, and the actualization of the self and various ego capacities through action and relationships—a broad life goal of contemporary American culture.

Notes

1. America and Americans in this chapter refer to the United States where my psychoanalytic work has been based. Generalizations made about Americans probably apply in the main to the dominant sociocultural and psychosocial modes of Canadians as well, but not necessarily to Central and South Americans, whose family patterns and psychological makeup in certain ways may be more similar to those of Indians.

2. Erik H. Erikson, *Childhood and Society* (New York: W. W. Norton, 1950).

3. See Takeo Doi's *Anatomy of Dependence* (Tokyo, San Francisco, New York: Kodansha International Ltd., 1971); and Sudhir Kakar's *The Inner World: A Psychoanalytic Study of Childhood and Society in India* (Delhi, London, New York: Oxford University Press, 1978).

4. My own experience in India was primarily in Bombay and secondarily in New Delhi, Ahmedabad, and Bangalore. In Bombay, I conducted short-term psychoanalytic therapy with thirteen Indian patients for periods of one to six months on a two- to five-times-a-week basis. These patients came from highly heterogeneous backgrounds reflecting the cosmopolitan nature of Bombay. These five women and eight men all spoke fluent English, came from the middle- and upper-middle classes, and were from five different religious communities: Hindu upper caste, Parsees, Moslem Bori and Agha Khan communities, Christian, and Jewish. Regionally, they came from Maharastra, Gujarat, the Punjab, and Goa. More homogeneity entered into their educational backgrounds as most of them were college graduates over half of whom had done postgraduate work and specialization, a few having achieved some recognition in the arts. Their age range was from nineteen to sixty-three, with the majority in their middle to late twenties and thirties. With only one exception, all of these patients were functioning anywhere from reasonably competently to highly creatively in their work situation and/or families. They were thus very much like others of the educated urban middle- and upper-middle classes, and could by no means be considered deviants or significantly disturbed members of Indian society. This therapeutic work has been supplemented by seeing two South Indian male patients in Bangalore in very short-term therapy. And by having two other North Indian women patients (from Himachal Pradesh and the United Province) in psychoanalytic therapy for a few months each in New York City. Both of these women had a very high level of postgraduate specialization and careers.

This intensive clinical psychoanalytic work was supplemented by other important data that derived from several sources: supervising two psychoanalysts, three students of psychoanalysis, several social workers, and a few psychoanalytically oriented psychiatrists on their Indian patients—some of whom were from lower castes as well as scheduled castes, and who did not necessarily speak English; co-counseling with two female social workers from the Indian Council of Mental Health three groups of female college students for several sessions at three colleges in Bombay with quite different student bodies ranging from traditional lifestyles to moderately modern ones; and sitting in on individual counseling sessions at St. Xavier's college with a psychoanalyst, Mr. Chinwalla, conducting these sessions. Still another important source of clinical data was attending case conferences at a great variety of institutions that included the B. M. Institute of Mental Health in Ahmedabad (the foremost psychoanalytic mental health center in India at the time), the Psychiatry Department of the All-India Institute for Medical Sciences in New Delhi, the students of the Indian Psychoanalytic Society in Bombay, the Indian Council of Mental Health, the Social Service Department of the Atomic Energy Commission, and the Tata Institute for Social Services—all in Bombay, and the National Institute for Mental Health and Neuro Sciences in Bangalore where I also attended group therapy sessions composed of patients and family members from several different families.

Throughout my clinical experience in India I had continuous opportunity for ongoing discussions with other psychoanalytic therapists and various social scientists—particularly from the Centre for the Study of Developing Societies in New Delhi with which I was also affiliated. Supplementing all of this was the large number of lectures I gave, some of them concerning my work, where various mental health professionals and/or social scientists would make valuable comments or critiques. This included meeting daily for a week's time with the senior staff at the B. M. Institute of Mental Health to discuss a variety of questions and issues about the Indian psyche and relationships with which I was grappling—an invaluable experience.

In contrast, I have well over fiteen years' experience in psychoanalytic work in New York City with a wide variety of persons from different ethnic groups and social classes, most of whom I have seen for at least three years. I have also supervised a number of students in psychoanalytic training, have taught courses at two psychoanalytic institutes for a number of years, and have been director of the Training Institute and Chairman of Scientific Programs at the National Psychological Association for Psychoanalysis in New York City, the largest multidisciplinary psychoanalytic institute in the United States.

5. An excellent example of this type of approach is Warner Muensterberger's summary paper on psychoanalytic-anthropological work on separation and symbiotic processes in non-Western societies: "Psyche and Environment: Sociocultural Variations in Separation and Individuation," *Psychoanalytic Quarterly* 38 (1969): 191–216.

6. Heinz Hartmann, *Essays on Ego Psychology* (New York: International Universities Press, 1964).

7. Erik Erikson, *Identity, Youth and Crisis* (New York: W. W. Norton, 1968).

8. Heinz Kohut, *Analysis of the Self* (New York: International Universities Press, 1971).

9. D. W. Winnicott, *The Maturational Processes and the Facilitating Environment* (New York: International Universities Press, 1965): Esther Menaker and William Menaker, *Ego in Evolution* (New York: Grove Press, 1965); Hans Loewald, "The Nature of the Therapeutic Process," *InternaJournal of Psycho-Analysis* 41 (1960); and comments made by Heinz Kohut at a symposium of the American Psychoanalytic Association, December 1979.

10. *Jiva Atma or Finite Self*, ed. Swami B. H. Bon Maharaj (Vrindaban, India: Institute of Oriental Philosophy, 1963).

11. Splits in the organization of the self have been discussed at length by Kohut in *Analysis of the Self*, and also in *Restoration of the Self* (New York: International Universities Press, 1977.)

12. André Beteille, "Family and Social Change in India and Other South Asian Countries," *Economic Weekly* (February 1964).

13. Veena Das, "Masks and Faces: An Essay on Punjabi Kinship," Contributions to *Indian Sociology* 10 (1976): 1–30.

14. Michael Moffitt, *Untouchability in a South Indian Community* (Princeton, Princeton University Press, 1977).

15. Francis L. K. Hsu, "Psychological Homeostasis and Jen: Conceptual Tools for Advancing Psychological Anthropology," *American Anthropologist* 73 (1971): 23–44.

16. Takeo Doi, *The Anatomy of Dependence* (Tokyo, New York & San Francisco: Kodansha International Ltd., 1973).

17. Sudhir Kakar, *The Inner World: A Psychoanalytic Study of Childhood and Society in India* (Delhi, Oxford, and New York: Oxford University Press, 1978), pp. 86, 124–25.

18. S. K. Pande, "The Mystique of Western Psychotherapy: An Eastern Interpretation," *Journal of Nervous and Mental Diseases* 46 (1968): 425–32.

19. Personal communication from Mrs. Loveleen Posmenteir, a psychoanalyst and member of the National Psychological Association for Psychoanalysis.

20. Personal communication from Dr. B. K. Ramanujam, formerly clinical director of the B. M. Institute for Mental Health in Ahmedabad.

21. Personal communication from Professor A. K. Ramanujan of the University of Chicago.

22. The self-object refers to the psychological meaning of the other for oneself, not necessarily the actual relationship that is going on.

23. Kohut, *Analysis of the Self* and *Restoration of the Self*.

24. Personal communication from Professor Neki, formerly president of the Indian Psychiatric Association. Professor Neki's point is that the individual in India individuates in practices such as meditation or prayer apart from social relationships, which then has a profound social impact.

25. Personal communication from Dr. Sobhan Lal, an Indian psychiatrist who is receiving psychoanalytic training in the United States.

26. Kakar, *The Inner World*.

27. Das, "Masks and Faces."

28. Kakar, *The Inner World*. Exceptions would have to be made of certain ethnic groups in America from southern Europe and Africa, as well as Jews and Armenians.

29. Margaret Mahler, Fred Pine, and Annie Bergman. *The Psychological Birth of the Human Infant* (New York: Basic Books, 1975). Edith Jacobson, *The Self and Object World* (New York: International Universities Press, 1964).

30. Personal communication.

31. I was conducting a discussion of this film, which was part of the regular film program for colleges run by the Indian Council for Mental Health in Bombay.

32. Mahler, Pine, and Bergman, *The Psychological Birth of the Human Infant*.

33. Muensterberger, "Psyche and Environment."

34. D. W. Winnicott, *Maturational Processes.*

35. For a more thorough discussion of transitional objects and the separation and individuation processes, see *Between Reality and Fantasy*, ed. Simon Grolnick and Leonard Barkin (New York: Jason Aronson, 1978).

36. D. M. Bassa, "From the Traditional to the Modern: Some Observations on Changes in Indian Child Rearing and Parental Attitudes," in *The Child and His Family in a Changing World*, ed. E. J. Anthony and C. Chiland (New York: John Wiley, 1978).

37. Anandalakshmi, *Socialization for Competence* (Delhi: Indian Council for Social Science Research, 1978).

38. David Riesman, Reuel Denney, and Nathan Glazer. *The Lonely Crowd: A Study of the Changing American Character* (New Haven: Yale University Press, 1951).

39. Personal communication from Dr. Parmar, Psychology Department National Institute for Mental Health and Neuro Sciences, Bangalore.

40. Personal communication from B. K. Ramanujam.

41. A. K. Ramanujan, "Is There an Indian Way of Thinking?" Unpublished paper presented at a Social Science Research Council Committee Meeting on "The Person in South Asia," Chicago, September, 1980.

42. Milton Singer, *When a Great Tradition Modernizes* (New York: Praeger Publishers, 1972).

43. Muensterberger, "Psyche and Environment"; Kakar, *The Inner World.*

44. Personal communication from Udayan Patel, a psychoanalyst in Bombay.

45. This formulation emerged from discussions with B. K. Ramanujam.

46. This observation was confirmed by a number of psychoanalysts. For fuller descriptions see Kakar's *The Inner World* and D. M. Bassa's "From the Traditional to the Modern . . ."

47. Personal communication from Dr. Erna Hoch, a psychiatrist with many years of experience in India.

48. McKim Marriott, "Hindu Transactions: Diversity Without Dualism," in *Transaction and Meaning, Directions in the Anthropology of Exchange and Symbolic Behavior*, ed. B. Kapferer (Philadelphia: ISHI Publishing, 1976).

49. Personal communication from B. K. Ramanujam.

IV
Poetry, Politics, and the Sense of Self

6

The Self-Person of Surrealism

Sarah Lawall

> Let us remember that the idea of surrealism tends simply towards the total recuperation of our psychic force by a means that is nothing else than the dizzying descent in ourselves, the systematic illumination of hidden places and the progressive darkening of other places, perpetual promenade in the middle of forbidden zones.[1]

Surrealism, according to this famous definition from the Second Manifesto, is a probing of inner depths to take possession of our full self, a plunge into darker zones of the subconscious not for any exclusive interest they may have but because they make up a less recognized half of human experience. Surrealists constantly focus on the discovery, liberation, and development of the self, and on the possible ways for this self to enter history. Yet there is another well-known passage from the First Manifesto that seems to deny the importance of individual human beings (or rather the existence of individual selves other than the speaker) when André Breton claims that "the simplest surrealist act consists in taking revolvers in hand and, descending into the street, shooting at random into the crowd as long as one can" (*Man.* 78). Clearly there is a great difference in value between *selves,* with their recuperable psychic force, and *persons,* identified by their exterior appearance and social situation. Breton is counting on the proposal's shock value to startle the reader into paying serious attention, but when he later defends himself he reverts to an implied distinction between self and person. This simplest act is "not at all incompatible with the belief in that glimmer that surrealism tries to reveal in our depths"; rather, it expresses despair with the leveling and humiliation caused by social systems. It is a test of imagination and strong feeling, showing whether a person is "endowed with violence" in the first place, and has the sense of "not-accepting" that is so important in developing a free imagination (*Man.* 79). Taken together, the two passages show a tight but uncomfortable relationship between the idea of self as a spontaneous, active inner awareness capable of thought, emotion, and growth, and that of person as a socially situated identity, shaped and reflected by outer circumstances and people.

Surrealism may dislike the way society shapes a person and not a self, but it does not isolate itself from recognizing that influence. Beginning in Dadaist revolt against bourgeois habits of mind, surrealism issued many a manifesto attacking the abuse of legal, penal, governmental, and psychiatric authority; spoke out against war and oppression; flirted with Marxism as a pragmatic extension of its own absolute quest; and worked for social reform through the liberation of the mind from stereotyped ideas and constricting civilizational values. It recognizes the need to insert oneself in history but, paradoxically, it must do so while asserting the self and resisting the pull of historical definition—definition as a person. In one sense, this is a contradiction in terms if the categories *self* and *person* exist at all: Breton himself exists as a historical figure, a person and even a personage, as he was well aware. However, the acceptance of this situation is another matter, and individual surrealists struggled to maintain themselves as selves, in perpetual growth and action, and to insert this concept of a spontaneous, revolutionary, fully aware consciousness into the process of history.

For our purposes, it may be useful to situate surrealism in general terms inside a civilizational perspective and to relate it to some of the concepts suggested by Vytautas Kavolis in "Logics of Selfhood and Modes of Order."[2] Inside the cultural logic described by Kavolis, surrealism takes its place as a form of neo-Romanticism: common to both movements are the rejection of formal constraints, an emphasis on the self developed to its fullest potential, glorification of the individual versus the crowd, the figure of a visionary genius (the artist or prophet who may shock his contemporaries but is a truly human and profoundly moral prophet: Shelley's "legislator of the world"), a certain mysticism revolving around the desire for a transfigured everyday life, and a practice of involving oneself in social comment and often revolutionary action. Such an ancestry was certainly recognized by the surrealists, whose leader Breton once commented that they were the "prehensile tail" of Romanticism (*Man.* 110).

The story becomes more complicated when we move to specific frameworks for the self inside cultural logic. Although the most comprehensively applicable framework suggested by Kavolis is that of "coincidence-logic" (inasmuch as the self—however uniquely felt—is considered potentially in tune with the structure of the universe), several aspects of surrealist experience touch on other metaphysical presuppositions. Briefly, Kavolis proposes four major frameworks for the logic of the self: "*a unique pattern of enduring internal coherence,*" "*coincidence of the subjectively sensed core of experience of the empirically concrete individual with the essential structure, or fundamental quality, of the universe to which the concrete individual is oriented,"* "a submerged luminosity . . . that gives a hint of its presence only in moments of the most vivid, or purest, *peak experiences,"* or "a process of *casual encounters,"* a passively experienced manipulation of the self by historical contingencies. He adds:

> The unique-pattern and coincidence logics presume a self that has an enduring structure . . . the peak-experience and casual-encounter logics presume a self that has an unstable, processual structure. The peak-experience and coincidence selves are "transcendent" in the sense that the true self is located outside the ordinary everyday activities of the individual (and is not fully, without residue, expressed in them); the casual-encounter and unique-pattern selves are "immanently" located within the ordinary everyday activities of the individual. . . . (Kav. 48–49)

The four models exist at a highly abstract level of civilizational analysis, even though they have been arrived at heuristically. Kavolis hypothesizes further that there is a probably cyclic evolution from casual-encounter logic to peak-experience, coincidence, and unique-pattern logic, the cycle beginning again once a civilization has experienced all four stages of selfhood. Since these stages—as cultural models—cover a range of civilizational observations over great periods of time, during which one attitude will imperceptibly blend with and shade off into another, it is not surprising that the application of the models to a particular movement will demonstrate one dominant attitude with contributing aspects from others. Thus peak experience has great significance for the surrealists: they are on the watch for those magical occasions, in love or the shock of surprise or coincidence, when the self suddenly experiences the "marvelous" and exists in a miraculous perspective known as the "sublime point." Mutuality is ideally felt in the peak experience of shared love, experienced by the monogamous androgynous couple. With its emphasis on the preordained fusion of two individuals (the androgyne), and on the bodily achievement of a visionary state, the surrealist peak experience is part of a coincidence-logic that reveals connections with a natural universe when formal constraints are abolished. There is another way in which aspects of the "casual-encounters" logic seem to apply: in rejecting the kind of transcendental mysticism that saw divine reasons for everything, Breton and his friends emphasized the random and material nature of their experience—welcoming, in fact, the eruption of chance into their world as a means of combating deceptively coherent world views. Chance and casual encounters are really co-opted in this approach, however, which merely absorbs the sense of otherness and materiality that is part of all experience, and prepares its incorporation into a coincidence-logic. In this logic, the surrealist self—although undergoing imaginative metamorphoses—remains basically stable, a single subjective self relating consistently to the world and to other people. Although it rejects transcendentalism, living a supremely realistic existence according to the revealed patterns of dialectical materialism,[3] surrealism still measures everything by the "marvelous" perspective that refocuses and transfigures everyday existence.

At a more intuitive and less explicit level of organization, says Kavolis, we find the global comprehension of order and disorder: symbolic frameworks that have "particularly important implications for the organization of individual identities" (Kav. 50). Concepts of order and disorder penetrate the cultural logics and show some of the same combinatory richness. With surrealism, for example, there is the incorporation of significant disorder inside a larger implied pattern, much as coincidence absorbs casual encounters. Of the four patterns of order hypothesized by Kavolis: "lawful Nature," "spontaneous Nature," the "factory," and the "work of art," surrealism has most in common with a subset of lawful Nature. The apparent chaos and calculated disruption of Dada-surrealism exist either as an obverse of initial patterns, or as an attempt to redress an unnatural imbalance. Early surrealist activities show a straightforward pattern of trying to turn ordinary expectation topsy-turvy: art exhibits entered through a public lavatory; lectures announced at which the speakers squabble and insult the audience; a mock trial held of an eminent writer who is represented by a tailor's dummy; the interpretation of madness as truer vision; and a general attack on all the traditional ideals of religion, family, patriotism, and Cartesian logic that provided unquestioned models for behavior. Insofar as these demonstrations are reactions, they are governed by the original expectations of order. In addition, their calculated rupture constitutes what Kavolis calls a "sacred disordering" and a "miraculous intrusion" into overly codified behavior, allowing previously repressed elements to be reintegrated into a total experience (Kav. 49–50, 54). As the philosopher Ferdinand Alquié has said, the surrealists espouse "a principle of order and coordination distinct from reason."[4] Their emphasis on dreams and the subconscious (over conscious will), on eroticism (over Victorian proprieties), on free association (over cause-and-effect rationality), and on the acceptance of chance (over syllogistic logic) aims to reintegrate the "dark side" of human experience within a full human identity, and thus to reaffirm the true balance of natural law. Once again, there are shadings from other concepts of order: in one sense, the surrealist world— unpredictable, changing, full of chance encounters and subconscious pulls—implies a spontaneous universe unfettered by natural law. Certainly there is no notion of divine order, or a God-given hierarchy among men. However, if the paradigm of spontaneous Nature is truly spontaneous— not allowing for rights, obligations, or criteria of judgment—then it cannot really account for the surrealists' moral humanism and their goal of a fully realized human being capable of experiencing the "marvelous." Possibly the "factory" model is implied in the surrealist love for games, and their fascination with transforming raw (or conventional) materials into new and strange shapes. There is indeed an emphasis on transient experience, and a rejection of fixed forms in favor of perpetual creation, but this creation does not "produce." Rather, it is a developmental activity allowing the self to explore its different possibilities. Ultimately the surrealist self transcends production as it transcends the work of art: both factory and work of art offer finished forms judged "well-made" by formal or external criteria, and thus do not correspond to the idea of an individual interior order. Marxist critics may be correct that surrealist ideals reflect the absolutist individual assumptions of the same Judaeo-Christian tradition they reject: in spite of glimpses of an irrational, unpredictable, materialist universe they retain the image of a potentially unified human individual exploiting his sur-roundings rather than being subservient to the processes of history.

The previous generalizations about surrealism are fairly accurate and supported by documentation. Nevertheless, surrealism is probably matched only by existentialism in the number of popular misinterpreta-tions to which it has been subject (aided, of course, by the surrealists' constant attempt to avoid codification) and it is useful before proceeding further to outline our boundaries of reference. Surrealism is not merely a grotesque and impotent revolt of adolescent minds against the sound com-mon sense and even sounder morals of their ancestors; it is rather a move-ment with historical, philosophical, and cultural roots that constitutes the most important influence in literature and art since Symbolism. Yet there is no one historical definition of the surrealist period. In addition to the numerous quarrels, exiles, withdrawals, and reformations of the initial surrealist group (dating from Breton's *First Manifesto* and the official jour-nal *La Révolution surréaliste* in 1924), there is no agreement as to when—or whether—the movement actually ended. Maurice Nadeau, in a 1957 addi-tion to his *Histoire du surréalisme* (1944), considers that the movement had played its part by the time of World War II.[5] Yet Breton, the chief surrealist figure, continued to speak of "surrealism in its living works" ("Du surréalisme dans ses oeuvres vives," 1953) and to encourage the formation of new surrealist groups until his death in 1966. One of Breton's new-followers, Jean-Louis Bédouin, published another study to follow directly upon Nadeau's: *Vingt ans de surréalisme, 1939–1959 (Twenty Years of Surreal-ism, 1939–1959).*[6] Some take Breton's death as a terminal date for surreal-ism; yet groups on both sides of the Atlantic either consider themselves surrealists or disavow the label (as unsurrealistically fixed) while reaffirming the spirit of the movement. Herbert Gershman's *The Surrealist Revolution in France* provides a chronology running from the surrealist origins in Dada up to 1968. J. H. Matthews, in *Toward the Poetics of Surreal-ism*, analyzes contemporary as well as early evidence, and the Canadian poet Jean Benoît surely took his surrealism seriously on December 2, 1959, when he ritualistically branded himself with the letters S A D E in the presence of his friends.[7] Surrealism is very much alive in our day, both in specific groups and as an attitude of radical interrogation. For our own purposes, however, we concentrate upon the early surrealist group, usually taken as defining the movement, and especially the work of Breton, whose lifelong dedication to surrealism makes him, according to Alquié, the "es-sence and norm for the philosophy of surrealism."[8]

Another complication that arises in describing the surrealist self is that the surrealists frequently tested it in relation to other movements of libera-tion, and explored different ways of affirming their surrealist identity. When these ways involved commitment to national politics, or the submis-sion of intellectual freedom to more pressing needs (the abandonment of the autonomous self), those concerned usually ceased to consider them-selves—or to be considered—surrealists. Yet often the dividing line is not clear, especially if the initial move outside the group came as an attempt to express the self in appropriate political action. Such was the commitment of Louis Aragon, who considered himself a true revolutionary and refused to hide behind claims of artistic freedom when he was brought to trial for his revolutionary poem "Front Rouge." And Paul Eluard, who joined the French Resistance in 1940 and whose patriotic and didactic poetry after that time was far from his first surrealist mode, still believed in the essential continuity of his surrealist convictions enough to ask Alquié in 1945 to write an article showing the connections between surrealism and the Resist-ance.[9] Although the surrealists' goal was a revolution of the mind, with an individual rather than a political focus, that did not prevent their being tempted by the possibility of extending the self into effective social action through other more pragmatic ideologies. Nor is it easy to consider this temptation a compromise, for the refusal to act can also be seen as a refusal to *exist* in accord with supposed principles. Jean Schuster asserts that sur-realist groups from the 1920s to the 1960s actually prepared the student revolts in Paris in May 1968,[10] but this perspective was not available to the early surrealists and they often sought more immediate support in commu-nism and a related Hegelianism whose process of dialectic seemed close to their own emphasis on transformation, and whose theory of history of-fered an objective materialist base for their own intuitional approach. How-ever genuine these attachments were, they were never permitted to regulate the surrealists' essential criterion of absolute freedom of the imagination. When the attempt to enter history threatened to define their modes of being, to change self into person, those who continued to call themselves surrealists withdrew from the competing faith and the others withdrew from the surrealists.

Surrealism is usually seen as growing out of the Dada movement which flourished from 1916 to 1922 in Zurich and Paris, although some would see two distinct and enduring movements, with Dada always more negative and centered on the absurd. Certainly the chief figures of surrealism: Breton, Soupault, Péret, Eluard, Aragon, and Desnos, were also active in Dada, and Tristan Tzara, a founder of Dada, was a surrealist for a number of years. But Dada is particularly known for a spirit of absolute revolt, a gigantic refusal aimed at the whole cultural baggage of traditional logic and morality, and at political, religious, and artistic proprieties. The violence of Dada's attack sprang from a poignant historical consciousness on the part of the young intelligentsia who had either fled or taken part in World War I that they were not being consulted in matters of life and death but rather expected to follow the worn-out traditions of a moribund society. "This war was not ours," says Tzara; "enduring it, we felt the falseness of its sentiments and the mediocrity of its excuses."[11] The Dadaist Manifesto of 1918 reacted to this falseness by proclaiming nonsense, destruction, and aimlessness. "DADA MEANS NOTHING . . . Let every man cry: there is a great work of destruction and negation to be accomplished. Sweeping away, cleaning out . . . Without goal or plan, without organization: untameable madness, decomposition."[12] Tzara's *Approximate Man* (1931) describes a lost, alienated, fragmented, and imperfect self:

> I speak of the one who speaks who speaks I am alone
> I am only a little sound I have several sounds in me . . .
> approximate man like me like you reader and like the others
> heap of noisy flesh and echoes of conscience.[13]

Despite the "ineffable fullness surrounding us with the impossible" and the envisioned "nocturnal peace strong fragrance nocturnal peace," Tzara's self is insecure and unstable ("facing others you are another than yourself . . ." *ApMan* 51) and unable to believe in its own reality: "I think of the warmth spun by the word / around its center the dream / called ourselves" (*ApMan* 44). At the mock trial at which Barrès was to be condemned for crimes against the human spirit, Tzara as witness tried to subvert the trial by proclaiming "we are all a group of slobs, and . . . little differences (big slobs or little slobs) have no importance."[14] Tzara called this total anarchy a "new intellectual heroism . . . a moral movement,"[15] but ultimately he was not satisfied with what he called Dada's unproductive rebellion and turned to the pragmatic political action of orthodox communism. Breton, the judge at the trial, wished to use the opportunity to pronounce a serious condemnation of Barrès' compromise and moral cowardice. Disagreeing with Tzara, Breton proposed to give Dada's "negative spirit an executive power,"[16] and to change the context of revolt from a despairing negative gesture—however pure—to a specific moral commitment. This commit-

ment to the systematic liberation of human imagination would provide a
focus for the self and a rationale for its survival. It is probably not fruitful
to try to distinguish Dadaism from surrealism beyond the general and
certainly simplified view: for one thing, texts of the two movements have
too many points in common. Both stress revolt, antirationalism, spontaneity, the destruction of traditional norms, the freeing of the unconscious
mind, and a political and cultural internationalism. Surrealist revolt would
develop, however, by exploring the concept of the liberated imagination,
and of *desire*, a characteristic surrealist term that expressed both the erotic
overtones of the liberated unconscious and a constant, freely metamor-
phosing, optimistic extension of the self toward the unknown and the
Other.

Imagination and desire shape the concept of human being in surrealist
thought. In this secular ideology, the awakening and fulfillment of the full
being are the main criteria of value. Dualism is rejected: both the dualism
of subject and object that separates a person from the surrounding world
now become an object of contemplation, and the Platonic dualism that
separates human nature into higher and lower faculties and cultivates reason to realize human potential. Any definition of the human condition, said
Breton, must take into consideration the two worlds of dream and reality,
subconscious and conscious experience. Certainly the surrealists were not
alone in this discovery, and Breton, whose wartime experience with
shellshocked soldiers at the psychiatric center of St. Dizier had given him
insights into the "other world" of madness and nightmare, constantly mentions Freud as the key to a new understanding of the human mind. Yet
theirs is a peculiarly moral view of the new psychology, for they refuse to
accept complexes, aberrations, or sexual drive as explanations for human
conduct, and choose rather to see in them the many channels used by the
mind in developing its own freedom. Their search for imaginative freedom
was matched by a simultaneous impulse of desire, a less easily articulated
(because irrational) concept that implies a state of eagerness and curiosity,
an urge for possession, an intense, almost-mystical attraction for the "marvelous" revealed in the exclusive abandonment of love, or in the chance
configurations of everyday life seized by intuition at one of those visionary
moments or "sublime points" that were the goal of surrealist activity. As
both of these concepts involve attitudes rather than categorical definitions,
and thus remain true to the surrealist insistence on freedom and metamorphosis, they constitute guidelines for a movement that must be seen in
action, exploring the strength and validity of its intuitions and their possible realization.

The *First Surrealist Manifesto* begins by describing the predicament of
modern man as he reaches adulthood: locked into a conventional routine
dictated by practical necessity, he is no longer able to envisage, as in child-

hood, "the perspective of several lives lived simultaneously," or to live any of life's "exceptional situations" (such as love) at full intensity. The imagination that modern man subordinated to practical necessity has abandoned him to mediocrity, and there is no return. "Beloved imagination, what I especially love about you is that you do not forgive" (*Man.* 12). As an absolute value, imagination requires complete dedication before it will yield its rewards: a limitless future, the power to take control of one's destiny and live life to the fullest. Imagination tells us what *can be*, thus opening up to us the possibility of growth and change; in terms that suggest a biblical sense of condemnation and exile in the world, Breton calls upon the imagination as the only thing that can "lift somewhat the terrible interdiction." It is the quintessential human quality, our own "legitimate aspiration" and the "supreme justice" (*Man* 13). This dedication to liberating essential humanity persists throughout Breton's works. As he says in *Arcane 17* (1945), the goal is to "evoke from human sensibility everything it can give" (*Arc.* 16). Science and technology cannot provide the ultimate liberation, for these rational pursuits more usually have contributed to our misery. Instead, the intuitive phenomena—"love, poetry, art"—restore human confidence and revitalize thought (*Man.* 32). The romanticism of this attitude should not obscure the fact that Breton is not speaking of transcendental aims: this is a secular mysticism,[17] a purely terrestrial awakening in which unconscious impulses energize the mind's full play and liberate an otherwise stifled individuality.

The assumptions of contemporary society directly negated individual human nature as the surrealists conceived it, and it became their moral duty to destroy the constricting formulas that framed the average person's life. Singled out are the bulwarks of conservative bourgeois society: family, nation, and religion. All means are good to destroy this abject trinity, says Breton, and there can be no compromise (*AFou* 136, *Man.* 82). The notion of family is too often used to codify spontaneous emotions and to prescribe acceptable or unacceptable forms of love (see the group statement, "Hands Off Love" defending Charlie Chaplin against his wife's accusations).[18] Or the family may be a setting for the most hideous cruelty and injustice and still be upheld by a society that finds its first interest in maintaining stable institutions, as exemplified by the celebrated trial of Violette Nozières, who was convicted of parricide and being an unnatural daughter for poisoning her parents after being repeatedly beaten and violated by her father.[19] Finally, the family was the first and most powerful shaper of thought and morality. Even beyond economic dependence and the traditional subordination of European youth to their parents (documented for women by Simone de Beauvoir), there was the early, insidious channeling of the imagination into accepted patterns. One of the most amusing passages in "Du temps où les surréalistes avaient raison" ("When the surrealists were

right," a group statement of 1935) is a series of letters translated from a
Pravda article titled "Respect Your Parents." These letters, from repentant
or righteous young Communists determined to set a good example, demonstrated to the surrealists "the completely conformist misery" and "process of rapid regression" into which the Russian Revolution had sunk. First
the idea of nation and then that of family has survived, they note bitterly:
all that is left is to reestablish religion and private property (*Hist.* 430–32).
Yet family, country, private property, and religion all alienate human beings from a sense of personal responsibility; the first three channel energies
into established economic or political structures, and the last directs any
hope for change into the otherworldly realm of religion. All formulate
ideals that transcend the individual—absolute values outside the self—and
are therefore set apart from living experience. Such experience, as the
existentialists would later say, cannot be frozen but must be accepted in all
its fluidity and change: totally alive at each moment, it is the only possible
context for the surrealist self.

If family, country, and religion all provide constricting models that
must be exploded to realize the self, what of art? Many critics have felt that
surrealism is merely another artistic movement, an interesting variation in
the great tradition and soon to be absorbed into academic history. Inasmuch as surrealist writing and painting are now commonly taught, there is
something to be said for this point of view. On the other hand, nothing
could be farther from the surrealists' view of themselves and their consistent aims. Tzara asserts that surrealist poetry is an "*activity* of the mind . . .
one can be a poet without ever having written a line . . . there is a quality of
poetry in the street, in a commercial spectacle, anywhere."[20] Anyone can be
a poet, for the criterion is a spontaneous lyric attitude, a visionary activity in
which the alert observer puts together elements of daily life in unaccus-
tomed juxtaposition—chance discoveries at the flea market, coincidences
whose recognition proposes a sudden new structuring of existence—and
"writes" with his or her life: perhaps the first instance of poetry as happening. The "beauty" of this poetry is the indescribable experience of the
marvelous: "the marvelous is always beautiful, any marvelous is beautiful,
there is even nothing but the marvelous that is beautiful" (*Man.* 24). Traditional artistic criteria like clarity and precision are "profoundly
insignificant," constituting an artificial veneer that misrepresents the human spirit and offers false ideals for admiration. "Behind the amorality of
style . . . we denounce the amorality of man" (*Hist.* 224). Surrealist writing
represents the true self through dreams, clusters of significant images,
random jottings, and the dictation of the unconscious. It rejects a linear,
coherent discourse just as the surrealist rejects logic and rationality as keys
to existence. Logic solves only "secondary problems," says the *First Manifesto:* "cannot dreaming be applied, also, to resolving the fundamental
questions of life?" (Man. 18, 21–22).

This oneiric idealism has its own prophets, saints, vision, and quasi-religious vocabulary. Breton claims in "Légitime Défense" ("Legitimate Defense," 1926) that "We are endowed . . . with the gift of speech and, by it, something great and obscure tends imperiously to express itself through us . . . each one of us has been chosen . . . from a thousand to formulate what must be formulated in our lifetime. It is an order we have received . . . as if we had been condemned to it through all eternity" (*Hist.* 235–36). It is a "mysticism against God,"[21] initially cut off from mundane matters: Aragon calls the Russian Revolution "at most a vague ministerial crisis" (*Hist.* 205), and although Breton promises "We will have utopia [*l'au-delà*—the "beyond"] in our own time," he also avoids any pragmatic commitments: "Who speaks of . . . making us contribute to abominable earthly comfort?" (*Hist.* 226). Later, when Aragon has become an orthodox Communist and Breton an admirer of Trotsky, the emphasis is on finding the proper political channels for surrealist revolutionary energy, rather than isolating oneself from involvement. Nonetheless, Trotsky, in one of his meetings with Breton, commented gently that the latter kept "a little window open on the 'beyond,'" (*Clé* 62), and it is clear from the surrealist insistence on the "marvelous," on revelation, and on sublime experience that there is a personal rather than societal vision at the core. Breton, listing a series of miraculous coincidences that led him to describe, in a poem of 1932 ("Tournesol") a 1934 meeting with his future wife, affirms "the clearly *revelatory* character" of such coincidences, in which "all things are given over to complete transparency, connected by a glass chain where not one link is missing . . . a dazzling contact of man with the world of things" (*AFou* 49). Surrealist art and poetry regularly display a transfigured world that is neither objective reality nor a God-given illumination, but a reassembly of familiar elements into a new "surreal" picture fusing viewer and viewed, or human subjectivity and nature. Thus, this short poem by Eluard, in which the lover's perspective fuses the image of the woman he loves with the life of the landscape:

> Nature is caught in the nets of your life.
> The tree, your shadow, shows its bare flesh: the sky.
> It has the voice of sand and the gestures of wind
> And everything you say moves behind you.[22]

It is the vision of such a world—freely imagined, sensuously present, fully integrated and harmonious—that surrealism aims to make possible for everyone. Practical politics has little to do with it: this is not a picture that can be transposed into urban renewal or agricultural reform, even though it may be easier to achieve such reforms when individual minds are capable of similar ingenuity. Nor is it religiously inspired, reflecting a mystic truth whose origin is outside the world. This ideal vision is purely subjective, but can be communicated on the imaginative level though the magical power of language: "Earth is blue like an orange / Never a mistake words do not lie."[23]

But imagination can be lost. The danger, says the *First Manifesto*, is that adulthood obscures the importance of imagination—and perhaps even the ability to recognize it. Conforming to the role of responsible adult in a bourgeois society, pressured into a routine, repetitive existence that imperceptibly closes off avenues to the unknown, we become content to relate everything to familiar stereotypes and to resist the possibility of surprise or change. Every new experience is measured by (and thus reduced to) preexisting categories, and we greatly overestimate the importance of what is already known compared to what remains to be known (*AFou* 49). The ways that we can envisage reality are consequently much diminished, unless we take active steps to revitalize our perspective. The surrealists experimented with many ways to loosen the hold of habit and rationality: dream, hypnosis, automatism, games, group creativity responding to "objective chance," and erotic love. Rejecting custom and logic, they solicited the special perspective of the unconscious mind or of madness. Breton's experience as assistant in the psychiatric clinic of St. Dizier, and the surrealists' general interest in psychoanalysis, as Freud's works were translated and popularized, suggested that there was a whole world of the unconscious imagination that could be tapped if the appropriate techniques were devised. Madness itself, "the madness they lock up" (*Man.* 13), seemed as legitimate an attitude as sanity. In an open "Letter to the Head-Doctors of Insane Asylums" (1925), the surrealists claimed that asylums were merely jails and workshops for those who did not conform: "We affirm the absolute legitimacy of their conception of reality . . . you have only the advantage of superior force" (*Hist.* 212). As expected, this attitude did not find much favor with practicing psychiatrists, who felt that it overlooked the pain and unhappiness of many mental illnesses and could even lead to a revolt in the asylum. Breton's *Second Manifesto* is preceded by an article and discussion reprinted from the "Medico-psychological Annals" in which a group of psychiatrists complain about his *Nadja,* a copy of which had been given to a doctor by an inmate who had underlined the following passage: "I know that if I were insane, and locked up for several days, I would profit by a remission in my delirium coldly to assassinate any one of them who was close at hand, preferably the doctor. . . . Then maybe they would leave me alone" (*Man.* 72). The lesson of Nadja is rather ambivalent, for although the heroine's commitment to total liberty is admired (she accepts her madness and does end up in an asylum), Breton makes it clear that he is unable to follow her example.[24] Madness seems to be a symbol (like the revolver shots mentioned at the beginning); its value as an alternative view of reality is available only to one who can compare, who can move in and out of the alternate state and thus actually control the processes of imagination.

If Breton could not actually abandon himself into madness, he did try to adopt its perspective as much as possible by writing, with Paul Eluard, a simulation of five states of mental illness from mental weakness to dementia praecox. *The Immaculate Conception* (*L'Immaculée Conception,* 1930) also imagines other frames of the self by simulating consciousness during various stages of life including conception, life in the womb, and death. In its programmatic aspect, *The Immaculate Conception* already reflects conscious control and thus a certain artificiality, but it is best known for its attempt to espouse the rhythms of the self through the stream-of-consciousness method of automatic writing. This spontaneous "dictation of thought," or "psychic automatism," takes place whenever one writes what comes to mind—quickly, abundantly, without any corrections or preconceived end. It is available to anyone who wants to recover the depths of his or her imagination, for the uncontrolled flow of words is supposed to evoke those elemental clusters of images that reflect our basic drives and bring us back to a common mythology. (Breton never really considers the problem that what rises to the surface may also be the most stereotyped, habitual references engendered by the society and not a primitive self.) Psychic automatism can be produced by other circumstances too, and surrealists used both the retelling of dreams and experiments with hypnosis as a means of releasing the voice of the unconscious from rational control. Soon hypnosis was no longer necessary, and during the famous "period of sleepwriting" (1922) a number of surrealists claimed to be able to fall asleep at will and then to speak at length and answer questions.

Although automatic writing was supposed to put one in contact with a larger sense of reality, it did so only by a completely subjective plunge into the self. Other strategies reached outside, either putting the surrealist in contact with the group or forcing recognition of objective chance. Surrealism has been accused of being otherworldly in that it reaches from the self directly to the "beyond," and avoids pragmatic action in the world for a glimpse of fulfillment in some sublime moment or far in the future. To a certain extent this is true but there is an important difference in the fact that the surrealist "beyond" is composed of earthly reality and human perceptions. Surrealist methods for reaching outside the self usually aim at joining several selves, creating an anonymous production to release the true voice of the unknown; they call upon random happenings and chance discoveries to impose a new (but still subjective) perception on the group. Shared automatic texts (Soupault and Breton, *Les Champs magnétiques/ Magnetic Fields,* 1919; Breton, Char, Eluard, *Ralentir Travaux / Slow Down, Men at Work,* 1930) and games like the "exquisite corpse" in which members of a group take turns writing lines of a poem (or sections of a drawing) on pieces of paper that are folded to hide the previous work and then passed, draw their disconcerting effect from the impression of a communication that is both human and unreal. It is a group activity that is suddenly objective and anonymous, intertwining several personalities inside a larger framework that seems to speak from beyond, challenging the reader to derive his or her own interpretation of the whole and thus—incidentally—forcing the reader back into a subjectivity that momentarily had been put into contact with otherness. In the game of "one in the other" ("l'un dans l'autre"), which makes ever greater use of group interaction, participants choose a particular image (for example, a chestnut or a wild boar) to propose to a player who is secretly identifying with another image (such as a soap bubble or chocolate bar). The latter player now describes himself as a chestnut (or boar) but with such slanted detail that the second image is gradually implied. The game ends when the previously unrelated images are inextricably joined, and the group finally identifies the player's hidden identity. Both the game of shared creation and the game of chance, in which players grope toward hidden relationships, are methods for the surrealist player to gain knowledge of what exists outside. Objective chance can fill the same role as partners in a game, for it supplies the uncontrollable, unpredictable intervention from outside that forces the limits of subjective understanding. The surrealist is always on the lookout for an unusual incident, such as a coincidence, the suggestive aura of bizarre objects found in a flea market, an unexpected meeting that holds mysterious promise implying a sudden breach in the wall separating what we seem to know from what really exists. The *"problem of problems,"* according to Breton, is in drawing the links, "elucidating the relationships between 'natural necessity' and 'human necessity,'" between materiality and human consciousness (*Ent.* 136). Thus one must remain open to the promise of the unknown and increase the number of occasions for the unexpected to occur.

This dogged quest for a breach to the outside suggests, perversely enough, that the opening never really occurred, or that if it did occur it was not exploited. The most visibly exterior of the surrealists' achievements is the fact of multiple speech or group creation, where the claims of a single voice are lost in a larger, anonymous expression. It is a fascinating strategy to carry out Lautréamont's declaration that "poetry must be made by all, not just by one," and has surely influenced both contemporary group-created art and the "happening," which involves the audience as well as the initiating artist. Yet the multiple speech is "heard" on the level of the marvelous, by individuals who are reacting not to each other but to a magical greater voice which has suddenly been created. The dialogue is still carried on between the self and its own creation, set on a cosmic level.

It would be easy to label this return to the self and its mirrorings as pure narcissism and immaturity, but it is also important to recall the philosophical underpinnings of what is a genuine—if shortcircuiting—quest for knowledge and philosophical understanding. The preoccupation with authentic perception, the attempt to shake off the constraints of pre-conceived ideas, the inquiry into the boundaries of the knowable self and the impingement of other selves and alien materiality, are all accepted parts of contemporary phenomenology and existential psychology.[25] If the surrealists seem to return to the self in the face of the two most important challenges they recognize (action in society and love), absorbing everything into patterns of selfhood instead of yielding partial sovereignty, it is only after a concerted attempt to burst subjective limits. Paradoxically enough, and despite their rejection of Cartesian duality, the surrealists return to a belief in the self as the only basis for interpreting experience. They understand by incorporating otherness, by seeing it in self-reflexive terms. Much of the surrealist landscape is thus dominated by a single "paranoiac" vision that invests the world with its own subjective mythology ("Paranoiac-criticism," popularized by Salvador Dali, recommends a visionary perspective relating everything to personal desires and obsessions.) The fusion of woman and nature in the Eluard poem "Nature is caught in the nets of your life" distorts reality according to the poet's choices and sensual values (not in pure geometric forms, for example, to compare Guillevic's *Euclidiennes*.) In "Vigilance," by Breton, the poet achieves a highly personal revelation by doubling his own individuality. Setting fire to his former self, he watches the familiar furniture take on monstrous (but visually related) new shapes: "The furniture gives way to animals of the same size who look at me fraternally / Lions in whose manes are swallowed up the chairs / Sharks whose white belly embodies the last shudder of the sheets." Moving farther into embedded layers of the imagination, the cricket described by Breton in the last lines of "Tournesol" welcomes his author into the transfigured world he has just conceived: "André Breton, he said, pass."

Objects can put up only passive resistance to becoming part of a subjective vision; people tend to react more strongly. The surrealists have been criticized, and convincingly, for failing to envisage the partner in love as a self in (usually) her own right; the partnership is reduced to that of an initial self and another person who exists as part of an emotional landscape. From the time of the *First Manifesto*, when Breton used the inability to love as his chief example of what is lost when imagination departs and the self stops growing, love has been the favored surrealist topic and has embodied the highest surrealist aims. Erotic images and themes dominate the poetry, painting, and film of the surrealists, invoking an ecstatic, irrational, and trancelike state in which the lover explodes habitual constraints to experience sublimity: *amour fou,* mad love, or *amour sublime,* sublime love. This is an outlaw love of total freedom, abandoning the self utterly to an experience that cannot be reduced to logic or traditional family patterns. It has no laws or calculation, but is instead related to magic, dreams, the supernatural, and objective chance: all the antirational areas. It presupposes a tremendous drive to reach outside oneself toward the Other, a drive embodied with both erotic and metaphysical overtones in the surrealist concept of limitless desire.

Love in the strict sense, says Breton, is a "total attachment to a human being, based on the imperious recognition of the truth, of *our truth* 'in a soul and in a body' which are the soul and the body of that being" (*Man.* 142). It is now that the problems begin, for despite the apparent recognition of individual truths, descriptions of surrealist love seem constrained by a series of cultural myths. The governing image is that of the androgyne, the Platonic myth of two halves of a single identity that seek each other throughout life (Breton: "This precipitation of one toward the other by two systems held separately for subjective" in "L'air de l'eau"). Unlike Platonic love, this love exists through the body: "Love, the only love that is, carnal love . . ." (*AFou* 85), and also unlike the Platonic original, surrealist love is reduced from a broader sexual scope to a pairing of man and woman. Both male and female artists develop this concept of the androgyne, but with different emphases and implications. Xàvière Gauthier points out that the current version of the androgyne myth was also shaped by Jakob Boehme, who considered the female half originally part of Adam (Adam's rib), and thus saw the search for primordial unity as an attempt to reintegrate the female impulse into the male. Gauthier adds to this observation a telling passage from Eluard's "L'amoureuse," which describes the beloved in exactly those terms: "She has the form of my hands / She has the color of my eyes / She is swallowed up in my shadow."[26] There is clearly a question, then, as to whether the other half of the androgyne is complementary or supplementary. Benjamin Péret, in his *Anthologie de l'amour sublime,* [*Anthology of sublime love*] describes woman as "the complementary being capable of giving human life its full meaning," but continues to define this complementarity as follows: ". . . according to the degree in which she embodies more completely man's secret aspirations, inciting him to give free rein to his capacity for sublimation."[27] On the other hand, the painter Léonor Fini emphasizes women and suggests the masculine side of androgyny by making them bald. Fini's is a more evenly balanced creation as she is "in favor of a world where there is little or no sex distinction."[28] Joyce Mansour reverses expectations by applying a feminine perspective to the erotic fantasy worlds of male surrealism; she writes poetry of extreme sensuality and erotic tension, but with a certain cynical humor that puts the fantasies into question: "All my beauty drowned in your blank eyes / Death in your belly which eats my brain / All this makes a strange lady out of me."[29] Breton describes reciprocal love as a quest in which both men and women seek their perfect complementary image, but the sense of complementariness clearly depends on the lover's own personality and desire. "Reciprocal love . . . is a disposition of mirrors that send back to me, under the thousand angles that the unknown can take for me, the faithful image of the one I love, always more amazing in her divination of my own desire, and more golden with life" (*AFou* 106).

It may seem paradoxical that this unique, complementary love may be felt by the same person for a series of partners. This is not only clearly the case for the main figure of surrealism, but Breton explains it as the continuation of the quest for the perfect partner, loved completely in each of her incarnations. More pragmatically, it may be that the androgynous love of surrealism has mythic rather than real status. For the men, the perfect partner is "terrestrial salvation" in *Arcane 17,* a modern Beatrice leading her lover to an earthly paradise; the enigmatic figure of the mysterious passer-by in "Tournesol," hinting at revelations from Beyond; the protean Rrose Sélavy (Rose is Life, Eros is Life, and so on) of Duchamp and Desnos, a feminine incarnation of metamorphosis and chance; Mélusine, the child-woman; beauty, poetry, and imagination all wrapped up in one female image. Inspiring "mad love," she is linked to an enchantment that transfigures the universe, enabling us to "recognize the marvelous precipitate of desire . . . enlarging the universe, making it somewhat less obscure . . . the beginning of a supremely dazzling contact by man with the world of things" (*AFou* 16, 49). In other words, she is mythically defined as the magical quality of love, which, in turn, is seen as a method for reaching the marvelous.[30] When not defined strictly as the partner in love, the preferred image is Mélusine, the "child-woman" of *Arcane 17* whose intuitive grace, irrationality, and pacifism are to replace the repressive structures of man. Mélusine is not yet full woman, the morning star of the tarot card that combines Eve, Mélusine, and "is now woman complete" (*Arc.* 74), but she has a special contemporary value for the surrealists because she is the pure agent of change. She represents the aspect of woman that is most needed today. "In her and only in her resides, in a state of absolute transparency, the *other* prism of vision" that denies male despotism and rationality (*Arc.* 69). The real woman of everyday life, says Breton, is repressed by society and its dominant male vision and must "find herself" (*Arc.* 60): a declaration that could take its place in many a feminist manifesto. However, Breton qualifies the apparently feminist value of his statement by commenting that it is up to the artist (not women in general) to "bring out to its fullest everything that relates to the feminine world system as opposed to the masculine system" (*Arc.* 62). The male artist has become the spokesman for imposing a "feminine" system of values. *Nadja* is a case in point, for the heroine of the title, who is supposed to symbolize the liberating power of free, "mad" imagination, asks Breton to write a novel telling her story: "You will write a novel about me, I tell you. Don't say no . . . Something of us must remain" (*Nadja* 115). She does, in fact, take her place in Breton's own story, which begins (after Montaigne) "Who am I?"

It is amusing and perhaps not quite fair to notice the cultural stereotypes that persist in this image of woman on a new kind of pedestal. A surrealist round table discussion that Breton called "extremely free" (and was exclusively male) sounds like a self-conscious stag session in which the participants polled each other on their attitudes toward love and preferences for sexual positions. When Aragon pointed out that their perspective was necessarily limited, his observation met a resounding silence. Breton, teased for his refusal to admit pederasty as a form of love, threatened to leave.[31] In *Mad Love,* despite the abandon of the title, Breton cites Engels to the effect that monogamy is "a superior form of sexual relationship . . . the greatest moral progress" of modern times (*AFou* 87).

These attitudes have their source in traditional views of the family and, when linked with a mythic view of male and female natures and complementarity, they make it difficult for the male surrealists to endow their descriptions of women with any individuality. In fact the surrealists tend to divide their understanding of women into two large categories that visibly reflect Victorian images of "good" and "bad" women. According to Péret, the important categories are "the child-woman and the witch" (Péret 27). Xavière Gauthier copiously documented these two aspects and their subsets in *Surréalisme et sexualité. [Surrealism and Sexuality]*. On the one hand, there is woman as Mother Nature in her various aspects: woman seen as flower (typical images of young child and virgin), as fruit (compared to fruit, often being eaten), as close to the earth (mother; a natural principle mediating between man and things; a muse inspiring the artist), as a star (divine and celestial being). On the other, there is the scriptural "mulier instrumentum diaboli," the tool of the devil: faithless and unreliable, a predatory animal, prostitute, femme fatale, clairvoyant, and sorceress.

The women of surrealism adopt this mythic pattern for their own uses: not the model of the "child-woman" that Bona de Mandiargues calls "a doll, a pin-up, or a strip tease artist" (Orenstein, 20), but the more powerful image of sorceress, femme fatale, and Magna Mater. Since imagination and creativity are so important to the surrealist ethic, it is not surprising that the women of surrealism should attempt to define a creative role for themselves that has not been preempted by men, interpreters of Nadja and Mélusine. This creative role seems to be precisely the exploration of the female identity that is not really recognized by the male artists (except as catalyst or mirror). They use the myths and archetype of woman as reference points in a search that (characteristically, for surrealism) probes the unconscious to reveal the authentic self. Fini paints huge mother-goddesses, fertile but untouchable creatures who dominate in their nude sexuality. Leonora Carrington "delves for the new horizons that we discover when we are in touch with our psychic powers and with a fuller knowledge of our interior. . . ," and Remedios Varo "depicts woman as alchemist, voyager, inventor, scientist, explorer, and cartographer of a world that intersects with our own in imperceptible ways" (Orenstein 17, 20). Throughout, it is an active image of the female self, profoundly linked to the archetype of the all-creating Magna Mater, and thus attuned—in a different manner from the recognition of the marvelous—to natural law and the hidden structure of the universe.

Gauthier argues that all these aspects of woman—the archetypal creativity emphasized by surrealist women and the anguishing dichotomy felt by men—refer to a single psychological structure, which is that of mother and child. This mother is core and explanation of the universe, nurturing presence or frightening withdrawal, symbol of a lost unity which must be recaptured. In all capacities, for the surrealists, "the relation to the mother is the structuring imprint of the relation to the world" (Gauthier 285). This larger mythic structure may well be accurate from a psychological point of view; certainly it is well documented. This would account for both the psychological dependence and the need for exclusive control shown by surrealist men and the women's exploitation of the Magna Mater archetype. It is also possible that these views of women are metaphors for an understanding of the self. In a largely masculine movement, women come to be metaphors for the object of curiosity and desire, for otherness and the possibility of relating to it. "The problem of women is all that is marvelous and troubling in the world," says Breton (*Man.* 141), and certainly his self-consciousness in describing reciprocal love as a "disposition of mirrors" and his constant quest for the self (*Nadja*'s "Who am I?") reflect a philosophical anxiety that must be coupled with psychological explanations. Surrealist women adopt the archetypal structures of the masculine myth and use these structures to focus their own search for identity. In either case, the result of this mythic search is a further encapsulation in the self, a practical alienation from the other, and the denial of any authentic sharing of individuality between men and women.

Such individual relationships bear directly on self-awareness, but another, more publicized challenge came when the surrealists tried to align themselves with a group consciousness for direct political action. The surrealists' flirtation and later split with the Communist party is well known, but it has a particular interest because it reflects not only the surrealists' rejection of political constraints and an identity imposed by the outside but also a contemporary split in Marxism itself as to the role of individual and group. The surrealists were drawn to communism because they saw in it a way to overturn an established, corrupt order and create a utopian future where everyone would be raised to his and her highest potential (much like Trotsky's vision in the closing pages of *Literature and Revolution*). They sought to bring together their "revolution of the mind" with political revolution, and they had some rather sophisticated notions on ways to advance social consciousness. Nonetheless, there was never any real exploration of the links between the revolutionary surrealist self and its integration into activist political history, for the surrealists (like Trotsky) were suspected and expelled from the party by those who held more conservative Marxist views. Relations between surrealism and communism cannot be taken, therefore, as an acid test of the surrealists' ability to integrate selfhood and historical personality; nor, because of their intense pacifism and distrust of European nationalism does their refusal to join the army in World War II tell much more. On the other hand, the controversy at the time provides a good opportunity to follow the surrealists' view of self and history.

The first link between surrealism and international communism is the belief in revolution, and yet, despite their common enemies, the surrealists initially did not relate their concept of pure revolt to the events in Russia in October 1917. In the early editions of *La Révolution surréaliste*, the vision is of Terror, modeled on the French Revolution and defined with a casual disregard for social aims. Desnos, in "The Revolution, That is, the terror," proposes wholesale slaughter of heads of families, philanthropists, priests, soldiers, people who return lost wallets, mothers of large families, savings bank members, the police, the inventors of serums against epidemics, and all those who feel pity, so that "natural selection" may bring about a world in which there are more important questions than "cultivating cereals" and people will finally start thinking about "Eternity."[32] In spite of Desnos' joyful thoroughness, this obliteration of a whole list of approved bourgeois virtues does not add up to a program of political action. Aragon seems closer to grasping the political implications of this Terror: "There is no morality other than the morality of Terror, no liberty other than implacable dominating liberty . . . There will be chains for the enemies of liberty. Man is free, but not men."[33] Aragon would later follow the totalitarian implications of this view into the Communist party and away from surrealism,[34] but for the moment both he and the other surrealists upheld a notion of pure revolution that surpassed—and avoided—any real implication in historical process.

The declaration "La Révolution d'abord et toujours!" ("Revolution First and Forever!" 1925), signed by the whole group of surrealists defines their activity as "the revolt of the mind" committed to a revolutionary ideal separate from history. "We do not accept the laws of Economy and Exchange, we do not accept the slavery of Work, and, in a still larger domain, we declare ourselves rebels against History" (*Hist.* 217). Pure revolt cannot be chained to any given historical moment, no matter how sympathetic it may seem: thus Artaud scathingly criticized Breton, Eluard, Péret, Unik, and Aragon in 1927 for joining the Communist party and turning their backs on the true revolutionary value of surrealist activity, "which normally could take place only inside the brain" (*Hist.* 275). The "true revolutionaries," says Artaud, are those who believe in individual liberty and sense intuitively "the horrible relativity of any human action" (*Hist.* 280). There is a split between this idea of pure revolt, individually experienced, and the idea of concerted action toward political revolution; much the same distinction has been made between the idea of authentic or pure anarchy and support of a particular revolutionary cause.

Before 1925, the surrealists' revolt was similar to the Dada revolt: anarchic, individual, silent about any of the major political issues of the time. As Herbert Gershman points out, there is no mention by the surrealists in 1922 of the Soviet-German treaty at Rapallo or of Mussolini's march on Rome; in 1923, of France's occupation of the Ruhr, the Fascist coup in Spain, or the Hitler putsch in Munich; and in 1924 of the death of Lenin.[35] Only in 1925, as the surrealists of *La Révolution surréaliste* engaged in debates and discussions with the Marxist journal *Clarté*, did they begin to envisage revolution in the form of planned political action. The "Declaration of January 27, 1925" suggests that the Revolution will take place "if necessary, with material hammers" (*Hist.* 219). The agenda of a meeting in April 1925 took up the question of "revolutionary or surrealist principles" without reaching any accord except that surrealism was not an abstract or poetic movement, and was really capable of changing minds (*Hist.* 220). Breton reviewed Trotsky's biography of Lenin and began to speak of a "revolutionary reality"[36] at the same time that the joint declaration "Revolution First and Forever!" stated "we are not utopian thinkers: we conceive of this Revolution only in its social form" (*Hist.* 217). Yet the surrealists' claim to autonomy in their own field survived and was the source of a major split among members of the movement. Pierre Naville, who with Péret was editor of the first three issues of *La Revolution surréaliste*, became an active Communist party member and criticized the surrealists for their political naiveté and self-indulgence in not subordinating themselves completely to the revolutionary cause.[37] Artaud, of course, did not agree with Naville and was expelled from the movement in November 1926 for indulging in "literary activities." In 1927 a group of five letters announced the adherence of Aragon, Breton, Eluard, Péret, and Unik to the Communist party, an adherence that was short-lived for some but indicated the surrealists' hope that they had found a politically effective outlet for the spirit of revolt.

There is a dual context for this parallelism of pure revolt and social revolution. First, there were common enemies. In addition, the surrealists were persuaded that the metaphysical bases of Marxism were identical with their own. Even before the surrealists were aware of Marxist doctrine, they (and the Dadaists before them) were attacking the same bourgeois society. The narrow habits of mind they associated with bourgeois thinking seemed to take on solid, attackable form in contemporary economic, political, and religious structures: church, nation, family, judiciary, army, and capitalism all suppressed the imagination, limited freedom, and stunted human development. "Open the prisons . . . disband the army" cries the second *Révolution surréaliste* (*Hist.* 208), and the third issue warns the Pope that "we have nothing to do with your laws, index, sin, confessional, rabble of

priests" (*Hist.* 210). "Revolution First and Forever!.," despite its ahistorical
notion of revolution and of redemption coming from the East,[38] condemns
the whole capitalist system for diminishing human dignity, and does so in
clearly Marxist terms. In Western society, the declaration states, human
relationships are reduced to money, and "human dignity brought down to
the level of exchange commodity." The poor become salaried slaves, and
"high international finance" oppresses the people of all nations (*Hist.* 216).
The common enemy, says Eluard in a later speech, is the "Internationale of
profit," "a morality which, to maintain its order and prestige, knows only
how to build banks, barracks, prisons, churches, and brothels."[39] A year
before, Breton had accused the judicial system of encouraging "the crowd's
ancient and sordid lynch instinct," and professional psychologists of sup-
porting the system by locking up nonconformists and testifying to such
absurdities as a category of mental illness that enhances rather than di-
minishes responsibility (*PosPol.* 23). With such a coincidence of enemies,
there is small wonder that the surrealists rallied to a cause that promised to
be the social wing of their revolution of the mind.

Even after Breton, Aragon, and Eluard left the Communist party in
November 1927 (Aragon and Eluard to return at later dates), they considered themselves sympathizers and fellow travelers, and tried to support
the party's aims so long as these aims did not directly contradict surrealist
principles. The group statement "Contre-attaque" in 1935 describes the
class struggle as historically true and as the "source of essential moral
values" at the same time that it affirms "the study of social superstructures"
as the new "base of all revolutionary activity" (*PosPol.* 142). Well after his
final rupture with the Communist party, Breton commented that the surrealists never lost their belief in Marxism-Leninism as the proper tool for
the social transformation of the world, and also that they had never intended to present their own political program. Marxism offered, he said,
"the greatest chance for the liberation of classes and oppressed peoples . . .
we had as yet no reason to suppose that its tip was poisoned" (*Ent.* 134, also
123).

If the tip was poisoned for the surrealists, the reason is that the orthodox reproaches they had to combat were aimed not only at recalcitrant
individuals but also at the way the *core* of surrealism—its belief in the
development of the self—could contribute to social revolution. Of course,
some personalities were involved: Breton, generally accepted as the leader
of the surrealists, felt that his abilities were wasted when he was asked to
compile statistics (such as on steel production in Italy), and that the movement itself was misunderstood and insulted by being asked to prove its
loyalty (*Man.* 98–99). But the real problem came with the Communist
party's denial of intellectual and artistic freedom. On a purely practical
level, the surrealists could not accept the twists and turns of party policy,
and the way that, for example, it manipulated public opinion before and

after the Franco-Soviet pact of May 2, 1935. The party's encouragement of French national pride after the pact, praising especially a cultural heritage which the surrealists found bourgeois and profoundly unrevolutionary, was accompanied by open anti-German propaganda. Such propaganda not only set the French against the German proletariat (a negation of both surrealist and Communist internationalism for the political gain of a third country) but also insulted the intelligence of those who were asked to forget their previous commitment. It was in clear contradiction with the claims of personal responsibility, recognized as such by Breton and, as he says, "anyone whom political passion has not made lose the integrity of his judgment" (*PosPol* 69). Passion, to which the surrealists characteristically yield as a matter of principle and method, must support and may not interfere with personal integrity.

Social action, Breton says, is "only one of the forms of a more general problem that surrealism has sworn to raise and which is *human expression in all its forms*" (*Man.* 108). Surrealism contributes to social revolution by facilitating self-expression through the revolution of the mind. Here, for all their mystical vagueness about glimpsing the marvelous, the surrealists were not only close to the Trotskyite wing of Marxism but also had some rather sophisticated ideas about helping the self develop in modern civilization. Breton's criticism of modern French education is a case in point, and expresses a view heard recently from educators who are concerned about the way textbooks preserve and reinforce class-oriented stereotypes and civilizational values. The main fault Breton finds with current education is that it prevents proper self-development by offering selected material and prescribed manners of teaching that constrict the child's freedom of judgment. Children are offered hypotheses and half-truths as dogma, he says, and are not shown how much is actually unknown. Their history books— even the illustrations—all focus on kings, saints, and military heroes who are presented as the significant reference points of human history. The texts offer a subliminal education that works via the unconscious, impressing traditional patterns of value on young minds that are supposedly only learning their letters (*Arc.* 42–45). There is more than one way of approaching a topic, Breton comments in a letter comparing French and American methods of teaching art. One needs both disciplined realism (here he quotes Rousseau on the importance of teaching by the study of nature), and exercises of pure imagination: both copying casseroles and studying Matisse. Full consciousness requires that there should be an alternation between the two (*Clé* 330–34). Breton's clear understanding of the way textbook and teaching style shape the mind reflects the surrealists' basic fascination with forms of expression which must be liberated as much as possible in order to liberate the human imagination itself. This liberation may coincide temporarily with any political revolution that attacks old habits of thought, but it ultimately makes its way according to more personal goals: development of the self through love, a liberated mind, and the magic of art evoking the marvelous.

Small wonder that surrealist artists attacked the concept of proletarian art and were attacked in turn by those conservative Marxists who upheld it. Surrealist beauty has little to do with social class, and is certainly opposed to traditional realist aesthetic norms. It is a dynamic concept that concerns individual poetic vision seized fleetingly in sublime moments: "Beauty will be CONVULSIVE or will not be" (*Nadja* 187); "Convulsive beauty will be erotic-veiled, exploding-fixed, magic-circumstantial or will not be" (*AFou* 21). It is a personal experience that requires the individual's full concentration and self-abandon, and can never be captured for any length of time or set into publicly available formulas. Such a fluid, subjective goal is far from the objective, content-oriented claims of proletarian art.

In rejecting proletarian art, the surrealists did not feel that they were betraying their Marxist commitments, but rather rejecting a particular brand of Stalinist orthodoxy. Breton collaborated with Trotsky on the manifesto "For an Independent Revolutionary Art,"[40] and cited both Trotsky and Engels to prove that he and his associates were still close to the historic principles of social revolution. Artistic production is an intellectual phenomenon, he says, and can only be valued in terms of the sovereignty of thought. Engels tells us that such thought is not fixed but dynamic and constantly evolving. Art, therefore, must reflect these evolutions in thought and not be bound by traditional forms. Avant-garde artists who wish to strike at bourgeois society must never allow themselves simply to represent what is before them (in traditional realist form), or they will easily be absorbed by the bourgeoisie (*PosPol* 20). Artists must be given the same freedom as scientists to experiment with their resources, to discover the real relationship between the leftist spirit and advanced artistic techniques.[41] In addition, and even if proletarian literature is badly needed, the "pre-revolutionary writer or artist, necessarily with a bourgeois education" is incapable of writing it (*Man.* 111–13).

Breton is echoing Trotsky when he points out the difficulty of equating artistic and political progress. Both men share the vision of an ideal state, a perfect maturity of human consciousness as goal and implied standard for everyday actions. Trotsky's utopian view of this future society, where children will imbibe science and art like light and air, "the first culture that is truly human,"[42] is close to the surrealist vision that anticipates a "sublime point" and the "marvelous." Both views presuppose the complete development of individual human beings whose enlightened interaction constitutes this ideal society: a long-range goal that seems unrealistic and even self-indulgent to the orthodox pragmatic perspective. Trotsky and Breton's manifesto on revolutionary art accuses the Stalinist regime of manipulating cultural expression to bring about a global "twilight hostile to the emergence of any kind of spiritual value" (*Clé* 44). Socialist realism, according to Breton, is a "means of moral extermination," an attempt to "crush art once and for all" (*Clé* 335, 339) in the hands of "the great negator and the principal enemy of the proletarian revolution," Joseph Stalin (*Hist.* 460). True surrealist art is properly revolutionary and contributes to human progress, but its touchstone is personal integrity rather than forced conformity to historic events.

The title of the second surrealist journal, *Surréalisme au service de la révolution,* turns out to have a double edge. Intended to proclaim surrealist subordination to the Communist program for social revolution, it more accurately reminds us that surrealism *means* revolt and yields to none in its definition. Revolt is necessary because existing human structures are always imperfect: the acceptance of reality always limits our understanding of what could be, and therefore limits our imagination. On an initial level, one must revolt against any social structures that repress and diminish the mind: tradition, censorship, inhibitions, religious beliefs that promise fulfilment in another world. On another level, revolt for the sake of revolt is necessary to keep alive the possibility of change and growth: "The principle of *opposition* must be fortified. Ideas that triumph are all on the brink of disaster" (*Man.* 170). In this principle of unrelieved opposition to a higher goal, the surrealists appear as a band of secular mystics, hermits who exile themselves to a permanent fringe in an always-imperfect society in order to testify to unfilled possibilities and set the example of a purer devotion. Their anarchy has a direction: it moves away from anything that codifies and reifies, and toward the development of a self whose very outlines depend on the process of the search. Without the openness of this quest, it could be mere self-indulgence—the willful assertions of a predefined personality. Instead, it is more accurately an asceticism of the self, a condition of "moral asepsis" (*Man.* 250) that rejects all compromises with the known to become part of the evolution of consciousness.

The asceticism of the self, when the self is still being defined, is not easy to maintain in a pure state. First, there is the falling-away of those who believe they have found truer ways of expressing themselves and their relation to the world: Tzara and Aragon with the Communists, Eluard and Char in the Resistance. Then there are the hidden pulls of cultural habit: the bourgeois puritanism of which Breton was often accused, the myopically male perspective of the surrealist founding fathers, the strain of mysticism inherited from the Romantics and Symbolists alike. Yet the chief goal and the risk to that goal continue to be defined in the same terms: the goal as the development of a fully realized, individual self in tune with the universe, and the risk as the diminishing and codification of that potential self through loss of imagination and the pressure of exterior forces. The danger of reification is always present, freezing women into love objects or the magical child-woman, freezing activists as political pawns, freezing successful artists as objects of aesthetic consumption, freezing surrealists into

anticipated frameworks of "surrealist" activity. (Hence, perhaps, the refusal of contemporary "surrealist" Claude Courtot to accept the name,
while he recognizes the heritage.)[43] "Ideas that triumph" become law,
generating a fixed pattern of relationships and set models for identity. For
the surrealists, then, these ideas must be challenged by a disordering activity that is part of a subtler order, a rupture that reaches for the marvelous,
an ecstatic link with Being that provides opportunities for the self (still in
the body) to expand toward perfect coincidence with the essential structure
of the universe.

Notes

1. André Breton, *Manifestes du surréalisme* (Paris: Gallimard, 1969), p. 92. Breton is widely
recognized as the founder and chief spokesman for surrealism; since several of his books are
mentioned here on numerous occasions, references are made according to the following
abbreviations: *Manifestes: Man. Position politique du surréalisme* (1935; Paris: Bélibaste, 1970):
PosPol. L'Amour fou (Mad Love) (1937; Paris: Gallimard, 1966): *AFou. Arcane 17* (1945; Paris:
Union générale d'éditions, 1965): *Arc. Clé des Champs (Key to the Fields)* (1952; Utrecht: Pauvert,
1967): *Clé. Entretiens (Interviews)* (Paris: Gallimard 1969): *Ent.*
Unless otherwise indicated, translations from the French are my own.
2. Vytautas Kavolis, "Logics of Selfhood and Modes of Order: Civilizational Structures
for Individual Identities," in *Identity and Authority: Explorations in the Theory of Society,* Roland
Robertson and Burkart Holzner, ed. (Oxford: Basil Blackwell, 1980), pp. 40–60, 268–71,
284–87.
3. Hegel's negation of transcendence, and the historically rooted transformations of the
dialectic process, appealed to those who rejected bourgeois society and its vision of a measured, logical, absolute truth. In "Limits Not Frontiers of Surrealism" (in *Surrealism,* ed.
Herbert Read, London: Faber and Faber, 1971), Breton formulated this acceptance of dialectical materialism: "Adhesion to the theory of dialectical materialism, which the Surrealists
adopt in all its points: supremacy of matter over thought; adoption of the Hegelian dialectic as
the science of the general law of movement applied to the exterior world as well as human
thought; the materialist conception of history. . . ." (p. 100).
The Hegelian thesis, antithesis, and synthesis seemed the perfect historical expression of
transformations tending toward full consciousness and—best of all—culminating in poetry
(*PosPol* 109–110). Yet Ferdinand Alquié is undoubtedly right when he says that the surrealist
position is basically different from Hegelianism in its emphasis on individuality over history,
on the immediate experience rather than the mediating concept, and on a consciousness
capable of judging history rather than on history as the creator of consciousness. Ferdinand
Alquié, *The Philosophy of Surrealism,* trans. Bernard Waldrop (Ann Arbor: University of Michigan Press, 1965), pp. 31–43, 64, 70–71.
4. Alquié, *Philosophy,* p. 151.
5. Maurice Nadeau, *Histoire du surréalisme* (Paris: Seuil, 1964), p. 191. The second half of
the Nadeau volume (pp. 195–498) presents a series of surrealist documents, references to
which are abbreviated in the text as *Hist.*
6. Jean-Louis Bédouin, *Vingt ans du surréalisme, 1939–59* (Paris: Denoël 1961).
7. Herbert Gershman, *The Surrealist Revolution in France* (Ann Arbor: University of Michigan Press, 1974), pp. 138–69. J. H. Matthews, *Toward the Poetics of Surrealism* (Syracuse, N.Y.:
Syracuse University Press, 1976), and the article "Surrealism in the Sixties," *Contemporary
Literature* 2,2 (Spring 1970):226–42.

8. Alquié, *Philosophy*, p. 3.

9. Alquié, *Philosophy*, p. 163.

10. Matthews, *Toward the Poetics of Surrealism*, p. 224 note 21.

11. Tristan Tzara, *Le Surréalisme et l'après-guerre* (Geneva: 1966), p. 17. Richard Hülsenbeck, who had fled Germany for Switzerland, said of his associates in Zurich that none of them "had much appreciation for the kind of courage it takes to get shot for an idea of a nation which is at best a cartel of pelt merchants and profiteers in leather, at worst a cultural association of psychopaths who, like the Germans, marched off with a volume of Goethe in their knapsacks, to skewer Frenchmen and Russians on their bayonets." Cited in J. H. Matthews, *Introduction to Surrealism* (University Park: Pennsylvania State University Press, 1965), p. 19.

12. Tristan Tzara, *Sept manifestes dada, Lampisteries* (Paris: Pauvert, 1963), pp. 21, 33.

13. Tristan Tzara, *Approximate Man and Other Writings*, trans. Mary Ann Caws (Detroit: Wayne State University Press, 1973), pp. 43–48.

14. Nadeau, *Histoire du surréalisme*, p. 36.

15. Tristan Tzara, *Le Surréalisme et l'après-guerre*, p. 24.

16. Nadeau, *Histoire*, p. 36.

17. Anna Balakian, in *The Literary Origins of Surrealism, a New Mysticism in French Poetry* (New York: New York University Press, 1965) discusses another aspect of this mysticism, its "road to the absolute."

18. *La Révolution surréaliste* 9–10 (1927):1–6.

19. Maxime Alexandre, "A propos de morale" ("On Morals"), *La Révolution surréaliste* 12 (December 1929):49.

20. Tristan Tzara, "Essai sur la situation de la poésie," in *Le Surréalisme au service de la révolution* 3–4 (1931):15–23.

21. Alexandre, "A propos de morale," p. 50.

22. Paul Eluard, *Capitale de la douleur* (Paris: Gallimard, 1926).

23. Paul Eluard, *Capitale de la douleur* (1926).

24. André Breton, *Nadja* (Paris: Gallimard, 1964; first 1928), pp. 165–69, 176 note.

25. Ferdinand Alquié says of the surrealists that "they never neglect the intentional nature of consciousness." (*Philosophy*, p. 153)

26. Xavière Gauthier, *Surréalisme et sexualité* (Paris: Gallimard, 1971), pp. 96–97.

27. Benjamin Péret, *Anthologie de l'amour sublime* (Paris: Albin Michel, 1956), pp. 69–70.

28. Cited by Gloria Orenstein in "Women of Surrealism," *The Feminist Art Journal* (Spring 1976):16.

29. Joyce Mansour, "Les machinations aveugles . . .," in *La Poésie surréaliste*, ed. Jean-Louis Bédouin (Paris: Seghers, 1964), p. 218.

30. See also the section on surrealism and André Breton in Simone de Beauvoir, *The Second Sex*.

31. *La Révolution surréaliste* 11 (March 1928):32–40.

32. Robert Desnos, "La Révolution, c'est-à-dire, la Terreur," in *La Révolution surréaliste* 3 (April 1925):26–27.

33. Louis Aragon, essay under "Sciences morales," in *La Révolution surréaliste* 3 (April 1925):26–27.

34. See "L'affaire Aragon" in Nadeau, *Histoire*, pp. 143–49.

35. Gershman, *The Surrealist Revolution in France*, p. 85. See also Robert S. Short, "The Politics of Surrealism, 1920–36," *The Journal of Contemporary History* 1, no. 2 (1966):3–25.

36. André Breton, "Léon Trotsky: Lénine," in *La Révolution surréaliste* 5 (October 1925):29.

37. Pierre Naville, *La Révolution et les intellectuels* (Paris: Gallimard, 1927).

38. A perennial theme with roots in Romanticism, but particularly evident in *La Révolution surréaliste* 3 (1925) with its Artaud-inspired "Address to the Dalai Lama" and "Letter to the Buddhist Schools."

39. Paul Eluard, "L'Evidence poétique," in *Oeuvres complétes,* (Paris: Gallimard, 1968) 1:520–21. Eluard also cites Péret: "O you who are my brothers because I have enemies!" (p. 520).

40. "Pour un art révolutionnaire indépendant": according to Breton, the 1937 manifesto was written by Trotsky and Breton, but Diego Rivera's signature was substituted for Trotsky's at the latter's request (*Clé* 49, footnote).

41. Breton is suggesting many of the same ideas as Walter Benjamin (especially the latter's "Artist as Producer"): that a truly revolutionary art must adopt modern techniques and media, and not try to convey progressive thoughts in the fixed forms associated with a bourgeois, reactionary past.

42. Leon Trotsky, *Literature and Revolution,* trans. Rose Strunsky (Ann Arbor: University of Michigan Press, 1966), p. 14. Trotsky's 1923 "Revolution and Culture" is quoted by Breton (*Man.* 114).

43. Claude Courtot, in a July 23, 1969, letter to Mary Ann Caws: "Intentionally, we have decided to renounce *provisionally* and *officially* the label 'surrealist,' in order to free ourselves of a weighty heritage. . . . It is no less certain that *surrealism* remains a living movement that surpasses us all and has no need of fingerprints, identity cards, or other anthropometric indices to affirm its existence, deliberately outside the law." Letter cited in Caws, *The Poetry of Dada and Surrealism* (Princeton, N.J.: Princeton University Press, 1970), p. 8, footnote 7a.

7

Some Varieties of Metaphor in American Images of Selfhood

Corinne Lathrop Gilb

Concern about the connections between civilization and selfhood raises the questions of the relation between the actual self and societal definitions of the self and of the relation between the actual self and cultural images of selfhood. These in turn suggest a third question, which is my theme, of how the cultural images relate to the societal (including political) definitions. Evidence from the American past appears to suggest that the cultural images of selfhood are not replications of the societal definitions, though they are not totally unrelated. Instead, whereas societal definitions emphasize the individual's partialness vis-à-vis the broader context, oneself as person, and as social construct, cultural images of the self attempt to restore wholeness both within the self and for the self even while it is in conjunction with its total context. Although societal definitions focus on rights, obligations, status, and function, cultural images may be concerned with relationships between body and soul, mind and emotion, the male and female principles within the self, and hence of the relationships between time and eternity, self and other, public and private, the world and nature, and man and God. Because of the American "civil religion," the two kinds of definitions have been linked in some fashion. However, cultural images of the self often attempt to serve not to reinforce the societal definition but rather to compensate for the deficiencies it legislates.

The broadness of the topic raises issues about the nature of the evidence. Societal definitions of selfhood (or personhood) are provided in the law articulated by American courts concerned with white males at neither extreme of the social scale. To summarize as succinctly as possible the relevant trends in American case law over the last three hundred plus years; in seventeenth-century New England, status defined the person; the law emphasized individual statuses rather than individuals as such. Said John Winthrop: "God Almighty in his most holy and wise providence hath soe disposed of the Condicione of mankinde, as in all times some must be rich, some poore, some highe and eminent in power and dignities; others meane and in subieccion."[1] Status was taken into account in the earliest allocation of town lots. Voting rights depended on freeman status, church membership, or (later) property ownership. Sumptuary laws regulated the kind of clothing that could be worn by persons of various status positions. Criminal penalties varied according to status. Courts reinforced a variety of prescriptive rights.[2] The general purpose of the law was to keep people in their places in a social order that God had ordained. But law-enforcement mechanisms treated individuals as if they were at least in part idiosyncratic, with status reinforcing rather than undermining their personal uniqueness.[3]

By the nineteenth century, some men saw the self as the seat of pain and pleasure, the locus of will based on interest or instinct. The frontiersman and the early free enterpriser might make of every encounter a test of self, as if the self were the sum of its victories or defeats. Mid-nineteenth-century law seemed to favor ego-defined and ego-managed selfhood. The advent of universal white male suffrage was one evidence of this, since voters were no longer expected to act as passive channels for God's will but rather actively to express their own desires and interests. Many saw the self as built up and extended by the reach of power, of command over land and possessions. The law now assumed that land was an instrumental or productive asset. The essential attribute of property ownership was the power to develop one's property regardless of the injurious consequences to others.[4] In place of a former doctrine defining negligence as failure to perform one's duty, the nineteenth-century law defined negligence as carelessness and then added the concept of contributory negligence so that men "could not be held liable for socially useful activity exercised with due care."[5] Around the mid-nineteenth century, the law of corporations initially favored competition before it came around again to reinforcing various restraints on competition. Most important of all, nineteenth-century contracts came to be interpreted solely in terms of the will of the parties involved and "all pre-existing legal duties were . . . subordinated to the contract relation."[6] The purpose of legal certainty was now to help individuals plan their affairs more rationally.[7] In the realm of consumer law, caveat emptor prevailed.

In the twentieth century the law has reverted to its reinforcement of statuses within the framework of a renewed emphasis on the relation of statuses to the common weal, but now the statuses are not so idiosyncratic as they were in the seventeenth century, but instead have come to be based on membership in rather large generic groups or categories. For consumers as a whole, strict liability of manufacturers has replaced caveat emptor. The law can compel one to join a trade union or, under the National Industrial Recovery Act of the early 1930s, it could compel a company to join a trade association. Today, one has all sorts of job rights that are not expressly stated by contract, as well as rights to information and to nondiscrimination because of sex or race. Today, the law is more concerned with clarifying roles and group rights and obligations (the rights of women, children, racial groups, the handicapped, the elderly, criminals, and victims; the obligations of employers and professionals) than it is with reinforcing any concept of freewheeling autonomous selfhood. Private ownership of property has been circumscribed by all sorts of easements and public obligations, frequently in the name of environmental protection.[8]

When we turn to the other side of the ledger and look at images in the arts, we see quite a different story. To be sure, in each era, didactic literature articulated and justified or deplored the changing socio-economic and legal definitions of personhood or selfhood. Quite another set of concerns appears in the works of three representative poets, all from the Northeastern part of the United States, all Protestant, and roughly out of the same tradition, but dispersed over time from the seventeenth century to mid-nineteenth century to the twentieth century. The three poets are Ann Bradstreet, Walt Whitman, and Wallace Stevens. What they illustrate is a continuity of themes about the self that do not precisely match the law's dialectic, because their central concern has been with the ontological position of the self and its relation to the Absolute. They do illustrate that there has been a marked increase in ontological precariousness, if we take as evidence changes in the metaphors of selfhood. For Bradstreet, the self was a little city or country; for Whitman, it was leaves of grass; for Stevens, it was the possessor of a blue guitar, the imagination. There is something solid about being a little country, especially if that country is believed to be a microcosm of the universe. To be leaves of grass is at least to be rooted in Nature. But for the self to depend on what it can make of itself on the blue guitar of imagination is to rest on much less solid ground.

Differences between social (i.e., legal) and cultural definitions of selfhood were least marked in the seventeenth century. Seventeenth-century English law as well as theology thought that the little body of man corresponded exactly to the larger body of the world and the still larger body of the universe. All were composed of the same elements: earth, water, air, and fire. As John Donne wrote, "I am a little world made cunningly of elements." Man, world, and universe each had its individuality, yet each was involved with the others and all partook of God.

For all their sense of original sin and human fallibility, American Puritans shared John Donne's view of man as a microcosm of the universe, but they also believed that the individual was a microcosm of his country or city. Poetess Anne Bradstreet, daughter of one New England governor and wife of another, could write:

"As a man is called the little world, so his heart may be called the little commonwealth, his more fixed and resolved thoughts are like to inhabitants, his slight and flitting thoughts are like passengers that travel to and fro continually; here is also the great court of justice erected which is always kept by conscience, who is both accuser, witness, and judge."[9]

Puritans repeatedly invoked the image of a city as an armed camp, a controlled environment, outside of which nothing gained form. Economic activities within a city were regulated to serve the common interest. Bradstreet's use of the word "commonwealth" implied that the self was a microcosm of the political economy of which it was a member, which is to say that all of the self's parts had a responsibility to the whole self, the whole in turn being responsible to God. The poet's view reinforced the legal view of the individual self as a being defined by status rights and obligations, but the poet—more than the law—emphasized selfhood's wholeness; a wholeness that could not have existed without its replication of the patterns that existed in the larger wholeness of which it was a part.[10]

Running parallel to these ways in which American Puritan thought resembled English thought were other ideas that reinforced the transformation of America into a distinctly different set of ideas and institutions. Robert Bellah, in *The Broken Covenant,* notes that the idea of reform was central to Christianity, "the idea of conversion, the turning from evil to good, from self to God," and that the Reformation was a heightening and intensification of all these themes.[11] Sacvan Bercovitch, in *The Puritan Origins of the American Self,* speaks of "the baptismal efficacy of the ocean crossing."[12] Since in the Bible the wilderness was tied to the renewal theme, Americans thought of themselves as the chosen people, and of their America, the wilderness, as the locale of rebirth. Rebirth, renewal, in early times, meant a reinforced orientation to God, but the Founding Fathers of the late eighteenth and early nineteenth centuries spoke not of God but of "Providence," "Infinite Power," and so forth.[13] The American Revolution was a "born again" experience, but much of the emphasis had been translated from sacred into secular terms; into a "civil religion." The reformation of the self by renewing its ties to God could be transmuted into repeated reformation of the civil/moral commitments of the secular society, as, for example, when slavery was abolished. The idea of renewal did not require the idea of God. Also, there was nothing in the "civil religion" that required a regulated mercantile economy; free enterprise was possible.

Because of changes in the economic system, by the 1850s it was before the law and in emergent economic practice rather than in poetry that the self was a little commonwealth, and this no longer implied that the individual must occupy a specialized social role in order to fulfill the obligations of membership in a larger civic Commonwealth. Instead, everyday emphasis was on the natural autonomous man whose economic desires and even greed were part of the plan of the natural universe and automatically served a social and national purpose. (If original sin persisted in social manifestation, the remedy was spasmodic social and political reform.)

In the middle third of the nineteenth century, the metaphors that poets used for the self were not the same as those used in the law or in economic and political theory, though there were some analogies between the law's emphasis on individual autonomy and the Romantic concept of a monologic self-contained self whose outreaches were simply extensions or projections of inner feelings and who saw the whole world as grist for or projections of itself. In the nineteenth-century context in which Walt Whitman found himself, Romantics saw the self in terms of will, feeling, and action—incomplete, trying to gain completion by attempts to fuse with the ideal. It was its sense of incompleteness that led the self to action. For mid-19th century poetry, the self was problematic, probably because the economy and law had "liberated" the person from many constrictions.

Bercovitch argues that the Puritans regimented selfhood by insisting that each person should live up to the example of Christ. And, since America itself was "representative of universal rebirth," the whole country was expected to live up to Christ's example.[14] It was a collective person. Therefore, the concept of "Americanus" designated "a comprehensive social-divine selfhood that surmounts the anxieties of secular time, since the very notion of "social" has been transformed (by association with the idea of the new continent) into the realm of rhetoric—of sacred past and sacred future unified in self-celebrating imagination."[15]

Bercovitch also argues that for Ralph Waldo Emerson, as for Jonathan Edwards, the image of the New World invested the "regenerate perceiver with an aura of ascendant millennial splendor; and for both of them, the perceiver must prove his regeneration by transforming himself in the image of the New World."[16] The Emersonian triad was "American nature, the American self, and American destiny."[17] In short, Emerson's Transcendentalism was not far from earlier themes of rebirth and redemption. Although he stressed the individual, the idea of America as a collective person was an antecedent premise.

Trends toward democracy and hypothetical egalitarianism complicated the problem of selfhood. John O. Lyons, in *The Invention of the Self,* points out the impact of the seventeenth and eighteenth-century revolutions: "There is a gamut in Liberty, Equality, Fraternity. The first frees the self to discover what it is to find Truth in its own memories, experiences, and reason. The second suggests a reservation, for to be equal with others is to imply that our Truth is conditional—it is only ours, or it is only true, as it conforms to that of others. And Fraternity insists that we merge our unique self with that of others, and deny ourselves uniqueness—perhaps the self itself."[18]

At the same time there was a transformation in the ideas about soul.

The Old World idea of the soul was of something that did not really belong to the self but was "a gift from out of the bag of eternity," placed in the individual's incompetent keeping, weighed upon by his animal flesh, and subject to manipulation by Church and State.[19] More modern thought tried to tie the soul and body together within skin-encapsulated ego-directed selfhood. New questions then arose about ties between flesh and spirit, time and eternity.

All of these questions or problems were alive in Whitman's world. Whitman began his "Song of Myself" with the image of a unitary separated self:

> Apart from the pulling and hauling stands what I am,
> Stands amused, complacent, compassionating, idle, unitary.[20]

In "Song of Joys" Whitman also celebrated the simple separate person:

> O to struggle against great odds, to meet enemies
>   undaunted!
> To be entirely alone with them, to find out how much
>   one can stand.
> . . .
> To be indeed a God![21]

But this was a vulnerable kind of self, subject to defeat, alienation, and despair, so Whitman set out on the open road on a journey to discover a larger, more viable self. And this entailed openness to and dialogue with external reality and with other people.

> There was a child went forth every day,
> And the first object he look'd upon, that object he became,
> And that object became part of him. . . .[22]

One does not move toward self-discovery through suppression, denial, or elimination, Whitman said. Instead, one moves toward completeness only by plunging into existence, by taking the risks of openness. Self-discovery is a process, a lifelong endeavor, a problematic journey.[23]

The I is historical, temporal, and transient. It participates in the change and development of the concrete world. As Whitman wrote: "This is the city and I am one of the citizens."[24] And: "In all people I see myself."[25]

In the dialogue with the world and others, Whitman began to find his larger self in "One's-Self I Sing" *(Leaves of Grass):*

> One's-self I sing, a simple separate person,
> Yet utter the word Democratic, the word En-Masse.[26]

Thus, Whitman surmounted the threats to the self from Fraternity, by re-identifying with "Americanus," in effect reaffirming the "civil religion."

For Whitman, as it was for earlier writers, the problem of the self was a problem of the relation of the soul to the body, for he believed that the soul was that aspect of God or the Absolute that every man possesses; the soul informs and gives meaning to the self; it relates the self to the eternal;[27] and the eternal constitutes the truly significant reality. Whitman's answer was that the division between the I and Soul is a microcosm of the division between temporal and eternal, so that the fusion of the soul and I can only occur on the same ground that the fusion of temporal and eternal takes place. In "Crossing Brooklyn Ferry,"[28] Whitman discovered that the absolute or spiritual was to be found in the moment through his encounters with objective reality and through communication with others. He transcended time by joining past, present, and future in the lived present moment. In the experience of the community mind and the wholeness of living, Whitman broke through to mythic time. When the eternal is concentrated in a particular moment of human time, the fusion of soul and I takes place, he said.

> There was never any more inception than there is now,
> Nor any more youth or age than there is now;
> And will never be any more perfection than there is now,
> Nor any more heaven or hell than there is now.[29]

> I am an acme of things accomplished, and I am an encloser of
> > things to be.[30]
> I hear and behold God in every object.[31]

> (I am large, I contain multitudes.)[32]

For Whitman, a leaf of grass came to be a symbol of the totality of life, the journey-work of the stars, a symbol of the unity of life, God, and death, a uniform hieroglyphic. It was above all a symbol of selfhood.

To a late nineteenth-century plutocrat, the self might be defined in terms of action and power (male) or ostentation (female). The middle-class person might define the self in terms of character (adherence to a code of "virtue"), decency, and improvement according to external standards. When a bureaucratized society was emerging, unwittingly helped along by middle-class reformists, psychologists William James and George Herbert Mead were defining the self in ways that emphasized individualistic detachment, individual willpower as a motive force, and individual percepts and constructs as shapers of pluralistic reality. James said that any individual had a variety of selves, ruled over by pure ego having no absolute oneness but a center that remained steadfast through shifting experience. Mead said that the "I" is that which wills and thinks "me," the self as object. The "me" is an organized set of social attitudes that the "I" assumes and introjects. Mead's model of the self was like that of a company with the "I" as manager and the "me" as the workers who had a later role as consumers.[33]

The total self was not a content but an activity. The ultimate unit of existence, he said, is the act, which takes place over time. The self is always in process.

The self these men defined was no runaway imperialist; it was tempered and meliorist. It was not solipsistic but rather in dialogue with other selves and internal circumstances. Desire and activity helped to expand the self. But the creativity of the self had to contend with boundaries imposed as a result of struggles and bargains with other people. It was just at this time that the law was beginning to shift away from nineteenth-century individualistic patterns.

Twentieth-century American literature about the self has been divided. On the one hand some white Southern writers and certain ethnic writers have hunted for the self among traditions that are slipping away, all the while suspecting that selfhood might somehow be beyond tradition.[34] On the other hand, writers in general—these included—have taken the self to be more of a problem than ever. Lyons' diagnosis is: "From the Romantic period to our own day literature has largely been concerned with the methods by which men disguise from themselves the gap in their beings where the soul once resided."[35] "A man's fear before the Romantic age was that his soul would be corrupted or . . . some . . . devil would abscond with it. The modern fear is very different. It is that this private and precious self might be duplicated in another, and so our unique individuality would be denied."[36] The mask of the personality "is a protection from the void within," as well as a protection against the world.

Although the law now imputes status, in the name of job rights, and wraps the individual in a net of reciprocal obligations and protections, writers have seemed to feel that the self is fragmented, lost, caught in a plight, and in danger of disintegration. And one reason seems to be that the macrocosm has lost its anthropomorphic identity. God and nation are no longer role models for selfhood. Man is not one with or a miniature of the universe. Despite the influence of Keynesian economics, the political economy is not really a commonwealth. The nation-state is not self-contained, and the interdependence of the world is a hostile independence. There is no suitable model for the self either in civics or in Nature.

Wallace Stevens, who died in 1955, may not be an entirely representative poet for the twentieth century, but he does express something of the new mood. Although he was an entirely different kind of man from Whitman, his poetry bears Whitmanesque traces. The key difference is a loss of belief in any kind of Absolute. From Bradstreet through Whitman through Stevens, more and more responsibility for creating the self and its meaning has been placed back on the individual human self. Thus Stevens has written that our divinity lies in our capacity for

> Celebrating the marriage
> Of flesh and air.[37]

because the earth is "all the paradise we shall know." We are alone in this world; no benign spirit watches over us:

> We live in an old chaos of the sun,
> Or old dependency of day and night,
> Or island solitude, unsponsored; free,[38]
> The lean cats of the arches of the churches,
> That's the old world. In the new, all men are priests.
> . . . .
> . . . God and the imagination are one . . .[39]

This is not to say that Stevens believed there was no reality external to ourselves. But what Stevens desired was an encounter with reality on terms of equality. The world is a beast, a lion, a monster, which might be mastered and purified by imagination. ("The Man with the Blue Guitar"):

> That I may reduce the monster to
> Myself, and then may be myself
>
> In face of the monster, be more than part
> Of it, more than the monstrous player of
>
> One of its monstrous lutes, . . .[40]

In "The Auroras of Autumn",[41] Stevens depicts the consciousness as a male force, with the strength of subjectivity and individuation, playing the ardent lover of reality, which has a female nature, the mother principle. In Stevens's poetry, it has been said, "the world is variously and continually realized by a concretion of the possibility it holds for individual experience." "Burgeoning within and projected without, the self creates the nature of its occurrences through its individual vision of things."[42] In "The Sail of Ulysses," Stevens portrays

> The self as sibyl, whose diamond,
> Whose chiefest embracing of all wealth
> Is poverty, whose jewel found
> At the exactest central of the earth
> Is need.[43]

And, in "Credences of Summer," he describes:

> Three times the concentred self takes hold, three
>   times
> The thrice concentred self, having possessed
>
> The object, grips it in a savage scrutiny,
> Once to make captive, once to subjugate

> Or yield to subjugation, once to proclaim
> The meaning of the capture, this hard prize,
> Fully made, fully apparent, fully found.[44]

The self is an artifact. As Stevens said in "Tea at the Palaz of Hoon," "I was the world in which I walked."[45] And, in "Notes Toward a Supreme Fiction,"

> There is a month, a year, there is a time
> In which majesty is a mirror of the self:
> I have not but I am and as I am, I am.[46]

One of the primary servants of the self is imagination, for which Stevens used the symbol of the blue guitar. It is imagination that enables us to soar beyond the self. The paramount concern of the imagination is the relationship of things, the order to which everything belongs and expects of this order a cosmic harmony. The imagination must remain faithful to things as they are. The act of the mind and the object are distinct existences united by the relation of compresence. But then

> . . . The blue guitar
>
> Becomes the place of things as they are.[47]

Stevens is not saying that the reality of the self is created out of abstractions. Rather, he puts his greatest faith in sentience:

> With my whole body I taste these peaches.[48]

To be released from abstraction, he wrote in "The Latest Freed Man" is

> To have the ant of the self changed to an ox.[49]

The self is the center of the world it conceives and experiences, the pure center to which everything must be related in the present moment of consciousness in the eternal vivid moment of time. Each moment has a fresh universe. The self is forever perishing, but the "idea of man, of the hero, of God—all are projections of self and examples of the spontaneous act of personification by which man continually interprets the world."[50] The richness of each moment, the degree of eternal in the moment, and therefore the moment-by-moment quality of selfhood depended on the reach of imagination. In "Examination of the Hero in a Time of War," Stevens extols:

> The highest man with nothing higher
> Than himself, his self, the self that embraces

The self of the hero, the solar single,
Man-sun, man-moon, man-earth, man-ocean,[51]

And the ultimate hero, Stevens said, is he who practices best the art of imagination, for it is he who reaches through to the ultimate order of things.

How high that highest candle lights the dark.

Out of this same light, out of the central mind,
We make a dwelling in the evening air,
In which being there together is enough.[52]

There is an ultimate order or harmony of things but there is not just one truth; there are many truths. As Stevens wrote, in "On the Road Home,"

It was when I said,
"There is no such thing as the truth,"
That the grapes seemed fatter.
The fox ran out of his hole.[53]

What do we make of this fragmentary evidence? Simply this, that whereas present-day socioeconomic, political, and legal structures tie individuals into an ever more complex interdependent system, the American poet has become increasingly aware that he creates his own universe though he has not ceased to believe that he creates it out of something that is bigger than he is. There is more of an analogy between twentieth-century Stevens' concepts of self and mid-nineteenth century legal-economic treatments of the individual, than there is between Stevens' thought and present-day legal conceptions. In contrast to Whitman's time, it is clear that the public world has ceased to supply a viable metaphor for selfhood, though there is still considerable evidence of a civil religion. Though the contemporary American has statuses, an interdependent society, and a public/private fusion resembling some earlier patterns, he does not have a commonwealth of the sort in which Anne Bradstreet lived. Perhaps the individual must be his own God because he no longer has a commonwealth. Or perhaps the American no longer has a commonwealth and struggles to find selfhood because he no longer has a common god.

Notes

1. See Edmund S. Morgan, *The Puritan Dilemma, The Story of John Winthrop* (Boston: Little, Brown, 1953).

2. Sumner Chilton Powell, *Puritan Village: The Formation of a New England Town* (Middletown, Conn.: Wesleyan University Press, 1963), pp. 108–9; Richard L. Bushman, *From*

Puritan to Yankee (New York: W. W. Norton, 1967); George A. Billias, ed., *Law and Authority in Colonial America* (Barre, Mass.: Barre, 1965); George Lee Haskins, *Law and Authority in Early Massachusetts* (New York: Macmillan, 1960); James Morton Smith, ed., *Seventeenth-Century America* (Chapel Hill: University of North Carolina Press, 1959); George F. Dow, *Every Day Life in the Massachusetts Bay Colony* (Boston: Society for the Preservation of New England Antiquities, 1935); Richard B. Morris, *Studies in the History of American Law with Special Reference to the Seventeenth and Eighteenth Centuries* (New York: Octagon, 1963); Morton J. Horowitz, *The Transformation of American Law, 1780–1860* (Cambridge: Harvard University Press, 1977), p. 44.

3. See Eustace M. W. Tillyard, *The Elizabethan World Picture* (London: Chatto and Windus, 1943).

4. Horowitz, *Transformation of American Law,* pp. 36, 99; *Journal of Economic History* (supp.) December, 1943).

5. Horowitz, *Transformation of American Law,* p. 99.

6. Ibid., p. 209.

7. Ibid., p. 26.

8. See Corinne Lathrop Gilb oral history interview with Mathew O. Tobriner, Institute of Industrial Relations Library, University of California, Berkeley, dated 1960. Charles A. Reich, "The New Property," *Yale Law Journal* 73 (1964): 733; Francis S. Philbrick, "Changing Conceptions of Property in Law," *University of Pennsylvania Law Review* 75 (1938): 691.

9. Anne Bradstreet, *Meditations Divine and Moral,* #62, p. 286, Jeannie Hensley, ed., *The Works of Anne Bradstreet* (Cambridge: Belknap/Harvard University Press, 1967).

10. See also Ann Stanford, *Anne Bradstreet: The Worldly Puritan* (New York: Burt Franklin, 1974); Elizabeth Wade White, *Anne Bradstreet, "The Tenth Muse"* (New York: Oxford University Press, 1971).

11. Robert N. Bellah, *The Broken Covenant, American Civil Religion in Time of Trial* (New York: Seabury Press, 1975), p. 10.

12. Sacvan Bercovitch, *The Puritan Origins of the American Self* (New Haven: Yale University Press, 1975), p. 113.

13. Bellah, *The Broken Covenant,* p. 45.

14. Bercovitch, *Puritan Origins,* pp. 23, 108.

15. Ibid., p. 135.

16. Ibid., p. 152.

17. Ibid., p. 178.

18. John O. Lyons, *The Invention of the Self, the Hinge of Consciousness in the Eighteenth Century* (Carbondale: Southern Illinois University Press, 1973), p. 3.

19. Ibid., p. 4.

20. "Song of Myself," in Walt Whitman, *Leaves of Grass* (reprint of 1891–2 version) (Mount Vernon, N.Y.: Peter Pauper Press, 1944), p. 32.

21. "Song of Joys," in Whitman, *Leaves of Grass,* p. 142.

22. "There Was a Child Went Forth," in Whitman, *Leaves of Grass,* p. 271.

23. E. Fred Carlisle, *The Uncertain Self: Whitman's Drama of Identity* (East Lansing: Michigan State University Press, 1973), p. 7–8.

24. Whitman, "Song of Myself," in *Leaves of Grass,* p. 66.

25. Ibid., p. 43.

26. Whitman, "Leaves of Grass," p. 11.

27. Carlisle, *The Uncertain Self,* p. 58.

28. Whitman, "Crossing Brooklyn Ferry," in *Leaves of Grass,* p. 125.

29. "Song of Myself," in *Leaves of Grass,* p. 31.

30. Ibid., p. 69.

31. Ibid., p. 73.

32. Ibid., p. 74.